The Chinese Enterprise Globalization Series

Series Editors

Henry Huiyao Wang, Ph.D. is the Founder and President of Center for China and Globalization (CCG), a former Counselor of China State Council and Dean of the Institute of Development Studies at China's Southwestern University of Finance and Economics, Beijing, China

Mabel Lu Miao, Ph.D. is the Co-Founder and Secretary-General of CCG, a Munich Secretary Conference Young Leader, the Founder of Global Young Leaders Dialogue (GYLD) and the Deputy Director of the International Writing Center of Beijing Normal University, Beijing, China

This series contributes to the field of globalization and Chinese enterprises studies. It publishes completely up-to-date monographs dedicated to this topic. It also provides a wealth of the latest information regarding Chinese ODI. In addition to this data, the series stands head and shoulders above other work in this area due to its in-depth case studies on Chinese companies going global, all of which are based on thorough primary research.

The key words in TCEGS include but are not limited to:

- Going global
- Globalization
- ODI
- FDI
- Cross-border M&A
- One Belt One Road
- International talent
- Risks
- Challenges
- Outbound Investment
- Chinese enterprises
- Greenfield investment

Henry Huiyao Wang · Mabel Lu Miao
Editors

The Challenge of "Going Out"

Chinese Experiences in Outbound Investment

Springer

Editors
Henry Huiyao Wang
Center for China and Globalization
Beijing, China

Mabel Lu Miao
Center for China and Globalization
Beijing, China

ISSN 2524-5929 ISSN 2524-5937 (electronic)
The Chinese Enterprise Globalization Series
ISBN 978-981-99-3325-9 ISBN 978-981-99-3326-6 (eBook)
https://doi.org/10.1007/978-981-99-3326-6

This Springer imprint is published by the registered company Springer Nature Singapore Pte Ltd.
The registered company address is: 152 Beach Road, #21-01/04 Gateway East, Singapore 189721, Singapore

Foreword

Reflecting on 2020 and Looking to the Future

It could be said that the end of the honeymoon period of Chinese outbound investment was the detention of Meng Wanzhou in 2018 and the subsequent restrictions placed on Huawei driven by the United States. The increased influence of larger and more competitive Chinese companies abroad has resulted in increased challenges for Chinese companies looking to invest and grow outside China's borders. More intense scrutiny, more complicated public relations, and constantly changing regulations that are motivated by both economic and political considerations epitomize the environmental challenges that Chinese companies face when doing business abroad.

In 2020, following the outbreak of COVID-19, a government and public in the United States that was increasingly inward-looking caused trade tensions between China and the United States to reach an all time high and the challenges of expanding abroad, especially in developed economies, peaked. These tensions were exacerbated by two major inter-linked challenges. The first challenge was obviously the COVID-19 pandemic, which heavily impacted the worldwide economy and global trade, causing enormous losses for Chinese companies. The second challenge was the push back against globalization, which had already been a growing trend and was exacerbated by the pandemic. After more than three years, while trade continues, growth has slowed considerably. The World Bank recently lowered its expected growth rates across the board, which reveals a trend, but also presents Chinese companies, which are looking to other global markets to grow their own businesses, with new challenges and prospects that are not as bright as they once were.

From 1978 to the present day, China has sought to integrate itself into the process of globalization. After more than four decades of economic reform and opening-up of its domestic market, China has become a pivotal player in the world's economy. Notably, in 2020, when the global economy as a whole was on the downswing, China was one of the few countries able to maintain positive growth. During this time, China acted as the world's engine of trade, driving the growth of the global economy. This indicates how proactive participation by the Chinese business community is also important.

In my experience, Chinese companies can make a significant contribution to globalization in a number of ways. For example, I was once part of a global clean cookstove project. Established by the Clinton Foundation, the project aimed to liberate women around the world from the heavy burden of domestic work, and in particular, kitchen work. This project improved the well-being of both women and children and women were "liberated" from domestic chores and could give more attention to their children. I saw that it was well funded and successful due to a partnership with the United Nations. However, this is not a particularly innovative project or a project that requires incredibly advanced and expensive technology. If we look at rural China, we can see that cookstoves are already using other innovative forms of energy, including biogas, solar power, and wind energy. The competitiveness of Chinese companies in this area means that they could consider undertaking projects in rural China that could easily benefit its residents.

In December 2009, I attended my first global governance conference, the Copenhagen Climate Change Conference (COP 15). The Conference put climate change policy at the top of the world's political agenda. This was the latest round of multilateral communication after the signing of the Kyoto Protocol in 1997, with a focus on carbon reduction. Attended by over 100 world leaders, it was the biggest gathering of world leaders ever outside the United Nations headquarters in New York, while over 40,000 people around the world attended remotely. They represented governments, non-governmental organizations, and media, as well as other UN bodies. Although the international community had high expectations for this conference, it achieved limited results. Later, I attended the UN Climate Conference in Morocco as a representative among 100 entrepreneurs.

In recent years, during the Trump administration, the US government took a hard line stance in terms of its climate change policies. This can be seen in the limited number of commitments the US agreed to make in terms of climate change policies. The Trump administration also withdrew from a number of international agreements, such as the Paris Climate Accord. At the same time, the US accused China of not accomplishing enough in terms of reducing its impact on climate change. However, since the start of the twenty-first century, China has made substantial achievements in environmental protection. China's environmental protection efforts and green building projects should not only be promoted domestically, but also internationally, so as to tell China's "green story" within a global context.

In addition to actively participating in globalization, the ways in which Chinese companies adapt to local conditions in host countries should also be addressed. This includes examining how and why Chinese companies cooperate extensively with local companies and manage the interests of stakeholders when expanding overseas. As is the case for China's domestic market, mutual trust and respect for common rules are necessary. In recent years, many Chinese companies have met their Waterloo in the process of overseas expansion, which was mainly due to a lack of compliance. The reasons for this are not only the political factors brought about by changes in government and political instability, but they also reflect a lack of preparation by companies in terms of public disclosure and transparency. In certain aspects, the traditional rules of the game in China are consistent with modern industrial convention, but in some areas also certainly conflict with global integration. Therefore, I believe that adhering to consistent and fair rules and holding stakeholders accountable will pave the path to globalization for Chinese companies.

Beijing, China
July, 2023

Wang Shi
Founder and Honorary Chairman of
China Vanke Co., Ltd.
President of Vanke Foundation

Acknowledgements

We wish to express our sincere gratitude to our commissioning editors at Springer Nature Group and their team, particularly Yingying Zhang and Yan Li. Our professional team within the CCG Publishing Center also worked with each author to ensure each work we selected was both relevant and timely. The final outcome of their hard work is a source of pride for us and we would like to express our warmest thanks and appreciation to Joshua Dominick, Genevieve Bridget Donnellon-May, Yueyuan Ren and Yunfeng Bai, Weiwei Yu, Shaoli Hou, Jung-Yul Ogborne, and Beijie Tang.

We also wish to express thanks for the support provided by Beijing China Globalization Think Tank Foundation.

Lastly, we would like to thank our readers for their continued support and encouragement. Your continued readership gives us the confidence and drive to continue to produce innovative and insightful publications like this one.

Henry Huiyao Wang, Ph.D.
Mabel Lu Miao, Ph.D.
Center for China and Globalization (CCG)

Introduction

Outward investment by Chinese enterprises has remained a growing trend in recent years and is encapsulated in the phrase "*zou chu qu*" or "going out". China's large population and rapid growth rate have provided Chinese companies with fertile soil for growth for decades, but for companies that have reached a certain scale or found domestic markets saturated, new opportunities in markets around the world provide more room for growth and attractive challenges. Official support for outbound investment has ebbed and flowed over the years, but it remains a key strategy for the Chinese government and many Chinese companies, both large and small.

In the two decades since China's accession to the WTO in 2001, China has grown at an increasingly faster pace and become more and more integrated into the global economy. This is true in terms of high level decisions and legislation as well as day-to-day interactions with individual entities beyond China's borders, whether they be companies or governments. The capabilities and sophistication of Chinese companies in dealing with different issues in the course of "going out" serve as a barometer of China's level of growth and maturity on its path toward globalization. This process was enhanced even further with the launch of the Belt and Road Initiative (BRI) in 2013, which should be seen as a proactive move on China's part to enhance mutually beneficial trade ties throughout the developing and developed world with a strong focus on infrastructure development. In 2016, China's outward direct investment hit a record high of US$196.15 billion, which comprised 13.5% of total global outward investment. The following year, the Chinese government strengthened reviews of outbound investors, which ultimately resulted in more mature and rational investment. This was also the first year that China's outward direct investment showed negative growth, but it still ranked third in the world at US$158.29 billion. In 2018, the total outflow of global foreign direct investment shrank, and fell for three consecutive years from 2016 to 2018, by which time China's foreign direct investment flow was US$143.04 billion, ranking second in the world. In 2020, affected by the severe impact of COVID-19, the world economy shrank by 3.3%, the first time the global economy saw negative growth since 2009. Global foreign direct investment also decreased by nearly 40%, while Chinese outward FDI reached US$153.71 billion, placing it first in the world for the first time. In 2022, China's net outward direct investment was US$163.12 billion. As of the end of 2022, a total of 29,000 chinese investors have established 46,400 enterprises located in 190 countries and regions worldwide.[1]

However, with an increased presence on the world stage, Chinese companies face an increasing number of obstacles and challenges. While it may not be the most enjoyable experience, the obstacles Chinese companies face, whether they be WTO sanctions, regulatory barriers, or cultural differences, serve as cathartic learning experiences for Chinese companies and it can be argued that they are actually a positive sign of China's increased integration with the world, demonstrating how Chinese companies are constantly adapting to different systems and models. As China and Chinese companies grow and change, both domestically and internationally, different challenges will arise and the ability to be flexible and adapt is essential.

Specific challenges facing Chinese companies that have already established themselves abroad or are planning to "go out" are manifested in several areas. These include changes in the overall business environment, the ongoing impact of COVID-19, evolving geopolitical issues, and an overall slowdown in the global economy. The overall business environment is characterized by increasingly protectionist policies and attitudes as well as a general distrust or disaffection with globalization, which has been key to China's development thus far. More recently, constantly evolving geopolitical issues have also exacerbated feelings of uncertainty, which makes it difficult for companies to decide where to invest. The Russia-Ukraine conflict is chief among these, disrupting energy and food supply-chains and severely impacting countries key to China's Belt and Road Initiative, a major driver of potential growth. Finally, the overall slowdown in the global economy and reassessments of estimated growth rates by the World Bank are constantly forcing Chinese companies to reevaluate their strategies to deal with newly emerging challenges. The looming possibility of stagflation is very real, with the World Bank also predicting that global growth will have slowed by 2.7% between 2021 and 2024. While China is expected to maintain a growth rate of a little over 5%, on par with the rest of East Asia, advanced economies are expected to see only moderate growth of around 2%, while the developing world, with the exception of South Asia, will not do much better. These factors combined make "going out" a difficult decision for Chinese companies to make and require them to avoid risk as much as possible and make smart decisions in terms of both geography and industry.

China's rapid development and objective success—whether measured in terms of the modernity of its cities, the sheer size of its economy, or its strength and influence n the world stage—China is now a leading player in the global economy and is increasingly being held to a higher standard. As a result, Chinese companies are experiencing different challenges vis-a-vis the China context as they "go out" with varying degrees of risk and reward in both the developed and developing world.

[1] Ministry of Commerce of the People's Republic of China, National Bureau of Statistics, State Administration of Foreign Exchange, "2020 Statistical Bulletin of China's Outward Foreign Direct Investment" and "2022 Statistical Bulletin of China's Outward Foreign Direct Investment".

Ultimately, the secret to success in going beyond one's own borders to invest or build a business is finding a balance. Naturally, this balance is always in flux and the ultimate outcome of "going out" for some Chinese companies may be drastically different from what they first envisioned, but the process provides successful companies with maturity and perspective, and unsuccessful companies with valuable lessons so that they can, as the ancient Chinese saying goes, "rise again from the Eastern Mountains".

We have divided this book into five main parts, focusing on issues in outbound investment and "going out" in a progressive manner, from macro to micro. Each of the contributors have their own unique insights and perspectives on the experiences of Chinese enterprises abroad, which we hope will prove useful not only for Chinese companies that are the movers and shakers in this sector, but also for administrators and potential partners of Chinese companies looking to gain a deeper understanding of the psychology, concerns, and goals of Chinese companies coming to their shores.

Part one, titled *Policy and Environment*, begins with an article by Xinquan Tu and Yifang Zhao that focuses on the topic of investment facilitation. Investing in a project in another country is a technical, risky, and potentially ruinous activity, which makes facilitation an indispensable tool for companies looking to "go out". Tu and Zhao provide an analysis of domestic facilitation policies, investment facilitation in host countries as well as insights into the global discussion on how to better facilitate investment.

This is followed by an in-depth look at the institutional environment of Chinese overseas investment and its impact from Guoyong Liang and Haoyuan Ding. This technical, detailed analysis gives a deeper look into the structural and systemic characteristics as well as the challenges unique to Chinese companies, which we hope will enhance the understanding of where Chinese entrepreneurs are coming from and how to better work with them in the course of investment.

Part two, titled *Underlying Trends and Influencing Factors*, moves into another level of this topic by looking at broader trends and other factors that influence Chinese enterprises looking to engage in overseas investment. This section begins with an article by CCG's own Enterprises Globalization Research Group that provides an overall analysis of outbound investment based on a questionnaire to understand the current situation of Chinese enterprises and the challenges they face, ranging from indicators of the basic state of investment to the impact of policy and the prospects of enterprises investing in BRI countries. This is followed by a second article by the Enterprises Globalization Research Group that looks at specific opportunities and challenges in the globalization of Chinese enterprises, which is taken from a series of panel discussions on political, economic, and academic issues. Part two concludes with a detailed look at financing structures and risk response from Shiwei Zhang and Xuejing Zhu, specifically focusing on overseas investment and M&A with detailed case studies and recommendations on strategies for dealing with foreign exchange and outbound capital risk.

Part three zooms in on the concerns surrounding legal issues and compliance in host countries. The diversity of structures with companies and the varying maturity of legal systems in host countries create a range of issues that must be addressed. The first article in this part is by Jihua Ding and focuses on the creation of compliance management systems to mitigate the risk of World Bank sanctions. An increasing number of Chinese enterprises investing abroad are affected by World Bank investigations and even sanctions, and Ding provides suggestions on how to avoid these risks, specifically work that enterprises can do in terms of setting up compliance systems and understanding compliance requirements in advance before they even invest. The second article in this part by Zhisong Deng and Jianmin Dai continues to focus on the importance of compliance, but this time from the perspective of anti-monopoly and data protection. The increased participation in outbound investment by China's state-owned enterprises has, more than once, raised red flags among regulators in terms of monopolistic practices and corporate relations. Knowing how to avoid or mitigate these risks is key for Chinese enterprises preparing to "go out".

Part four takes a closer look at opportunities and risks facing Chinese enterprises in more developed economies, namely Japan and the US. Jinghao Jin takes a close look at the huge efforts Japan has made to attract foreign capital and companies to Japan's shores, highlighting the opportunities that await Chinese enterprises willing to explore them, especially in different localities throughout the country. In the next article in this part, Weiwen He examines the long-term outlook for investment in the US, specifically overcoming some of the difficulties in light of US tariffs on China and the instability in US-China relations. He specifically highlights the advantages of greenfield investment, the huge opportunities that still exist outside so-called "sensitive areas", and the importance of connecting with local governments, businesses, and communities in the US, who generally welcome Chinese investment that results in jobs and revenue.

Part five concludes this volume with a look at two of China's greatest "going out" success stories—Geely and Fuyao. The team of Jihua Ding, Lingchen Guo, and Zhile Wang provided a comprehensive introspective into the path that Geely took to transition from a relatively low-key budget Chinese car maker to a real competitor on the global stage with a focus on localization, connecting with markets and communities, as well as maintaining a strong corporate culture, which are all key elements of Geely's success. The second piece in this section, and the last in this book, is a case study of Fuyao Group. The trials and successes experienced by this Chinese glass manufacturer from Fujian Province are typical of Chinese companies that want to build and grow a business beyond China's shores. The methods and strategies used by Fuyao are invaluable to Chinese enterprises that are looking to succeed abroad, but also serve as an important contrast to the trending "threatening" image of Chinese investment and companies that currently seems to be on the rise in the US and other countries around the world.

As editors and scholars, we are confident that readers of all backgrounds will be able to find something useful to take away from the content we've presented in this volume. The core theme throughout all of the pieces we've selected has been one of increased understanding and adaptation to new environments, whether it be in terms of legal compliance, corporate culture, or local engagement. If Chinese enterprises with a vision to "go out" follow some of the simple principles that are discussed here, it will not only make the process of investing overseas smoother and more successful, but also it has the potential to improve the reputation and standing of Chinese companies in the world.

July 2023

Henry Huiyao Wang, Ph.D.
Founder and President of Center for China and Globalization (CCG)
Mabel Lu Miao, Ph.D.
Co-Founder and Secretary-General of CCG

Contents

Risks and Opportunities in Investment

Notable "Going Out" Case Studies

About the Editors

Henry Huiyao Wang, Ph.D. is the Founder and President of the Center for China and Globalization (CCG), ranked among the top 100 think tanks in the world. He is also Dean of the Institute of Development Studies of Southwestern University of Finance and Economics of China, Vice Chairman of the China Association for International Cooperation, and a Director at the Chinese People's Institute of Foreign Affairs. He is currently a steering committee member of the Paris Peace Forum and an advisory board member at Duke Kunshan University. He has also served as an expert advisor at the World Bank, IOM, and ILO. He pursued his Ph.D. studies at the University of Western Ontario and University of Manchester and he was a senior fellow at Harvard Kennedy School and a visiting fellow at Brookings Institute. He is the chief editor of the Springer Nature book series China and Globalization, Chinese Enterprise Globalization and International Talent Development in China. His books in English include *Globalizing China* (2012); *China Goes Global* (2016); *Handbook on China and Globalization* (2019); *Globalization of Chinese Enterprises* (2020); *Consensus or Conflict?: China and Globalization in the 21st Century* (2021); *The Ebb and Flow of Globalization* (2022); *Understanding Globalization, Global Gaps, and Power Shifts in the 21st century: CCG Global Dialogues* (2022); *Strategies for Chinese Enterprises Going Global* (2023); and *Escaping Thucydides's Trap: Dialogue with Graham Allison on China-US Relations* (2023).

Mabel Lu Miao, Ph.D. is the Secretary-General of CCG, a Munich Security Conference (MSC) Young Leader, and the Deputy Director General of the International Writing Center of Beijing Normal University. She is also an Adjunct Professor at Huaqiao University and an Adjunct Researcher at Beijing Foreign Studies University. She received her Ph.D. in Contemporary Chinese Studies from Beijing Normal University and has been a visiting scholar at New York University's China House and the Fairbank Center at Harvard University. Dr. Miao is a co-author of many Chinese Social Science Academy blue books and Chinese Social Science Foundation research project reports. Dr. Miao has published a number of books in Chinese, which detail developments in China's outbound business and global talent. Her latest publications in English include *Blue Book of Global Talent*; *Annual Report on the Development of Chinese Students Studying Abroad*; *China's Domestic and International Migration Development* (2019); *International Migration of China: Status, Policy and Social Responses to the Globalization of Migration* (2017); *Transition and Opportunity: Strategies from Business Leaders on Making the Most of China's Future* (2022); and *Strategies for Chinese Enterprises Going Global* (2023).

List of Figures

An Analysis of Outbound Investment by Chinese Enterprises

Financing Structure and Risk Response in Overseas Investment and M&A by Chinese Enterprises

Investment and Cooperation Opportunities in Japan

List of Tables

Investment and Cooperation Opportunities in Japan

Looking at the Long Term and Overcoming Difficulties of Investing in the US

Building the World's Most Competitive Professional Supplier of Auto Glass: A Case Study of the Fuyao Group

Policy and Environment

The Evolution and Outlook of Investment Facilitation Issues

Xinquan Tu and Yifang Zhao

Abstract Negotiations on investment topics have stalled due to disagreements among WTO members. Investment facilitation is an area of concern, but it is also capable of avoiding controversial topics seen in other topics on investment. In recent years, inspired by the completion of the *Agreement on Trade Facilitation*, the international community has started to pay more attention to and research investment facilitation. This paper examines the evolution of topics on investment, analyzes the impact of and need for investment facilitation, the opportunities and challenges it faces as well as suggestions for future promotion. This paper argues that members of the international community should strengthen the implementation of and discussion surrounding investment facilitation, increase research and analysis related to investment facilitation and work toward reaching plurilateral agreements.

Keywords Investment facilitation · World Trade Organization (WTO) · Plurilateral agreements

As one of the main engines of economic growth, investment is a sensitive and complex issue in global economic development, and is often linked to issues of national sovereignty and policy space. The international community has been working to develop and implement multilateral rules on investment for decades, but has yet to reach an agreement due to the wide array of differing opinions among members. However, the increased intensity of economic globalization makes it even more urgent to formulate multilateral investment rules.

Under the larger topic of investment, investment facilitation focuses on information transparency, management effectiveness, and policy predictability within the investment environment. Compared with other sub-topics in investment, such

X. Tu (✉) · Y. Zhao
China WTO Research Institute, University of International Business and Economics, Beijing, China

H. H. Wang and M. L. Miao (eds.), *The Challenge of "Going Out"*, The Chinese Enterprise Globalization Series, https://doi.org/10.1007/978-981-99-3326-6_1

as investment protection and investment dispute settlement, it is less controversial and may be possible to development binding rules. In recent years, especially since 2013, when the WTO General Council passed the *Agreement on Trade Facilitation*, investment facilitation issues have sparked considerable research and discussion throughout the international community. By reviewing the evolution of topics on investment and analyzing impact and and necessity of discussions investment facilitation and the opportunities and challenges it faces, this article attempts to put forward thoughts on its further development.

1 The Evolution of Discussions on Investment Facilitation

The international community has been examining and discussing topics on investment for a long time. To understand topics related to investment facilitation, it is essential to begin by reviewing how these topics have evolved. Some Western countries, specifically the United States, initially wanted to negotiate and formulate a special agreement on investment issues during the Uruguay Round of negotiations. However, due to opposition from developing countries, investment-related rules were only partially included in WTO agreements, including the *Agreement on Trade-Related Investment Measures (TRIMs)* and the *General Agreement on Trade in Services (GATS).*

Unsatisfied with the Uruguay Round of negotiations, some developed countries continued to explore multilateral investment agreements. In May 1995, the Organization for Economic Cooperation and Development (OECD) launched negotiations on reaching a "Multilateral Agreement on Investment" (MAI) in an attempt to establish comprehensive, high-level multilateral investment rules covering investment liberalization, investment protection and dispute settlement. Nevertheless, negotiations eventually stalled due to internal disagreements within the group over issues including labour and environmental standards. In December 1996, under the leadership of developed countries, the WTO Singapore Ministerial Conference included investment in its agenda. It mandated the establishment of a working group to study the relationship between trade and investment and the possibility of a future multilateral agreement on investment. Since then, developed countries including Canada and Japan have tried to promote discussions on investment in WTO negotiations, but developing countries have resisted.

Given the debate between developed and developing members on whether to include investment in the negotiations, in November 2001, at the Fourth WTO Ministerial Conference held in Doha, it was decided that the Working Group on Trade and Investment would first continue to clarify issues such as the scope and definition of investment as well as transparency and non-discrimination. It was also agreed that negotiations on trade and topics on investment would commence at the Fifth Ministerial Conference on the premise of consensus. However, at the Fifth Ministerial Conference in Cancun in September 2003, developed and developing countries were still deeply divided on a range of issues including agricultural subsidies.

The confrontation over whether to launch negotiations on the "Singapore Issues", including investment, was particularly intense, leading to a fruitless conclusion. After several failed attempts, at the WTO General Council in July 2004, developed countries made concessions and agreed to exclude the topics on investment from the Doha Round of negotiations.

It was not until November 2013 that the WTO framework discussed topics on investment when the *Agreement on Trade Facilitation* forced the international community to rethink long-shelved topics on investment. In 2015, the United Nations adopted the Addis Ababa Action Agenda and the 2030 Agenda for Sustainable Development. It also called for increased investment in developing countries to bridge financing gaps in sustainable development, which attracted global attention. Subsequently, the United Nations Conference on Trade and Development (UNCTAD) released the *Global Action List on Investment Facilitation* in June 2016. By focusing on the topic of investment facilitation, this document proposed corresponding action guidelines in response to situations in which investment policies of the international community received less coverage on investment facilitation.

In September 2016, the G20 Leaders Summit established the Working Group on Trade and Investment and adopted the *G20 Guiding Principles for Global Investment Policymaking,* which contained articles on investment facilitation. In April 2017, 11 WTO members, including China, Brazil, Argentina, and Nigeria, formed the "Friends of Investment Facilitation" to further promote discussion of this issue and explore a path for the WTO to move forward on investment facilitation. In December 2017, at the WTO Ministerial Conference in Buenos Aires, trade ministers from 70 members signed the *Joint Ministerial Statement on Investment Facilitation,* calling for the initiation of structured discussions on investment facilitation within the WTO. In March 2018, the structured discussions were officially launched, with the participation of 71 WTO members.[1]

In summary, despite divisions among member states that initially caused negotiations on investment to stall, in recent years, inspired by the adoption of the *Agreement on Trade Facilitation*, the international community has begun to pay attention to and discuss investment facilitation. It is worth mentioning that China has played a crucial role in advocating discussion on topics of investment facilitation. In September 2016, when it served as host country, China promoted the *G20 Guiding Principles for Global Investment Policymaking,* which filled gaps in international investment rules. In October 2016, China took the lead in raising the issue of investment facilitation at the WTO, cleverly integrating trade, investment and development.[2] In April 2017, China established the "Friends of Investment Facilitation" group. China also led the *Outlines for BRICS Investment Facilitation* at the BRICS Summit in August and *the Joint Ministerial Statement on Investment Facilitation.* In addition, China mentioned in its position paper on WTO reform that WTO rules need to cover

[1] Khalil Hamdani, Investment facilitation at the WTO is not investment redux, 4 June 2018, https://www.ictsd.org/opinion/investment-facilitation-at-the-wto-is-not-investment-redux.

[2] Hong Junjie, China's push for investment facilitation issues gains broad support at the WTO, people.cn, Dec. 20, 2017, http://finance.people.com.cn/n1/2017/1220/c1004-29718958.html.

new issues appearing in the twenty-first century, which include investment facilitation. This document shows that China advocates investment facilitation, which is commensurate with its position as the second most significant contributor to outbound investment in the WTO (see Table 1).[3]

2 The Impact and Necessity of Investment Facilitation

By emphasizing "convenience", investment facilitation and trade facilitation are similar both in definition and scope. Trade facilitation aims to reduce trade costs and facilitate trade operations by enhancing the transparency of trade regulations, promoting freedom of transit, while streamlining import and export fees and formalities, which the *Agreement on Trade Facilitation* reflects. For example, the *Agreement* increases transparency by requiring member states to promptly release all information related to import and export procedures, establish special consultation points, and provide traders with opportunities to submit suggestions and seek consultation regarding streamlining import and export fees and formalities.

In addition, the *Agreement* stipulates that member countries should periodically review fees, reduce the type and number of fees, and establish a "single window" to allow trading companies to submit information and documents in one go. To ensure that all members can achieve and benefit from trade facilitation, the *Agreement* also provides developing countries, especially Least Developed Countries (LDCs), with special treatment in the implementation process and assistance and support for capacity building. It also encourages greater cooperation among and within members' border agencies. This process ensures transparency, efficiency, and predictability, which is a central tenet of trade facilitation. To this end, countries should reduce unnecessary red tape in administrative procedures and release relevant information in a timely and effective manner. Furthermore, the international community needs to provide developing countries with capacity-building support and encourage exchange and cooperation among members on various subjects to ensure that members can benefit from trade facilitation. These processes also apply to investment facilitation.

While there is no universal definition, several international organizations and forums have reflected on the essence of investment facilitation. For example, the Asia–Pacific Economic Cooperation (APEC), an early proponent of this discussion, considers investment facilitation to be actions taken by host governments to attract foreign investment and to achieve efficient management of investment at all stages of the investment cycle.[4] Similarly, both the OECD[5] and UNCTAD[6] define it as policy actions aimed at enabling investors to facilitate the establishment, maintenance, and

[3] UNCTAD, *World Investment Report 2019*.

[4] APEC Investment Facilitation Action Plan (2008).

[5] OECD, Policy Framework for Investment (2015).

[6] UNCTAD, Global Action Menu for Investment Facilitation (2016).

Table 1 The evolution of discussions on investment facilitation

Timeline	Events	Remarks
1986–1994	Uruguay Round of Negotiations	Investment rules sparsely mentioned in WTO agreements
May 1995	OECD launches negotiations on reaching a "Multilateral Agreement on Investment"	Stalled due to strong disagreements within the membership
December 1996	Singapore Ministerial Meeting	The establishment of a Working Group on Trade and Investment to study the relationship between trade and investment
November 2001	Doha Ministerial Conference	Agreed that negotiations on trade and investment shall be launched by consensus at the Cancun Ministerial Conference
September 2003	Cancun Ministerial Meeting	No substantive results were reached because of serious divisions among members
July 2004	The WTO General Council adopted the "July Package"	Topics on investment were excluded from the Doha Round of negotiations
November 2013	*The Agreement on Trade Facilitation* adopted	The first multilateral trade agreement since the Doha Round was launched, urging the international community to rethink the topics on investment
2015	The UN adopted the Addis Ababa Action Agenda and the 2030 Agenda for Sustainable Development	Called for increasing investment in developing countries to bridge their financing gap for sustainable development
June 2016	UNCTAD releases *the Global Action List on Investment Facilitation*	Focused on investment facilitation issues and proposed corresponding action guidelines
September 2016	The G20 Hangzhou Summit	Adoption of the *G20 Guiding Principles for Global Investment Policymaking* which included articles on investment facilitation
October 2016	China takes the lead in proposing the issue of investment facilitation at the WTO	China creatively integrated topics of trade, investment and development
April 2017	11 WTO members (inc. China) form the "Friends of Investment Facilitation" group	Pushed the agenda forward
August 2017	BRICS Summit	Issued *Outlines for BRICS Investment Facilitation*
December 2017	12th WTO Ministerial Conference	70 WTO members signed the *Joint Ministerial Statement on Investment Facilitation*

(continued)

Table 1 (continued)

Timeline	Events	Remarks
March 2018	71 WTO members jointly launch structured discussions	Aimed at identifying potential elements to advance the formation of a multilateral framework for investment facilitation and laying the groundwork for discussions at the 2020 Ministerial Conference

expansion of their investments. The international community has further discussed the action plan to move forward on investment facilitation. In its *Global Action List on Investment Facilitation*, UNCTAD proposed tentative guidelines for implementing investment facilitation, as shown in Table 2.

As an advocate of investment facilitation, China has also been actively promoting facilitation domestically in recent years. In June 2018, the State Council issued the *Notice on Several Measures for Active and Effective Utilization of Foreign Capital to Promote High-Quality Economic Development*, which called for substantial decentralization of the approvals process, the implementation of "one-stop processing" when registering businesses, and the registration of foreign enterprises beyond the negative list. It also called for making it more convenient for foreign enterprises to use funds and making entering and leaving the country more convenient for foreign citizens working in China.

In August 2019, the General Office of the State Council issued the *Notice on the Distribution of Key Tasks on Deepening the Reform to Streamline Administration and Delegate Power, Improve Regulation and Upgrade Services and Optimizing the Business Environment* during a national teleconference. This document set out specific requirements for the reduction of administrative licensing requirements set at the central and local levels, the reduction of industrial production licenses, the reduction of business start-up time, the governance of unreasonable fees, the development of nationally unified and simple regulatory rules and standards, and making government services more efficient. China believes that actively creating a convenient business environment is not only an inevitable requirement for China to deepen market-oriented reforms and expand its opening to the outside world, but that this is something consistent with China's goal of making its economy more competitive.

From the current discussions within the international community on this topic, the goal of investment facilitation is to provide convenience for investors and focus on promoting a transparent, efficient and predictable investment environment. Specifically, this means streamlining administrative procedures, enhancing information transparency, improving infrastructure, maintaining good stakeholder relations, and strengthening international cooperation in order to reduce "ground barriers" for investors in host countries. This will also prevent investment disputes and enable investors to facilitate the establishment, management and expansion of their investments, thereby promoting economic growth and sustainable development in host countries.

Table 2 UNCATD's action plan on investment facilitation

	Action plan	Examples of specific actions	Embodied principle(s)
1	Improve the transparency and accessibility of investment policies and regulations	Provide clear and timely information about the investment system	Transparency
2	Enhance consistency and predictability in the implementation of investment policies	Establish clear standards and management procedures regarding investment review, evaluation and approval mechanisms	Predictability
3	Improve the efficiency of investment management	Shorten the approval time and streamline the process of investment approval and business permit applications	Efficiency
4	Establish good relations with stakeholders	Have regular dialogues with stakeholders to discuss and solve investment-related problems	Transparency, predictability
5	Establish dedicated advisory and coordination bodies	Establish dedicated consultation points on investment policies to collect suggestions and opinions	Transparency, predictability
6	Establish regulatory and review mechanisms	Adopt diagnostic tools and indicators to measure the efficiency of relevant institutions	Predictability
7	Strengthen international cooperation	Establish dialogue mechanisms and partnerships among member authorities to jointly design, implement and monitor the process of investment facilitation efforts	Communication, cooperation
8	Enhance technical assistance for developing countries	Help developing countries to implement informatization in investment management	Capacity building for developing countries
9	Strengthen capacity building for developing countries to enhance the attractiveness of their policies for investment	Enhance the expertise of member Investment Promotion Agencies (IPAs) in promoting sustainable development-focused investments (e.g., in the environmental sector)	Capacity building for developing countries

(continued)

Table 2 (continued)

	Action plan	Examples of specific actions	Embodied principle(s)
10	Enhance the level of international cooperation in investment facilitation through signing international investment agreements and other means	Encourage home countries to provide outward investment support (e.g. investment guarantees), encourage investors to implement high standards of investment governance and responsible business practices, and encourage the establishment of consultation and cooperation mechanisms between such government departments as Foreign Investment Management Agencies and IPAs	Communication, cooperation

Table 3 Efficiency and cost of investment approvals for selected regions compared with OECD

	OECD	Middle East and North Africa	Sub-Saharan Africa	East Asia and the Pacific region
Business start-up procedures	4.9	7.6	7.4	6.8
Time (day)	9.3	20.7	23.3	25.9
Costs (% of national income per capita)	3.1	22.6	44.4	17.8

Source Credit Assessment Center of China Export and Credit Insurance Corporation *Report on the Status of Investment and Business Facilitation in Various Countries* (2018)

Why does the international community continue to study and discuss investment facilitation? The nature of this topic and the growing awareness of the international community on the importance of investment are the driving forces behind investment facilitation. There is a certain urgency to pushing investment facilitation. The APEC Investment Expert Group (IEG) published a report[7] in 2007 that identified eight significant barriers behind the border to international investment, three of which exist in the area of facilitation: over-regulation, policy uncertainty, and inadequate binding arrangements for contract enforcement. This suggests that the issue of an unfriendly investment environment has become a considerable constraint to the growth of international investments. Furthermore, according to the *Report on the Status of Investment and Business Facilitation in Various Countries (2018)* issued by the Credit Assessment Center of China Export & Credit Insurance Corporation, the investment environment in many countries, especially developing countries, suffers from complex, time-consuming and inefficient administrative approval procedures when compared with developed countries (see Table 3).

[7] Investment Expert Group (2007). "Enhancing Investment Liberalisation and Facilitation in the Asia–Pacific Region (Stage 2): Reducing Behind-the-Border Barriers to Investment".

As shown in the table above, the investment environment in some regions is less efficient and more expensive than OECD countries. An inefficient investment environment is not conducive to attracting foreign investment or using investment for the development of the host country. Nor is it conducive to the regular operation of foreign investors and the stable growth of international investments. Therefore, it is necessary and urgent that administrative structures are made more efficient for all parties involved. The international community recognizes the importance of investment in trade and sustainable development, and that the implementation of investment facilitation is an effective way to promote investment growth. As a source and facilitator of trade, investment is an essential engine of economic growth and a necessary guarantee for sustainable development. Sufficient high-quality investment can generate demand, introduce technology and increase employment in host countries, all of which drive a country's economic growth.

Many countries face challenges such as population expansion, increased poverty and job shortages, while also lacking the resources to cope with these challenges. UNCTAD estimates that developing countries face an annual financing gap of US$2.5 trillion[8] in their efforts to achieve Sustainable Development Goals (SDGs), while public investment and Foreign Direct Investment (FDI) are the two main channels to bridge the financing gap. Foreign Direct Investment (FDI), unlike public investment, does not create a public debt burden, which makes it an important source of financing for development in some countries. However, the *World Investment Report 2019* shows that investment flowing to underdeveloped countries remains below 3% of total global investment and that flows to transitioning economies fell by 28 percentage points from the previous year. These numbers show that some countries are less attractive to foreign investment, and therefore the conditions needed to achieve sustainable development.

However, as a less controversial sub-topic in investment, there is a real possibility of reaching an international consensus on investment facilitation. Topics on investment cover many areas including investment protection, investor-state dispute settlement, and market access. The history of negotiations on investment in the international community is complex and most of these areas are highly divergent and controversial, making it difficult to achieve consensus. In contrast, facilitation issues are less complex and sensitive, focusing on promoting a transparent, efficient investment environment, encouraging international cooperation, instead of changing existing investment laws in host countries.

Discussions and advocacy for investment facilitation in the international community can be seen in the successful *Trade Facilitation Agreement (TFA)* as well as failed experiences in previous negotiations on other investment topics. In practice, investment facilitation has won support from some developing countries, especially those with more outward investment or those dependent on foreign investment. This has made it possible to avoid large-scale differences and confrontation on broader topics of investment while also offering new perspectives and possible paths for growth in international investment and the formation of an international consensus

[8] UNCTAD, Global Action Menu for Investment Facilitation (2016).

on investment. This is supported by the fact that 70 WTO members jointly signed the *Ministerial Statement on Investment Facilitation* and the participation of nearly 80 members in the "Friends of Investment Facilitation" discussion process.[9]

In summary, the reason that investment facilitation has been studied and discussed is mainly because it is so urgently needed. The international community is also fully aware of the importance of investment for trade and sustainable development. Meanwhile, investment facilitation help us avoid more controversial and sensitive issues while opening up viable and effective new paths for investment growth and consensus building in the investment sector.

The potential for implementing investment facilitation is huge. Statistics show that from 2010 to 2016, 80% of the investment policies introduced by countries include support for special economic zones and investment incentives, of which only 20% focus specifically on investment facilitation. However, provisions for investment facilitation are still missing in multiple international investment agreements or simply too weak. The lack of attention paid to investment facilitation policies means that there is a lot of room to increase the impact of investment on economic development through the promotion of facilitation.

3 Opportunities and Challenges in Promoting Investment Facilitation

There are both opportunities and challenges in investment facilitation. Opportunities stem from an international context in which investment facilitation and liberalization have become mainstream in global investment policies, with more economies (including many developing economies) becoming interested in investment facilitation, which have prompted some countries to implement reforms that support investment facilitation.[10] These positive developments are conducive to continued international discussion and research on investment facilitation and reaching a possible consensus.

In April 2017, groups including MIKTA[11] and Friends of Investment Facilitation,[12] along with countries including Russia, China, Argentina and Brazil, submitted proposals to the WTO General Council on how to promote investment facilitation. In November 2017, "The Abuja High Level Forum on Trade and Investment Facilitation and Development", jointly organized by the Friends of Investment Facilitation,

---

[9] High-level Forum on Trade and Investment Facilitation and Development Held in Kazakhstan, Ministry of Commerce, Sept. 30, 2018, http://www.mofcom.gov.cn/article/ae/ai/201809/20180902792059.shtml.

[10] UNCTAD, *World Investment Report 2019*.

[11] MIKTA refers to the following group of countries: Mexico, Indonesia, Republic of Korea, Turkey, and Australia.

[12] At the time of writing, made up of 11 WTO members including China, Brazil, Argentina, Chile, Colombia, Kazakhstan and Mexico.

the Economic Community of West African States and the Government of Nigeria, attracted more than 30 African countries, many of which subsequently expressed their willingness to join the Friends of Investment Facilitation.[13] At the WTO Ministerial Conference held in December of the same year, trade ministers from 70 WTO members signed a Joint Ministerial Statement on Investment Facilitation, calling for a structured discussion on the subject. These members represented almost all informal organizations within the WTO, as well as a wide mix of developed countries and least developed countries.[14]

In September 2018, the Government of Kazakhstan and the Friends of Investment Facilitation jointly organized the "High Level Forum on Trade and Investment Facilitation and Development", which attracted representatives of 30 countries from Eurasia and the Middle East, including Turkey and Tajikistan. In March 2019, the G20 Think Tank Summit (T20) released a document titled *Towards G20 Guiding Principles on Investment Facilitation for Sustainable Development,*[15] which called for the G20 Summit to adopt non-binding guiding principles on investment facilitation. All of these discussions aimed to deepen countries' understanding of investment facilitation and to explore new possible directions, laying a foundation for developing a multilateral framework on investment facilitation.

It should be noted that it is primarily developed countries, which conduct more outward investment, that push for negotiations on investment in the WTO. As destinations for investment, developing countries are often worried that negotiations on investment issues (especially on topics like investment protection, investment liberalization and investment dispute settlement) might undermine their sovereignty. This is why developing countries have generally taken a more passive and conservative attitude. Today, many countries involved in studies and discussions on investment facilitation are developing economies and emerging markets. This is partly due to the fact that some developing countries (e.g., China, Mexico, Brazil) have become essential contributors to Outward Foreign Direct Investment (OFDI) and hope to attract foreign investment through investment facilitation. More recently, investment facilitation is often seen by developing countries as a way to speed up economic development.

However, investment facilitation still faces a number of serious challenges. First, a consensus has yet to be reached on binding multilateral rules. Some countries are resistant to this and oppose negotiating within the framework of WTO. In May 2017, the WTO General Council attempted to discuss trade and investment facilitation, but were challenged by a number of countries, mostly developing countries like as Venezuela and Uganda, which are net recipients of international investment.

There are two main reasons for this opposition. First was the legitimacy of a discussion on investment facilitation. They believed that investment lay outside the scope

---

[13] Nigerian Office for Trade Negotiations, Abuja Statement, November 4, 2017, http://www.notn.gov.ng/post_action/48.

[14] Felipe Hees, Investment Facilitation: leaving the past behind, December 3, 2018.

[15] Towards G20 Guiding Principles on Investment Facilitation for Sustainable Development.

of the Doha Round of negotiations under the "July Package" and the *Nairobi Ministerial Declaration*. Second, and more importantly, they still had doubts about investment facilitation, which they felt could potentially increase administrative burdens, hindering their ability to manage foreign investment or even undermining domestic policy and sovereignty. This was mainly due to the requirement that host countries proactively disclose information, simplify approval processes, incorporate foreign investment into policy and regulatory structures, and maintain good relations with stakeholders. Investment facilitation measures are also risky in the eyes of relatively conservative developing countries, which wary of foreign investment and concerned that foreign investment could erode their administrative decision-making power, thus damaging the domestic economy and society.

In the absence of progress on many existing issues in the Doha Round, especially those of great concern to developing countries, it was naturally felt that the introduction of negotiations on investment facilitation would divert energy and scatter resources. These countries, therefore, believed that the WTO should focus on achieving results in negotiations on existing issues rather than introducing new ones. Opposition from these countries has caused inevitable setbacks in negotiations and rule-making on investment facilitation.

Another challenge to the advancement and implementation of investment facilitation comes from the current protectionist headwinds in international investment, which are not in line with trends of facilitation. Of the 112 new foreign investment policy measures introduced in 2018 by the 55 economies counted in the *World Investment Report 2019*, 34% placed tighter controls on foreign investment, the highest level in nearly 20 years. In addition, countries have also strengthened their foreign investment reviews, with 54% of the new FDI restrictive policies implemented by countries from 2011 to March 2019 expanding the scope of reviews and 14% extending the review timeframe.

The *World Investment Policy Monitoring Report* released by UNCTAD in April 2019 also shows that many developed and developing countries have, to varying degrees, strengthened or expanded national security review and restriction procedures and measures for foreign investment in numerous areas. For example, the "Foreign Investment Risk Review Modernization Act" passed in the United States gives the Committee on Foreign Investment in the United States (CFIUS) greater authority in reviewing foreign investments. This document includes, for instance, language imposing mandatory declarations and extending review timelines. However, this is inconsistent with trends toward investment facilitation, thus creating more difficulties and challenges to promotion on a global scale. As demonstrated, while the implementation and discussion of investment facilitation is moving forward, there are still challenges in actual implementation.

4 Reflections on the Further Development of Investment Facilitation Issues

Given the current issues facing investment facilitation, the authors of this paper have put forward the following thoughts for its further development.

First, economies should continue to promote policies in favor of investment facilitation. Investment facilitation is a global trend and the overall level of investment facilitation in the world continues to increase. Many countries are also implementing investment facilitation reform measures. According to *Doing Business 2019* released by the World Bank, 128 economies worldwide carried out 314 reforms to optimize their business environments in 2017 and 2018. This figure was the highest number since 2003. In addition, the global average for the time required to register a business decreased from 47 days in 2006 to 20 days in 2019. The proportion of registration costs to per capita income also decreased from 76% in 2006 to 23%. Of all regions, Sub-Saharan Africa has seen the highest number of reform measures for seven consecutive years.

Although global trends to optimize business environments continue, in some countries, particularly developing countries, efforts to promote investment facilitation remain limited, which results in higher costs for investors. Economies should set up specialized agencies to explore measures and policies that optimize the domestic investment environment based on the actual domestic situation and the recommendations of international organizations. Countries should also include investment facilitation provisions in international investment agreements and free trade agreements. These agreements are binding and can provide institutional arrangements for signatories to improve investment facilitation.

Brazil has recently signed a new type of investment agreement with a number of economies called the *Cooperation and Investment Facilitation Agreement.*[16] Unlike previous agreements that focus on investment protection and promotion, this agreement focuses on investment facilitation and international cooperation. It also promotes the creation and expansion of investment facilitation rules in the international arena. The implementation of investment facilitation measures by economies and the signing of agreements that include investment facilitation provisions will lay the groundwork for expanding consensus and thus setting international rules on the topic.

Furthermore, economies should also participate in international discussions on investment facilitation in conjunction with "Friends of Investment Facilitation" and related international organizations. Similar to the "Real Good Friends of Services",[17] the "Friends of Investment Facilitation" is an independent sub-group of the WTO.

While it is difficult to eliminate doubts and objections that some WTO members have surrounding investment facilitation in the short term, it is even more challenging

[16] Cooperation and Investment Facilitation Agreement.

[17] Real Good Friends of Services.

to start multilateral negotiations and reach a consensus on multilateral rules on investment facilitation since they require the international community to adopt a more flexible, open, and inclusive discussion path. Economies should participate in transparent discussions organized by the "Friends of Investment Facilitation" that take into account the concerns participating countries, clarify misunderstandings, expand consensus, and continuously include new members in the discussion process. If members are able to reach a general agreement, negotiations could result in a plurilateral agreement, similar to how the *Trade in Services Agreement (TISA)* was reached. Seeking plurilateral agreements through internal discussions among members and opening discussions to members outside the agreement is a viable option for international rule-making when countries cannot reach a multilateral consensus. Major advocates of this model, such as China, Brazil, Argentina, and Russia, should organize and lead international discussions in this area. International organizations such as the WTO, UNCTAD and the World Bank, should also support discussions and strengthen research efforts to develop updated assessment reports and policy recommendations, which help the international community better understand the substance and importance of investment facilitation.

In terms of the specific content of these discussions, the international community should first clarify the scope and definition of investment facilitation. It should also specify what kind of technical support could be available for developing countries and balance responsibilities in investment facilitation. In responding to the concerns of developing countries that investment facilitation could be extended to controversial issues, the international community should also clearly define the boundaries between investment facilitation and issues such as investment protection and investment dispute settlement in studies and discussions on investment facilitation to eliminate at least some of the concerns that countries have. Such discussions should also draw on the experience of the *Agreement on Trade Facilitation* to support capacity-building in developing countries and attract more developing countries to join discussions.

Moreover, discussions should improve the balance of responsibilities. Current discussions on investment facilitation mainly focus on facilitating foreign investment and requires host governments to improve transparency and efficiency. Some countries are worried that these discussions could limit their policy space and sovereignty. Investors, home country governments, and host country governments are all essential players in international investment, and all have responsibilities in promoting investment facilitation. Home governments need to make regulations and support structures related to cross-border investors more transparent and more effectively regulate cross-border investments. Meanwhile, investors should establish and enforce standards of conduct. Incorporating the obligations of home governments and investors into investment facilitation issues and exploring institutional arrangements for shared responsibility, mutual assistance, and trust is necessary and feasible. At the same time, all countries should work together to promote sustainable development, allay the fears of developing countries, and ensure that foreign investment plays a positive role in the sustainable development of host countries.

5 Conclusion

Investment facilitation promotes transparency, efficiency, and predictability in investment and addresses "ground-level obstacles" encountered by investors. This issue has seen more research and attention in recent years due to the international community's growing awareness of the importance of investment. At the same time, investment facilitation serves to circumvent more controversial topics on investment, opening up a new path for reaching overall consensus. The conclusion of the *Agreement on Trade Facilitation* also serves as a source of inspiration and a reference for progress in this area.

At present, international rules on investment facilitation are at the research and discussion stage. However, in some economies they serve to guide policy and are attracting the attention of the international community. This demonstrates the valuable opportunities and broad prospects for advancing the topic of investment facilitation. Nonetheless, investment facilitation also faces challenges, such as outright opposition from some countries and surges in protectionist counter-currents in investment.

To this end, governments and international organizations should continue to strengthen the implementation and enforcement of investment facilitation policies, actively participate in related studies and discussions, and attract more members to join. The international community should make greater efforts to promote discussions on investment facilitation in order to reach a plurilateral agreement that provides for binding investment rules. The conclusion of an investment facilitation framework will very likely be a strong impetus for economic growth in developing countries and contribute greatly to global sustainable development goals.

Xinquan Tu Dean of China WTO Research Institute, University of International Business and Economics, Professor and Ph.D. research fields: World Trade Organization, as well as China-US economic and trade relations.

Yifang Zhao Master of China WTO Research Institute, University of International Business and Economics; research field: world economy.

The Institutional Environment of Chinese Overseas Investment and Its Impact Assessment: Analytical Framework, Empirical Study, and Countermeasure Suggestions

Guoyong Liang and Haoyuan Ding

Abstract This paper establishes an analytical framework for the institutional environment of international investment. On this basis, it uses an empirical analysis of its impact on Chinese firms' overseas investment. The econometric analysis of outbound investment data for listed companies from 2003 to 2016 shows that Chinese firms tend to invest in countries with better institutional environments and lower institutional risk, which implies that improving political systems can significantly promote investment. This paper also analyzes the recent institutional trends in investment and proposes countermeasures at the national and corporate levels.

Keywords Foreign direct investment (FDI) · Institutional environment · Political risk

Enterprises face institutional environments very different from their home countries when making investments abroad. This is generally due to differences in laws and policies and investment agreements between host and home countries. The laws and regulations on outbound investment in the enterprise's home country are also an integral part of the institutional environment for enterprises investing abroad. Institutional environments are generally complex when conducting international investment, and affect the performance of both overseas investment and operations. Chinese enterprises looking to speed up the process of "going out" must fully understand the institutional environment of overseas investment. The purpose of this paper is to establish an analytical framework on the institutional environment for international investment and analyze recent trends. Operational risk in overseas investment is an

G. Liang (✉)
UNCTAD, Geneva, Switzerland

H. Ding
Business School of Shanghai University of Finance and Economics, Shanghai, China

H. H. Wang and M. L. Miao (eds.), *The Challenge of "Going Out"*, The Chinese Enterprise Globalization Series, https://doi.org/10.1007/978-981-99-3326-6_2

important element that affects performance and is closely related to the changing and increasingly restrictive institutional environment in international investment. Therefore, this paper also empirically analyzes the impact of institutional environments on international investments made by Chinese enterprises, using the country risk index to provide a framework for the analysis of overseas investment practices and relevant policies.

1 Institutional Environment in International Investment: An Analytical Framework and Overview

Institutions are the rules of the game or in a society, more formally, are man-made constraints in society that shape human interaction.[1] Institutions can be either formal or informal and affect the behavior of individuals and firms. Formal institutions include laws, regulations, and rules, which include both written norms and unwritten rules. As a well-established code of conduct, an institution is relatively stable and long-lived. International investment institutions referred to in this paper are the specific systems of rules that govern investments by enterprises. They are generally formal and legally binding. Specifically, international investment institutions include regulations on market access, investor treatment and investment protection. In a broad sense, international investment institutions also govern general regulatory issues in the operational phase and host government policies that are not specifically related to foreign investors. A comprehensive understanding of the institutional environment in overseas investment requires a comprehensive analytical framework, including rule carriers and regulatory content that examine issues within temporal and spatial contexts. It also includes how investors are treated and an awareness of the potential impact on the operational performance of investments.

1.1 Carriers of the International Investment Regime: Domestic Laws and International Agreements

The international investment governance system takes into consideration each country's relevant domestic policies and the relevant agreements between countries: i.e., the relevant laws and policies of the host country (economy) and the home country (economy), as well as the international investment agreements signed between the two sides. Simply put, the former is domestic law, while the latter lies in the realm of international law.

Many laws and policies in a host country (the destination of international investment) affect the inflow of foreign investment at the macro level, entry at the industry

[1] Douglass C. North, "Institutions, institutional change and economic performance: institutions", *Journal of Economic Behavior & Organization*,1990–18 (1), 142–144.

level, and specific investments and operations of foreign enterprises at the micro level. Some laws and regulations specify the entry conditions for foreign investment, the treatment of foreign investors, and the protection of foreign investments. In contrast, others deal with investment liberalization and promotion, i.e. how to maximize the contribution of foreign investment to the country's economic development, and how to limit the negative impacts it may bring about. These are the main components of a host country's foreign investment policy system.

Some countries have chosen to enact specific laws to regulate FDI and are the core expression of a country's international investment regime. However, regardless how stable national laws and policies may be, changes may also occur. These adjustments may be either positive initiatives that welcome more foreign investment, improve treatment or enhance protection, or measures that introduce new restrictions or tighten foreign investment regulations. The laws and policies of the home countries of Transnational Companies (TNCs) may also affect international investment. In this regard, the main issue is based in regulations regarding the balance of payments capital account.

While developed countries generally liberalized their capital accounts in the 1970s and 1980s, developing countries continue to impose a certain degree of capital controls. These measures may affect portfolio investment and direct investment, including both capital inflows and outflows. Specific restrictions on FDI are mainly due to the desire to prevent large-scale capital flight and maintain sufficient foreign exchange assets.[2] During the 1990s–2000s, countries gradually relaxed restrictions on FDI by domestic enterprises, while some countries even introduced policies to encourage and promote outward investment. However, after the global financial crisis in 2008 and into the mid-2010s, when trends in anti-globalization intensified, restrictive measures on overseas investment increased. Restrictive measures included "reindustrialization" policies in developed countries, which sought to ensure TNC investment remained onshore and even sought backflow.

International Investment Agreements (IIAs) can be reached at bilateral, regional, plurilateral, and multilateral levels. Unlike international trade, there is no multilateral institution like the WTO to play an overarching supervisory role in international investment. Bilateral Investment Treaties (BITs) mainly establish rules and governance, while other agreements containing investment chapters and provisions are also beginning to play an increasingly important role. BITs refer to bilateral treaties between two countries that regulate and protect international investment, but other agreements (e.g., regional and bilateral FTAs) may also address investment-related issues. Several multilateral agreements and mechanisms like the Convention Establishing the Multilateral Investment Guarantee Agency (MIGA) and the Convention on the Settlement of Investment Disputes Between States and Nationals of Other States exist as guarantees for investment and dispute settlement. From a global perspective, the interweaving of thousands of international agreements make the governance of international investment look like a "jumble". As of 2018, there were more than

[2] UNCTAD, *World Investment Report 2019: FDI from Developing and Transition Economies: Implications for Development*, Geneva and New York: United Nations, 2006.

3,300 IIAs, which included more than 2,900 BITs and over 380 other agreements with investment chapters and provisions. Approximately 2,600 agreements are currently in force.[3] Despite varying in content, these agreements generally follow standard rules on the treatment and protection of foreign investors. These rules are a strong driver of international investment and one of the institutional cornerstones of globalization. However, such a large body of agreements is characterized by extraordinary complexity, overlap, and inconsistency, highlighting the need for reform.

1.2 Regulatory Content and Spatial/Temporal Dimensions of IIAs

Regulatory content of international investment agreements mainly outlines the definition of FDI, market access provisions, investor treatment, investment protection, and dispute settlements. These elements determine how host countries define foreign investors and FDI, which industries foreign investors may and may not enter, how to protect their investment and operational activities, and how investment disputes are resolved. Unlike dispute settlement in international trade, which is conducted on a state-to-state basis, the investor-state dispute settlement (ISDS) mechanism used in the investment sector is between enterprises (investors) and states (host governments). Currently, the International Center for Settlement of Investment Disputes (ICSID) is the leading international arbitration body for international investment disputes.

In terms of the temporal dimension, international investment can be divided into two phases—pre-establishment and post-establishment. For firms, this equates to the at-entry and after-entry phases for a particular investment destination, also known as the investment and operation phases. International investment is mainly concerned with the relationship between the source and the host country, and in exceptional cases may involve a third country. When considering investment paths, investments from one country to another may be made through a third country. This is called trans-shipping investment and specifically may involve offshore financial centers for tax purposes or special purpose entities (SPEs). In another case, a company from one country may also invest in its home country by establishing a branch in another country or region. This action is called round-tripping investment and is explicitly meant to take advantage of tax and other benefits provided by the home country to foreign enterprises.

The treatment of investors is an important issue in the international investment regime. Bilateral investment agreements provide different standards of treatment for foreign investors, such as Fair and Equitable Treatment (FET), Most-Favored-Nation Treatment (MFN), and National Treatment (NT). In national treatment, the host country provides foreign investors with treatment no less favorable than

[3] UNCTAD, *World Investment Report 2019: Special Economic Zones*, Geneva and New York: United Nations, 2019.

domestic enterprises, which explicitly includes both the pre-establishment and post-establishment phases. The former is essentially a matter of investment market access. In order to provide "pre-establishment national treatment" to foreign investors, the host country may place specific industries on a "negative list" to restrict foreign investment. In China's international investment policy, pre-entry national treatment and negative list management are relatively new concepts. In July 2013, China agreed to use this as a basis for substantive negotiations on a bilateral investment agreement with the US, but after six years, US-China investment agreement negotiations are still ongoing. However, pre-establishment national treatment and negative list management have been rolled out nationwide from their origins in pilot free trade zones. Adopted on March 15, 2019, China's Foreign Investment Law makes explicit provisions for implementing these new concepts, thus establishing their legal status.

1.3 Impact and Risk of International Investment Institutional Environments on Enterprises

Different institutional environments in international investment affect where enterprises choose to invest. The institutional environment of a host country will determine how and in what sector companies invest. It also influences the impact of the investment and how enterprises perform as there are different "transaction costs".

Entry modes are a crucial topic in research on international business practices, specifically whether an investor chooses to establish a sole proprietorship, a joint venture, or acquire an existing company in the host country. In an even broader sense, it can also involve exports and other non-equity forms of cooperation.

In a broader sense, industrial policy is also part of the institutional environment for investment in a broad sense and has a significant impact on the entry choices of enterprises. When industrial policies of both the home country and host country support companies, they are more inclined to enter overseas markets by setting up joint ventures.[4]

The greater the "cultural differences" between two countries, the more investors tend to use joint ventures or mergers. Kogut and Singh found that companies are most likely to choose joint ventures when first expanding in markets with significant cultural differences, while cross-border mergers and acquisitions are more common in countries with similar cultures.[5] A related concept is "institutional distance".[6]

---

[4] Du Jian and Zheng Qiuxia, "Joint venture or sole proprietorship?—The impact of industrial policy on the FDI entry pattern of Chinese MNCs" [J]. *Journal of Xidian University (Social Science Edition)*, 2017 (3).

[5] Bruce Kogut and Harbir Singh, "The effect of national culture on the choice of entry mode" [J]. *Journal of International Business Studies*, 19 (3): 411–432, 1988.

[6] Dean Xu and Oded Shenkar, "Institutional distance and the multinational enterprise", *The Academy of Management Review*, 27 (4): 608–618, 2002.

The stringency of host country policies and regulations is also something that affects how investors enter a market. The more stringent the restrictions, the more foreign investors prefer joint ventures to sole proprietorships or acquisitions. Developing countries tend to be more welcoming to foreign investors that invest in or establish new firms, while placing more restrictions on the acquisition of local firms in the host country to protect domestic national industries.[7] However, this is also becoming increasingly common in some developed countries.

The risks associated with international investment are manifested in two important ways: first, increases in restrictions and specific regulatory barriers to international investment; and second, in the uncertainties of international investment at both the international and national levels. Institutional risk can substantially impact investors in terms of both their investments and operational performance. Empirical studies show that the institutional environment of the host country has a significant impact on the outbound investment performance of Chinese MNCs. The size of the host country's economy is also positively linked to the overseas subsidiaries of Chinese MNEs while country risk is negatively related to performance.[8]

2 The Impact of Institutional Environments of International Investment on Chinese Enterprises: An Empirical Analysis Based on Country Risk and Institutional Factors

The ultimate outcome of any investment is determined by the rules in play, the strength of the parties involved, and the specific process in the real-world game. In economics, the main source of the rules are laws and regulations, while in international economics, international agreements serve as a more important source of rules. This is because the transactions involve market players from different countries, and the rules are made through agreements. At the same time, the laws, regulations, and related policies of the host and source countries (especially the former) are also essential components of this system of rules. This combination of international agreements and domestic regulations make up the international investment regime.

As mentioned in the previous section, risk is an important factor in the international investment regime that affects investment and business performance. In this section, we have chosen the International Country Risk Guide (ICRG), published by the PRS Group, as our measure of institutions to carry out an empirical analysis of the impact of the institutional environment on Chinese international investment. This index is widely used by international organizations including the United Nations (UN), the World Bank, and the International Monetary Fund (IMF), which use the

[7] Cao Linjing and Zhou Zhengfang, "Choice of two FDI entry modes: greenfield investment and M&A investment" [J]. *Inner Mongolia Science Technology & Economy*, 2006 (19): 92–94.

[8] Fu Zhu, "Cultural Distance, Entry Mode and Performance" [D]. *Southwestern University Of Finance And Economics*, 2010.

ICRG to assess a country's institutional development. Many scholars also use the ICRG composite index to measure a country's overall institutional level,[9] while some scholars prefer to choose a dimension or sub-index to reflect a country's specific institutional risk.[10, 11, 12]

The PRS Group forecasts and analyzes risk for 140 countries and regions worldwide every month. It divides country risk into two basic components: the ability to pay and willingness to pay, in which the former consists of economic and financial risks, and the latter is embodied by political risks. Thus, the ICRG index is composed of sub-indicators in three dimensions, namely political risk, economic risk, and financial risk, as well as a composite indicator. Among them, political risk involves 13 sub-indicators, while economic risk and financial risk include five sub-indicators each. The range of values for each sub-indicator reflect the weight of that element, while the ratio of the weight given to the three sub-indicators in the composite indicator is 2:1:1. The formula for the ICRG composite risk index (CR) is $CR = 0.5 \times (PR + ER + FR)$. Specifically, composite risk (CR) makes up 100% of the risk involved, while political risk (PR) accounts for 50% and economic risk (ER) and financial risk (FR) respectively account for 25%. The higher the score, the lower the level of institutional risk and the better the institutional environment in a country, and vice versa.

The existing literature generally uses country-level macro data to explore the impact of a host country's institutional environment on outward foreign direct investment (OFDI). But this section explores this issue using firm-level micro data to fill the research gap in this area. We have constructed the following econometric model:

$$OFDI_{ict} = \alpha + \beta Institution_{ct-1} + \gamma_1 Experience_{ict-1} + \gamma_2 X_{ct-1} + \theta_{it} + \theta_c + \varepsilon_{ict}$$

In this formula, *i*, *c*, and *t* denote the firm, country, and year, respectively. $\mathrm{OFDI}_{\mathrm{ict}}$ refers to the investment of firm *i* in country *c* in year *t*. We set two variables: one is a *dummy* variable to show whether the investment is made and the other is a *number* variable indicating the number of projects that are part of the OFDI. $Institution_{ct-1}$ denotes the composite indicator, three sub-indicators, and other sub-indicators of ICRG. $Experience_{ict-1}$ denotes whether firm *i* has had investment experience in country *c* before year $t-1$. X_{ct-1} is a set of country-level control variables that we selected including GDP growth, per capita GDP, and the share of values of imports and exports on GDP (Trade). All explanatory variables are lagged one period relative to the explained ones. θ_{it} and θ_c are fixed effects of the firm, year and country,

[9] Pierre-Guillaume Méon and KhalidSekkat, "FDI Waves, Waves of Neglect of Political Risk", *World Development*, 2012.40 (11), 2194–2205.

[10] Ivar Kolstad and Espen Villanger, "Determinants of foreign direct investment in services", *European Journal of Political Economy*, 2008. 24 (2), 518–533.

[11] Elias Papaioannou, "What drives international financial flows? Politics, institutions and other determinants", *Journal of Development Economics*, 2009.88 (2), 269–281.

[12] Yang Jiao and Shang-Jin Wei, "Intrinsic Openness and Endogenous Institutional Quality", NBER working paper (No. w24052), 2017.

respectively, and ε_{ict} is a random disturbance term, with standard errors clustered to the firm level.

OFDI data was obtained from two databases. Specifically, greenfield data came from fDiMarkets, while cross-border M&A data came from the SDC database. GDP growth rates, per capita GDP, and total GDP were obtained from the World Bank, while import and export data were obtained from the WMF. We first matched the two OFDI databases with the databases of CSMAR listed companies and then merged the matched data according to the stock codes of specific listed companies. Then, we expanded the corporate data based on information about the country and region where the investment occurred and excluded financial companies, as well as missing samples with conventional corporate control variables and country-level control variables. Ultimately, we obtained a total of 640,768 firm-year-country observations for 598 listed firms in 114 OFDI countries and regions for the period 2003–2016.

Table 1 reveals the regression results of the three ICRG sub-indicators and their Composite Rating. The results show that the ICRG coefficient is significantly positive regardless of whether the MNCs are engaged in OFDI or even a number of OFDI projects. This indicates that the more stable the institutional environment of the host country, the more enterprises tend to invest more in that country in both volume and number of projects. Considering the three dimensions of risk, the lower the host country's political and economic risk rating, the easier it is for firms to invest. Financial risk was not a significant factor. As for the control variables, experience investing in a host country, faster economic growth and lower per capita GDP in the host country make MNCs more likely to invest. The results also show that the share of total exports and imports in the national economy has no significant effect on the decision of an MNCs to engage in OFDI.

Furthermore, we explored the impact of specific institutional factors and risks on firms' OFDI decisions. This included government stability, socioeconomic conditions, investment profiles, and external conflicts in the host country. Political stability measures the extent to which the government implements publicly announced plans and the chances of regime change. Socioeconomic conditions refer to socioeconomic pressures that may limit the government's effectiveness or exacerbate popular discontent. Investment profile refers to investment risks not covered by other political, economic, and financial indicators and measures contract enforceability/probability of government expropriation, profits return and delayed payments. External conflict evaluates the various political risks involved in the host government's diplomatic activities. The empirical results in Table 2 show that the regression coefficients for government stability, socioeconomic conditions, and external conflicts are all significantly positive at the 1% level. The results also show that the effect of the investment environment on whether MNCs engage in OFDI is significant at the 10% level. These results suggest that the political system plays a noteworthy role in improving OFDI, i.e. the better the institutional environment of the host country, the more likely it is to attract foreign firms to conduct OFDI.

The findings of this paper are consistent with the existing literature. For example, for ICRG, Méon and Sekkat find that FDI is negatively affected by institutional

Table 1 Institution environment and OFDI of the host country

	(1)	(2)	(3)	(4)	(5)	(6)	(7)	(8)
	Dummy	Number	Dummy	Number	Dummy	Number	Dummy	Number
	Composite Rating		Political Risk Rating		Economic Risk Rating		Financial Risk Rating	
Institution	0.00419[a]	0.00313[a]	0.00773[a]	0.00583[a]	0.00217[a]	0.00161[a]	−0.000587	−0.000432
	(0.00094)	(0.00070)	(0.00136)	(0.00101)	(0.00046)	(0.00036)	(0.00046)	(0.00034)
Experience	0.0379[a]	0.0288[a]	0.0379[a]	0.0288[a]	0.0379[a]	0.0288[a]	0.0379[a]	0.0288[a]
	(0.00512)	(0.00396)	(0.00513)	(0.00396)	(0.00512)	(0.00396)	(0.00513)	(0.00396)
GDP growth	0.00499[a]	0.00381[a]	0.00440[a]	0.00336[a]	0.00472[a]	0.00362[a]	0.00630[a]	0.00480[a]
	(0.00111)	(0.00081)	(0.00111)	(0.00080)	(0.00111)	(0.00081)	(0.00117)	(0.00086)
GDP per capita	−0.00369[a]	−0.00274[a]	−0.00393[a]	−0.00293[a]	−0.00347[a]	−0.00258[a]	−0.00297[a]	−0.00221[a]
	(0.00064)	(0.00048)	(0.00066)	(0.00049)	(0.00062)	(0.00046)	(0.00060)	(0.00045)
Trade	−0.0007	−0.000697	−0.000975	−0.000907	−0.000307	−0.000404	−0.000189	−0.000317
	(0.00075)	(0.00057)	(0.00076)	(0.00058)	(0.00072)	(0.00055)	(0.00075)	(0.00058)
Firm-year FE	Yes	Yes	Yes	Yes	Yes	Yes	Yes	Yes
Destination FE	Yes	Yes	Yes	Yes	Yes	Yes	Yes	Yes
Observed values	624,098	624,098	624,098	624,098	624,098	624,098	624,098	624,098
R^2	0.032	0.032	0.032	0.032	0.032	0.032	0.032	0.032

P.S.: a, b, and c indicate significance at the 1, 5, and 10% levels, respectively

Table 2 The political environment and OFDI of the host country

	(1)	(2)	(3)	(4)	(5)	(6)	(7)	(8)
	Dummy	Number	Dummy	Number	Dummy	Number	Dummy	Number
	Government stability		Socioeconomic condition		Investment profile		External conflict	
Institution index	0.00300[a]	0.00227[a]	0.00366[a]	0.00273[a]	0.000868[c]	0.000739[c]	0.00783[a]	0.00582[a]
	(0.00059)	(0.00045)	(0.00062)	(0.00044)	(0.00052)	(0.00038)	(0.00137)	(0.00104)
Firm experience	0.0379[a]	0.0288[a]	0.0379[a]	0.0288[a]	0.0379[a]	0.0288[a]	0.0378[a]	0.0288[a]
	(0.00512)	(0.00396)	(0.00513)	(0.00396)	(0.00513)	(0.00396)	(0.00513)	(0.00396)
GDP growth	0.00484[a]	0.00369[a]	0.00530[a]	0.00404[a]	0.00617[a]	0.00469[a]	0.00457[a]	0.00351[a]
	(0.00113)	(0.00083)	(0.00116)	(0.00084)	(0.00117)	(0.00085)	(0.00110)	(0.00080)
GDP per capita	−0.00365[a]	−0.00272[a]	−0.00441[a]	−0.00328[a]	−0.00338[a]	−0.00254[a]	−0.00322[a]	−0.00239[a]
	(0.00062)	(0.00047)	(0.00065)	(0.00048)	(0.00064)	(0.00047)	(0.00061)	(0.00045)
Trade	−0.00037	−0.000451	−0.000898	−0.000845	−0.00042	−0.000499	−0.00109	−0.000985[c]
	(0.00072)	(0.00055)	(0.00074)	(0.00057)	(0.00072)	(0.00055)	(0.00075)	(0.00057)
Firm-year FE	Yes	Yes	Yes	Yes	Yes	Yes	Yes	Yes
Destination FE	Yes	Yes	Yes	Yes	Yes	Yes	Yes	Yes
Observed values	624,098	624,098	624,098	624,098	624,098	624,098	624,098	624,098
R^2	0.032	0.032	0.032	0.032	0.032	0.032	0.032	0.032

P.S.: a, b, and c indicate significance at the 1, 5, and 10% levels, respectively

risks in the host country.[13] In looking at Swedish manufacturing MNCs from 1987 to 1998 and ICRG indicators, Tekin-Koru[14] measures the institutional status of the host country, demonstrating at the firm level, the lower the institutional risk in the host country, the more greenfield investment and M&A is conducted by MNCs. This paper also demonstrates that Chinese firms prefer to invest in countries with better institutional environments and lower institutional risks at the micro-level.

3 Institutional Environment and Risks of Global International Investment: Current Trends and Coping Strategies

Since the early 2000s, Chinese outbound investment has snowballed, and overseas business interests have swelled. By the end of 2017, the number of offshore institutions and enterprises reached 39,000. The amount totaled US$6 trillion in assets while the stock of Chinese OFDI reached US$1.8 trillion. Meanwhile, new global trends in international investment agreements and various new developments in investment policies appeared at the national level. For instance, the restrictiveness and regulatory barriers to international investment have increased. Adverse changes for the international investment regime at both the international and national levels imply investment and operational risks for Chinese companies. Overall, China's vast overseas interests are increasingly exposed to various risks. Although complicated, there are two main concerns: (1) institutional obstacles to investing in developed countries and (2) institutional risks in developing countries. Both issues require a proper response from nations and enterprises.

3.1 New Trends in International Investment Agreements (IIAs)

Historically, IIAs have evolved from the "great expansion" starting in the mid-1980s to the "great adjustment" after the 2008 financial crisis. The adjustment is manifested in several aspects: the first is when quantity is reduced or improved. The second is the divergence of positions. On the one hand, some countries endeavor to promote investment liberalization, while on the other hand, some tend to take more conservative policy positions. The former is embodied in the gradual promotion of

13 Pierre-Guillaume Méon and KhalidSekkat, "FDI Waves, Waves of Neglect of Political Risk", *World Development*, 2012.40 (11), 2194–2205.

14 Ayça Tekin-Koru, "Asymmetric effects of trade costs on entry modes: Firm level evidence", *European Economic Review*, 2012.56 (2), 277–294.

pre-establishment national treatment, mainly led by the United States and other developed countries, while the latter is reflected by the withdrawal from existing agreements by the South and other developing countries. The third is the "rebalance of contents", expressed in the changes in the rights and obligations of investors and host countries, particularly the balance between private investor protection and sovereign state regulation. A more conservative policy stance and changes in investor-host country relations may imply significant institutional obstacles and risks.

After the global financial crisis, IIAs have also shown new trends. Firstly, there has been a rise in "regionalism". This is evidenced by the increasing drive to establish investment agreements and liberalization within and between regions, with regions playing a more active role in investment rule-making beyond the bilateral level. Second is a combination of free trade negotiations increasingly bundle trade, investment, and other issues. This has resulted in a new system of international economic rules. Third, international investment rules have undergone significant changes. Along with this "rebalance," agreements are increasingly focused on the regulatory power of host countries and policy space. In addition, beyond the traditional core of investor protection, IIAs have also begun to address new areas such as liberalization, facilitation, and investment promotion. At the same time, investment agreements have strengthened some sustainable development factors related to the environment, society, and labor.

Against the backdrop of the intensifying anti-globalization in recent years, the US has chosen yet again to favor bilateral international economic and trade rule-making over regional agreement. As a result, it has withdrawn from the Trans-Pacific Partnership (TPP) and stalled the Transatlantic Trade and Investment Partnership (TTIP). Since trade and investment are closely linked, this has inevitably influenced the development of global investment rules. Both Obama and Trump have chosen to leave the multilateral system behind and start again, only with notably different specific approaches. The Obama administration paid particular attention to the regional level, with the appearance of the so-called "Two-Ocean Strategy" as represented by the TPP and TTIP. Meanwhile, Trump's trade team attached greater importance to the bilateral level by implementing a "bilateral strategy" to gain an advantage in one-on-one negotiations and maximize their interests. Obama's approach solves problems of trade friction and differences mainly within multilateral rules, while Trump's approach pursued unilateralism, while at the same time challenging existing institutional arrangements and risks by launching a major trade war. Despite the US's "withdrawal," 11 countries signed the CPTPP (Comprehensive and Progressive Agreement for Trans-Pacific Partnership), while Regional Comprehensive Economic Partnership (RCEP) negotiations remain underway. This implies that there is still an impetus for setting economic and trade rules at the regional level. At the same time, bilateral FTA negotiations between developed economies have intensified. If the FTA between major developed economies breaks down, the global trade rules system will need to be restructured and could lead to the development of a new set of investment rules, and China would inevitably be adversely affected.

3.2 *New Trends in Investment Policy at the National Level*

From a global perspective, investment policies at the national level have always coexisted with promoting liberalization and strengthening restrictions, with the former reaching a higher proportion than the latter. A rebound in the proportion of restrictive measures, reflecting the rise of investment protectionism, was seen in 2016. Likewise, in 2018, there was a clear tendency for restrictive measures to intensify. The new restrictive regulations for foreign investors mainly targeted national security considerations, focusing on investments in infrastructure, core technologies, the military sector, sensitive business assets, and residential housing.[15] Restrictive measures have also been strengthened at the implementation level. In 2018, M&A deals blocked due to national security concerns totaled more than US$150 billion globally.

Chinese companies conducting outbound investment face increasing regulatory barriers overseas in the long-term. As measured by Guo Lu, after the financial crisis, overseas regulatory barriers have increased annually as the scale of outbound investment by Chinese enterprises has expanded.[16] Europe has higher regulatory barriers for Chinese companies investing in the region from a regional perspective. At the same time, the US has scrutinized investments from China and placed stricter regulations on Chinese companies investing in sensitive technology areas since the start of the trade war. Other Asian countries have slightly lower regulatory barriers to Chinese investments than the global average, and African countries have the lowest regulatory barriers to China. Chinese companies face complex political issues when investing abroad, especially in terms of state-owned enterprises, industries (natural resources, infrastructure, high-tech industries), and large-scale projects. The "political science" of overseas corporate investment stands out in two aspects: the institutional barriers to investment in developed countries and the institutional risks to investment in developing countries.[17] In the first sense, repeated setbacks Chinese companies have faced in acquisitions in the US and other countries reflect the protectionist tendencies of some developed countries. In the second sense, Chinese business interests are exposed to all kinds of political risks due to China's rise and its expanding global presence continues to expand.

Consistent with global trends, national security reviews are vital for developing countries to restrict Chinese investment. The US has been conducting national security reviews on foreign investment, specifically those by the Committee on Foreign Investment in the United States (CFIUS), established in 1975. Judging from the number of cases reviewed in recent years, the committee is particularly concerned with investments from China. The number of reviews is also disproportionate to the scale of investments. Since 2018, the US's security review of Chinese investments has become increasingly stringent. On March 22, the committee released the results

---

[15] UNCTAD, *World Investment Report 2019.*

[16] Guo Lu. "Regulatory barriers to Chinese enterprises' overseas investment in host countries—quantification, causes and countermeasures" [J]. *International Economic Cooperation,* 2018 (4): 30–34.

[17] See Guoyong Liang's speech at the Caixin Summit 2011.

of 301 investigations. Accordingly, US President Donald Trump signed a memorandum requesting the US trade representative take specific measures, including imposing tariffs. President Trump also requested that the Treasury Department and other departments consider restricting Chinese companies' investments in specific areas in the US. On August 1, the US Congress passed the Foreign Investment Risk Review Modernization Act which strengthened investment reviews and controls. Various EU member states have followed suit by imposing similar security reviews. In 2018, France and Germany expanded the scope of their foreign investment reviews which covered several new technology areas and held clear implications for China.

3.3 Responding to Institutional Risks and Protecting Business Interests: Countermeasures at Both Governmental and Corporate Levels

Protecting investors from institutional risks has been a central issue in international investment rule-making. In this regard, Bilateral Investment Treaties (BITs) have set up a basic institutional framework to provide investors with compensation for expropriation and capital transfer. BITs also play a role in settling disputes between investors and host countries because the agreements often invoke international arbitration mechanisms. In addition, the connection between domestic institutional arrangements and international agreements also protects investors: under the Overseas Investment Insurance System, investors are promptly compensated for losses due to political risks. Insurers are also granted subrogation rights under BITs to claim compensation from host countries. The US is the pioneer of this bilateral model. As an emerging outbound investment power, China faces common and individual challenges in protecting its business interests abroad. This means that relevant institutional changes should be holistically based on international experience to create a stable, transparent, flexible, and effective institutional structure. At the national level, governments should introduce special legislation for overseas investment. Regarding the introduction of foreign capital, China passed the Foreign Investment Law, which came into force on January 1, 2020. However, the processing of legislation on outbound investment should be sped up.

While signing new bilateral and regional investment agreements and expanding geographical coverage is positive, the content of the agreements should be further improved, and the quality of the rules should be strengthened. Effectively preventing institutional risks and protecting overseas business interests requires joint efforts by both the state and the market. The former should make improvements in the overseas investment insurance system, strengthening governments management and improvement of services throughout the course of investment and in economic diplomacy and economic and trade consultations. The latter mainly involves political risk consulting and related financial and intermediary services. To protect overseas interests, the Chinese government has established a relatively comprehensive mechanism for providing warnings, consular protection, as well as security, and interdepartmental coordination. However, there is a need to further improve the institutional risk response system with an eye on overseas business interests.

At the micro-level, Chinese enterprises that are going global should establish comprehensive institutional risk prevention and response mechanisms and should base their overseas investment operations in sustainable development of the economy, environment, and society in the host country, avoiding environmental, social and other sensitive issues that could trigger political risk. The M&A activities of Chinese companies in developed countries mainly focuses on acquiring technology and resources, which may conflict with the host country's policy objectives, thus creating high entry barriers and other institutional obstacles for Chinese enterprises. This is particularly evident in the US. Therefore, as Chinese acquisitions often face skepticism and even hostility, it may be advisable to encourage companies to implement large-scale investment projects in the US to build confidence in Chinese investment among communities in the host country by creating jobs. For example, there is great potential for Chinese investment in manufacturing in the US as exemplified by Wanxiang and Fuyao, while new territory in areas such as infrastructure could also be explored. This would establish a solid foundation for bilateral investment between the two countries if US-China economic and trade negotiations are to be successful and breakthroughs in bilateral investment agreement negotiations are made.

Guoyong Liang Ph.D., is an Economic Affairs Officer at the Investment and Enterprise Division of the United Nations Conference on Trade and Development (UNCTAD), as well as a Non-resident Senior Fellow of the Collaborative Innovation Center of China Pilot Free Trade Zone and Center for China and Globalization (CCG). He has written numerous works in the field of international economics and development, especially for international investment, where he has made pioneering research.

Haoyuan Ding Ph.D., is an associate professor, doctoral supervisor and assistant dean at the Business School of the Shanghai University of Finance and Economics. His research focuses on international economics and Chinese economy, being a recipient of the Shanghai Morning Glory Scholar and Pushan Academic Research Award for fruitful academic achievements in related fields. The content of this article only represents the author's personal views.

Underlying Trends and Influencing Factors

An Analysis of Outbound Investment by Chinese Enterprises

CCG Enterprises Globalization Research Group

Abstract 2017 saw a sharp decline in Foreign Direct Investment (FDI) worldwide due to a wave of anti-globalization. Overseas investments by Chinese enterprises also fluctuated during that year as entry thresholds for Chinese investors in developed countries rose, which marked the first decrease in overseas investment by Chinese enterprises in a decade. In order to better understand the current state of Chinese enterprises overseas and their role in the globalization process, the CCG Enterprises Globalization Research Group designed an annual "Chinese Enterprise Globalization Questionnaire". The purpose of the survey is to better understand the current situation and challenges that Chinese enterprises face, present empirical data on existing and planned Chinese overseas investments and provide a reference to relevant policymakers. It consists of five parts: (1) understanding the basic state of outbound investment by Chinese enterprises, including regions, industries, investment methods and profitability; (2) exploring the key factors affecting overseas investment; (3) exploring the problems Chinese enterprises face when "going out"; (4) identifying the impact of policy changes on enterprises; and (5) understanding the current state and prospects of enterprises participating in the Belt and Road Initiative (BRI).

Keywords Chinese enterprises · Foreign investment · Investment risk · Investment policy · The Belt and Road Initiative

CCG Enterprises Globalization Research Group (✉)
Center for China and Globalization, Beijing, China

H. H. Wang and M. L. Miao (eds.), *The Challenge of "Going Out"*, The Chinese Enterprise Globalization Series, https://doi.org/10.1007/978-981-99-3326-6_3

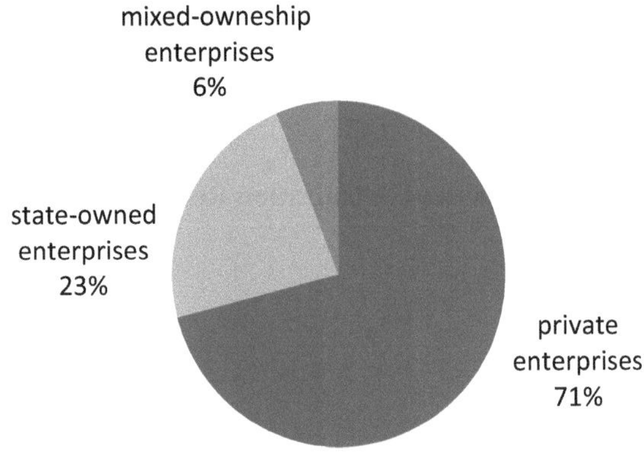

Fig. 1 Proportions of types of enterprises surveyed

1 Basic Information on Outbound Investment by Chinese Enterprises

1.1 Significant Increases in the Amount of Outbound Investment, Rapid Efforts by SMEs

Among the enterprises that participated in this annual survey, 71% were private enterprises, 23% were state-owned enterprises, and 6% were mixed-ownership enterprises. Through constant tracking, CCG found that the pace of overseas development by private enterprises has gradually accelerated, becoming the main force of overseas investment by Chinese enterprises (see Fig. 1).

Enterprises with overseas investments of less than US$5 million accounted for the most significant proportion of the total by the end of 2017 at 45%, a 5% decline from the same period in 2016. Enterprises with investments ranging between US$100 million to US$1 billion accounted for 15%, having risen by 5% year-on-year. In addition, companies with investments valued at US$5–10 million and US$10–50 million accounted for 9% each. After that, companies with investments in the range of US$1–3 billion saw a slight increase of 2% year-on-year. Finally, in FY2017, there was a significant decline in companies with large investments above US$3 billion, down by 57% year-on-year (see Fig. 2).

1.2 Overseas Investment Mainly in Southeast Asia and North Africa, SEA Markets to Remain Popular for 2–3 Years

Research shows that the majority of Chinese enterprises invest in Southeast Asia, accounting for 16% of all overseas investment by Chinese enterprises. This is followed by Chinese enterprises investing in North Africa (9%), the EU and Central

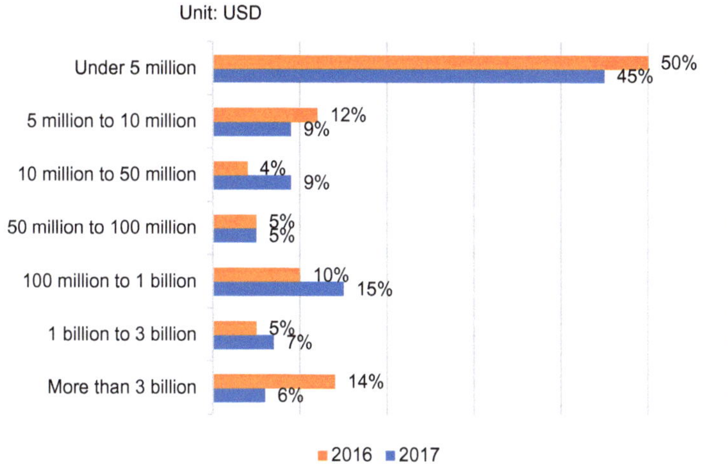

Fig. 2 Scale of outbound investment of surveyed enterprises

Asia (8%); and Latin America, West Asia, South Asia, Eastern Europe, and regions other than North Africa (7%); Australia and Central Europe (4%); and Canada and free ports like the Cayman Islands (3%) (see Fig. 3).

According to the survey, in the next 2–3 years, Chinese enterprises will most likely continue overseas investing in Southeast Asian countries, which is estimated to account for 10% of total future overseas investment by Chinese enterprises. This is followed by 7% in the US, West Asia, Latin America, the EU, and North Africa. As the BRI approaches its fifth year, increased anti-globalization in the US and other developed countries in Europe means that it is expected more Chinese enterprises will invest in the BRI economies in the future, with Southeast Asia and Africa expected to become investment hotspots for Chinese enterprises (see Fig. 4).

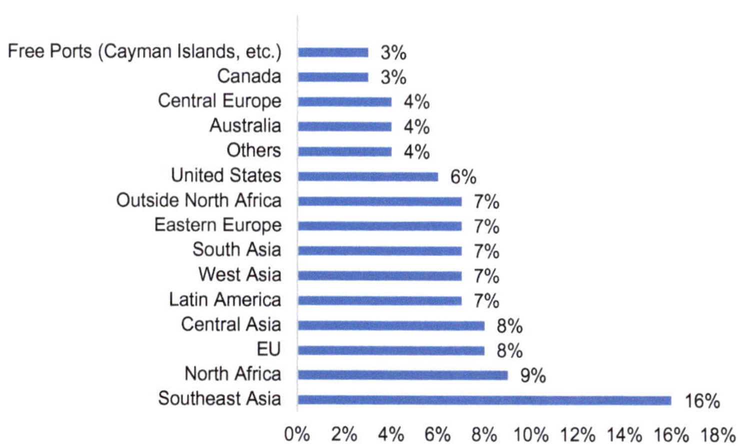

Fig. 3 Outbound investment by country (region)

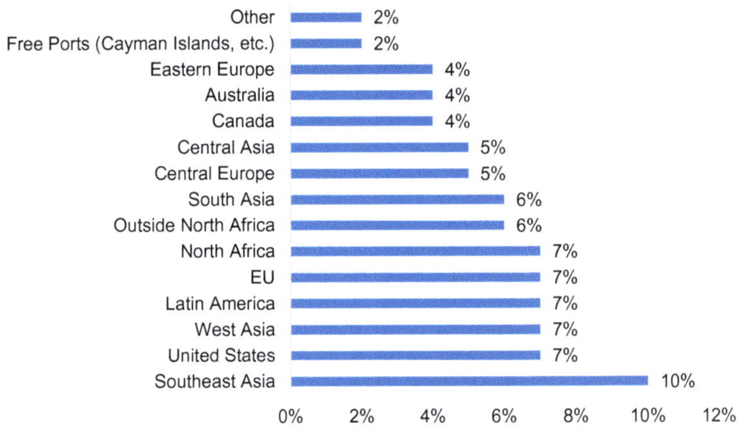

Fig. 4 Potential investment over the next 2–3 years by region

1.3 A New Model for Chinese Enterprises "Going Out"—Going Global as a Group

According to available data, when developing a "going out" strategy, more than half of the enterprises surveyed preferred to partner with Chinese enterprises, while 37% did not (Fig. 5).

When it comes to choosing local partners, 29% of the enterprises interviewed tended to cooperate with "local private enterprises"; 19% with "local state-owned enterprises"; 12% with "Chinese private enterprises (inc. Hong Kong, Macao, and Taiwan)" and 11% with "Chinese state-owned enterprises (inc. Hong Kong, Macao and Taiwan)" respectively; while 10% preferred "foreign enterprises investing locally". Lastly, only 8% of the enterprises maintained cooperative relationships with joint ventures (see Fig. 6).

Fig. 5 Intention of surveyed enterprises to partner with Chinese enterprises on a "Going Out" strategy

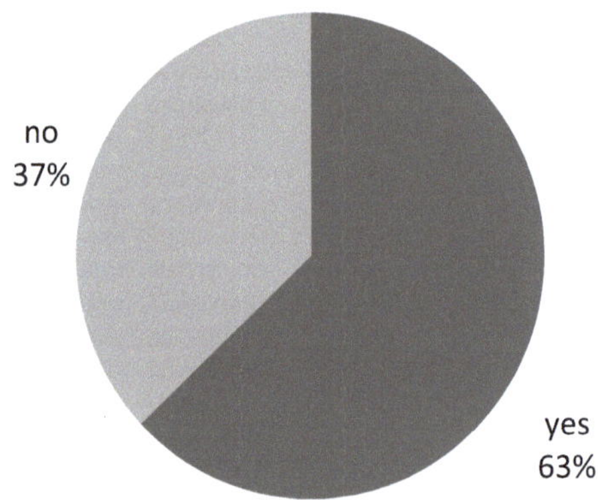

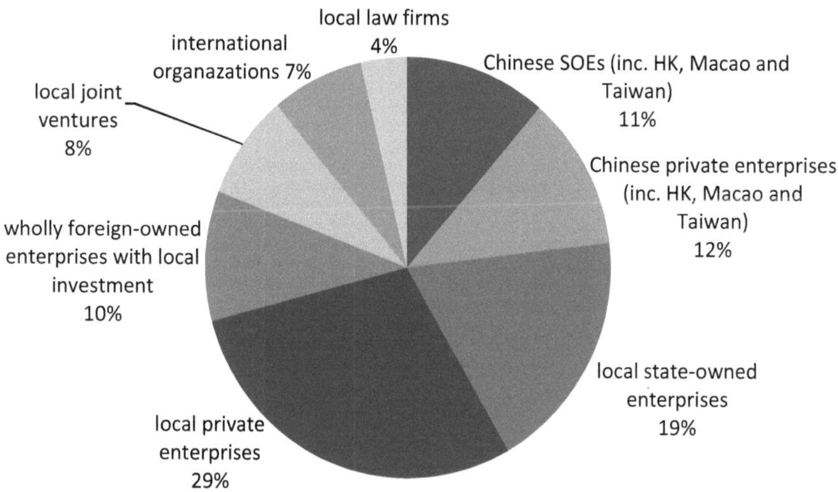

Fig. 6 Choice of investment partners in destination countries

1.4 Diverse Investment Portfolios—Construction and Mining Receive Most Funding

Overseas investment by Chinese enterprises was focused mainly in the construction and mining industries, each accounting for 12%. This was followed by agriculture, forestry, animal husbandry, and fisheries, accounting for 10%. Investments in transportation and infrastructure accounted for 9% of investment, while electricity, heating, gas, water, and drainage made up 7%. Software and information industries accounted for 6% while the remained was made up of various industries, each of which accounted for less than 5% (see Fig. 7).

1.5 More Overseas Representative Offices Established by Enterprises "Going Out", Investment Focused on Core Business

In terms of investment models, 47% of the surveyed enterprises established overseas representative offices; 39% preferred mergers and acquisitions; while only 14% tended to make greenfield investments (Fig. 8).

Of the companies that carried out M&A, horizontal, vertical, and mixed M&A were used equally, accounting for 33%, 34%, and 33% respectively (Fig. 9).

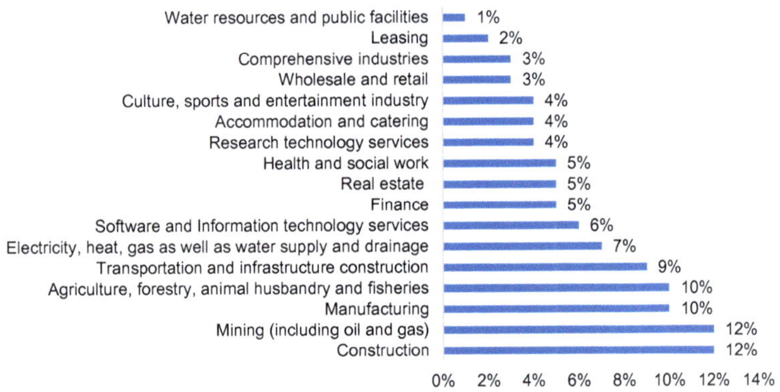

Fig. 7 Proportion of outbound investment by industry

Fig. 8 Main modes of foreign investment

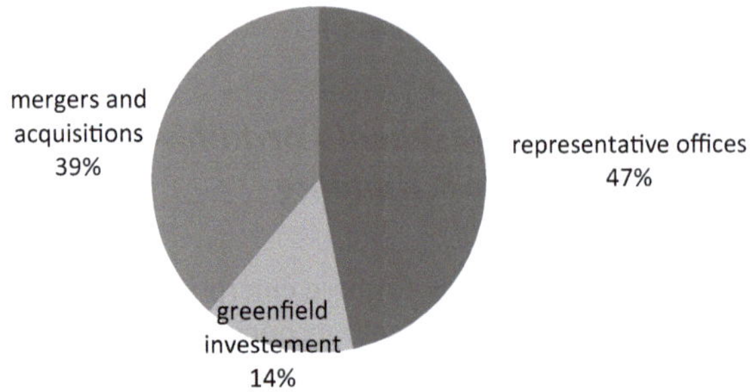

Fig. 9 Types of M&A used by surveyed companies

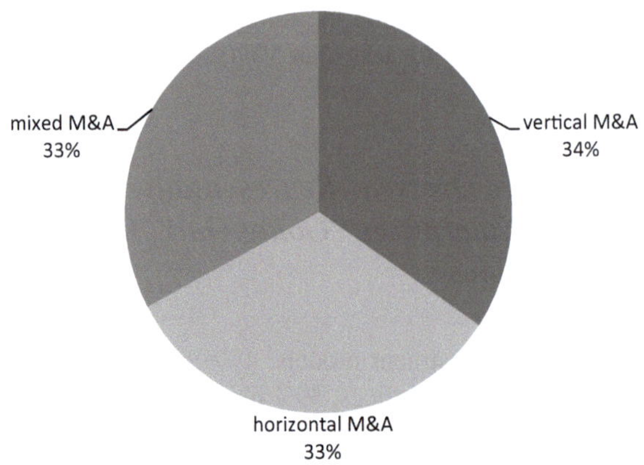

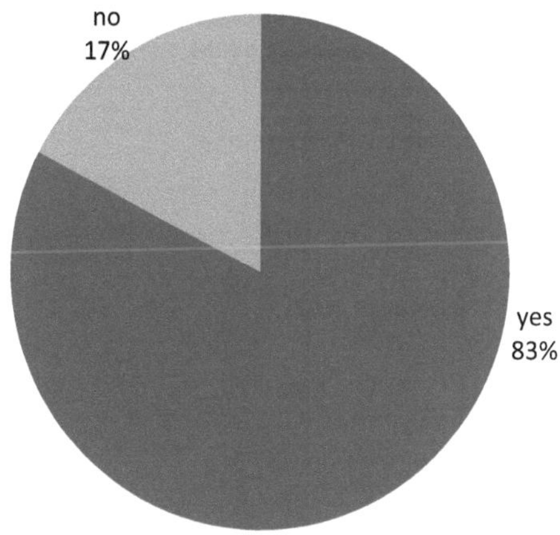

Fig. 10 Relationship between foreign investment projects and core business

According to the survey, 83% of the companies engaged in foreign investment projects related to their core business components, while 17% took the opposite approach (Fig. 10).

1.6 Main Financing Channels Include Corporate Profits, Bank Loans, and Equity Sharing

In terms of financing, 32% of the surveyed enterprises used existing profits to as a source for investment and financing. Bank loans were the second-largest source of financing and accounted for 25%. This was followed by "equity participation by investment partners" and "unofficial private financing", accounting for 12% and 11%, respectively. Both "capital market financing" and "government grants" accounted for 10% each (see Fig. 11).

2 Key Factors Affecting Outbound Investment

2.1 Domestic and Foreign Policy Support, Expansion of Upstream and Downstream Industrial Chains, Domestic Overcapacity and Market Saturation Remain Key Drivers

In terms of the main factors influencing Chinese outbound investment, enterprises felt that "domestic and foreign policies that support 'going out' and grant preferential treatment" (19%) was the main driving force in overseas investment, while 18%

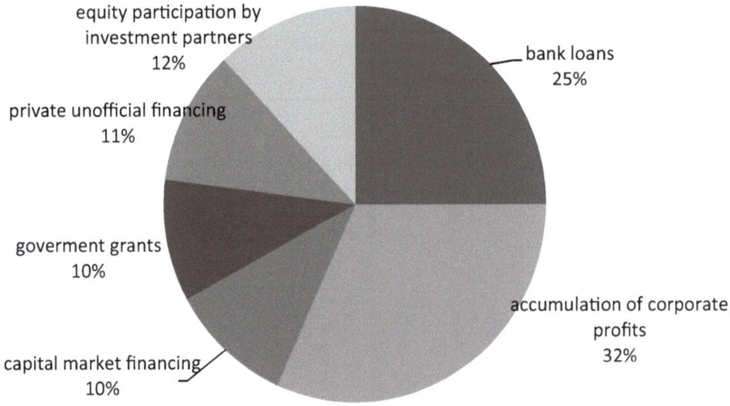

Fig. 11 Sources of financing

felt that "going out" was necessary to expand in overseas markets and upstream/ downstream industrial chains. 13% invested overseas to expand into new markets (see Fig. 12).

Both "preferential policies for attracting foreign investment in destination countries" and "bilateral and multilateral trade or investment agreements" are among the most critical factors that Chinese companies consider when going global. Due to China's increasing economic influence globally, countries are actively developing preferential investment policies to attract Chinese companies and support local economies. Chinese companies have also benefited from international bilateral and multilateral trade relations. The responses "seeking overseas resources such as high-end manpower, low-cost labor, parts, and raw materials" and "enhancing corporate brand influence" each accounted for 10% of all responses. This number suggests that

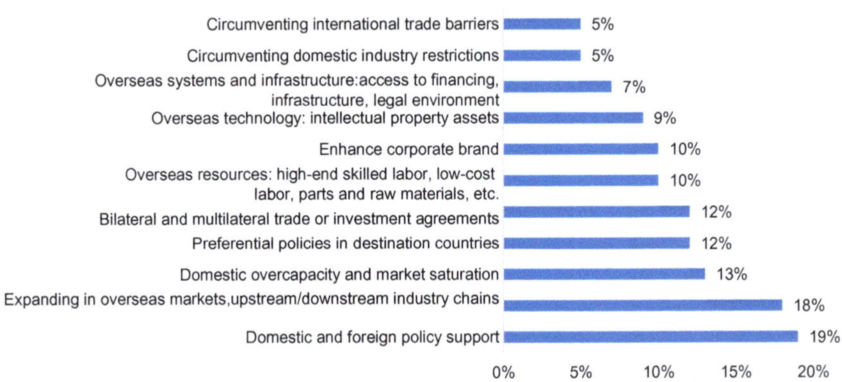

Fig. 12 Factors influencing surveyed companies to consider "Going Out"

Chinese enterprises choosing to "go out" are paying more attention to improving their soft power when investing overseas.

2.2 *Investment Willingness Influenced by 'Legal Approvals' and 'Freedom of Capital Flow'*

Responses showed that 16% of the enterprises surveyed said that they pay particular attention to "legal approvals" and "freedom of capital flow" when looking at the laws and regulations of target countries. This was followed by 14% of enterprises that focused on tax cuts and 12% of enterprises that paid more attention to to the "local financing environment" and "fairness in dealing with disputes" (see Fig. 13).

For Chinese companies wanting to "go out", the freedom of capital flow and the legal approvals in a host country are essential factors. Poor capital flow in the host country will greatly affect production and operations, and ultimately not be conducive to business development. However, with the rising wave of anti-globalization and increased protectionist sentiments, many host countries have strengthened foreign investment laws, which has become a new challenge for Chinese enterprises looking to invest overseas.

The tax breaks offered by host countries have also become a key factor for surveyed enterprises, as tax breaks and the profitability of overseas investments are closely linked. This makes favorable tax policies are an important factor in attracting foreign enterprises.

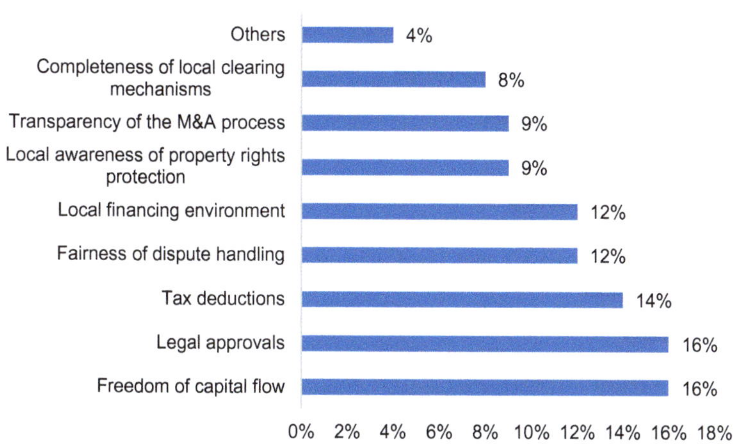

Fig. 13 Major considerations of respondents regarding investment laws and regulations in target countries

Fig. 14 Factors limiting international operations and development of surveyed enterprises

2.3 *Lack of International Talent and Vicious Competition Biggest Constraints*

Of the factors affecting the globalization and development of enterprises, the lack of international talent and competition from domestic counterparts are the most significant constraints to the overseas operations of Chinese enterprises, accounting for 12%. The next biggest factor was a belief among enterprises that unfamiliar cultural environments and their lack of international competitiveness influence their local business activities, accounting for 10% of responses. These were followed by "financing difficulties" and "poor corporate management" both of which accounted for 9% among the surveyed enterprises. Finally, unfamiliarity with local labor insurance and tax policies, the lack of experience in high-level cooperation at an international level, and the influence of local political trends each accounted for 8%. Other factors were more disparate (see Fig. 14).

3 Problems Encountered by Chinese Enterprises in Foreign Investment

3.1 *Poor Local Investment Environments, High Operating Costs, and Low Quality Labor*

On problems enterprises face in host countries, 17% of respondents said that there were "poor local investment environments", while 15% of enterprises said that cited "inadequate local infrastructure". 12% felt that "local labor unions are too powerful",

Fig. 15 Major problems faced by surveyed enterprises in target countries

11% believed that "local operating costs are high", and another 11% thought that "local labor force are lacking". Respondents who felt cited poor local financing environments, complex relationships with third-party organizations and strict local compliance reviews were lower at 9%, 7%, and 5%, respectively (see Fig. 15).

3.2 *Strengthening Local Ties to Counter Legal, Political, and Policy Risks*

In terms of overseas investment and operations, 15% of the interviewed enterprises consider "legal risk" the main risk. "Political turmoil and the risk of war" as well as "policy change" both ranked second at 13% each. Meanwhile, 10% of the enterprises surveyed felt that "macroeconomic risks" hindered their business activities in the region. "Government corruption" also accounted for 10%, while cultural risks, labor disputes, security reviews, or political obstruction accounted for 8% each (see Fig. 16).

According to the survey, 18% of surveyed enterprises responded to unexpected investment risks by "strengthening ties with Chinese embassies, foreign business organizations, and Chinese organizations". This was followed by 10% of enterprises that avoided potential risk by "fulfilling social responsibilities" to build trust with the local community. Meanwhile, 9% of the companies surveyed said having "cooperation with local enterprises in the host country" could reduce investment risk. In comparison, another 9% of respondents prefer to avoid investment risks by "strengthening self-defense and security measures" or "taking out overseas investment insurance". This was followed by hiring local employees, obtaining local government support, and seeking local legal protection, which accounted for 8% each. This was followed up by 7% of companies that chose to hire a third-party professional firm

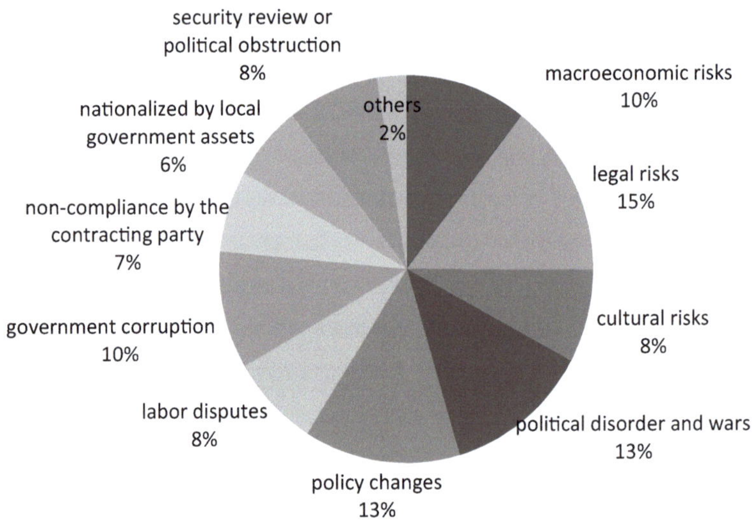

Fig. 16 Major risks encountered by surveyed enterprises when going global

to assess overseas risks for them, while 6% considered short-term investments or phased investment as an alternative way to mitigate risk (see Fig. 17).

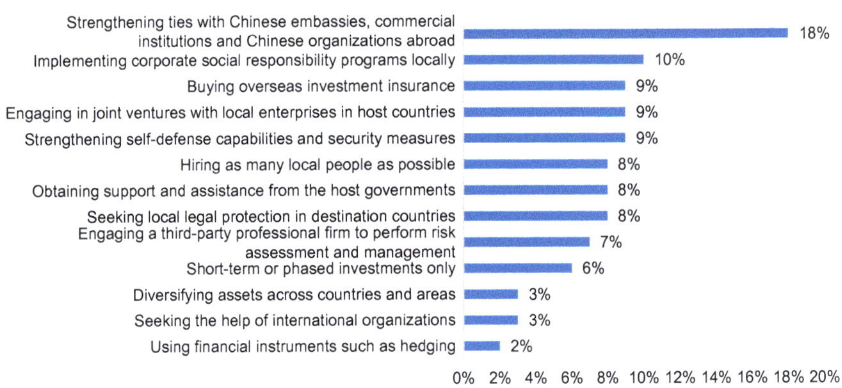

Fig. 17 Measures to cope with risks

Fig. 18 The percentage of local employees employed by surveyed enterprises

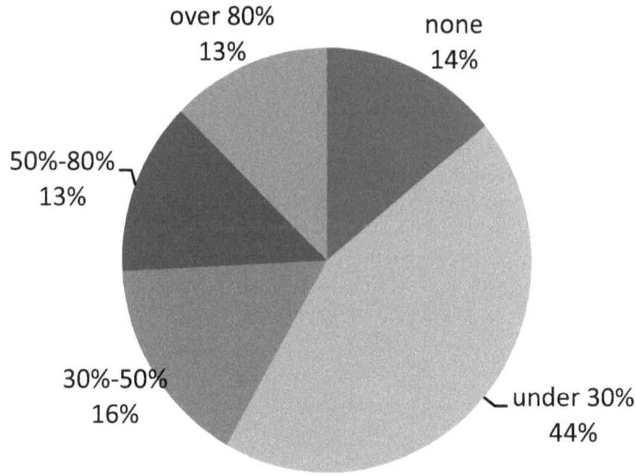

3.3 Limited Talent Localization in Host Countries

In terms of local employment, only 26% of the companies surveyed had staff made up of more than half local employees, while only 13% employed more than 80% local employees and 13% employed 50–80% local employees. 74% of the surveyed companies said that more than half their total staff was made up of non-local employees, of which only 16% employed 30–50% local employees, and 44% employed less than 30% local employees. 14% of the companies surveyed did not employ any local staff (see Fig. 18).

3.4 Slow ROI Levels Mean Only 30% of Enterprises Reach Expectations, over 30% Unsure of Returns

In responses on investment revenue, 25% of the enterprises surveyed said they achieved their original investment goals, while 6% saw profits that exceeded expectations. 22% of enterprises said their expectations had not been met and 15% of them were facing project losses. Meanwhile, 32% of the enterprises that were still in the development phase had yet to turn a profit (see Fig. 19).

3.5 Increasing Awareness of Corporate Social Responsibility in Overseas Investment

In terms of how companies manage corporate social responsibility overseas, the survey found that surveyed enterprises were keenly aware of the need to fulfill their

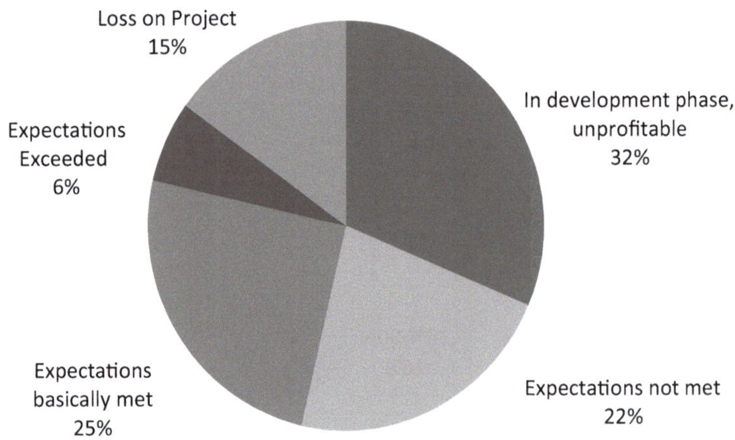

Fig. 19 ROI in foreign investments

social responsibilities when investing overseas. 23% of enterprises said they had established effective communication mechanisms with stakeholders; 20% had "a department and director specifically responsible for overseas social responsibility"; 19% "formulated overseas social responsibility objectives and management plans"; 15% described social corporate responsibility in their overseas development strategies; 12% prepared Corporate Social Responsibility (CSR) reports (or sustainability reports); and only 12% failed to carry out any corporate social responsibility activities overseas (see Fig. 20).

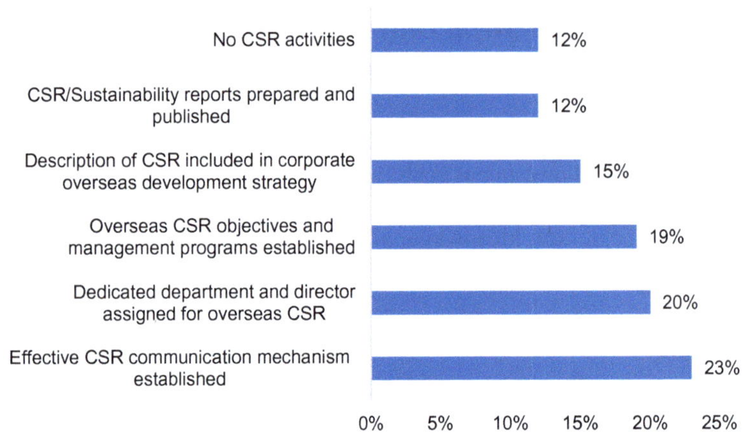

Fig. 20 Management and implementation of CSR efforts

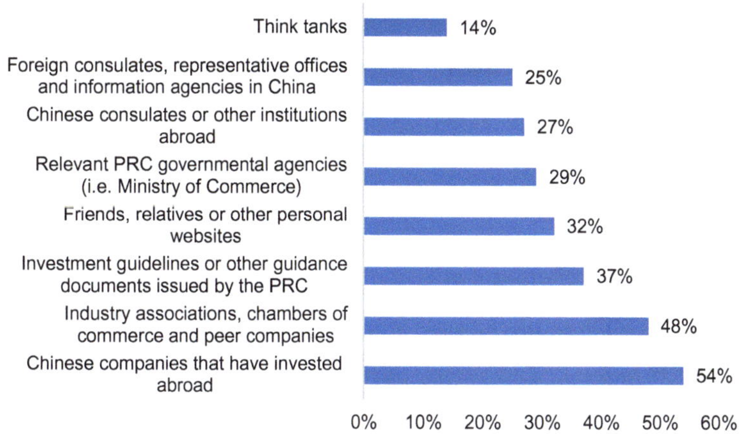

Fig. 21 Channels for overseas investment information

3.6 *Investment Information Mainly from Enterprises that Have Already Invested Abroad, Platform Services Need to Be Improved*

In responses regarding channels for information, 54% of the interviewed enterprises said that they obtained overseas investment information through "local Chinese enterprises that have already gone abroad", while 48% obtained information through industry associations, chambers of commerce and peer enterprises. The other three channels included "investment guidelines or other guiding documents issued by the state [PRC]" (37%), "friends, relatives or other personal websites" (32%), and "relevant national departments (such as the PRC Ministry of Commerce)" (29%) (see Fig. 21).

Fewer enterprises obtain information on overseas investment through platforms like institutions or agencies. Only 27% and 25% of enterprises respectively obtained information through "Chinese consulates or other foreign institutions abroad" and "foreign consulates, representative offices and information agencies in China", while only 14% of the enterprises used "think-tank platforms" as channels for information.

3.7 *Considerable Demand for Information Services on Global Markets and Host Country Laws/Regulations*

In terms of the demand for services, 57% of the enterprises surveyed said they needed information on international markets, accounting for the largest proportion. The percentage of companies that needed "legal and regulatory services in destination countries" was also high at 56%, while the next highest demand was for "industry

Fig. 22 Services demanded by surveyed enterprises investing abroad

information service for the destination countries", accounting for 46% of responses. Meanwhile, demand for "customer credit services", "debt recovery services" and "corporate public relations services" accounted for 31%, 26% and 25% respectively (see Fig. 22).

3.8 *PRC Government Still Needs to Improve Financial Support for Enterprises Investing Abroad*

According to the survey, 28% of surveyed enterprises did not receive any financial support from the government, while 18% received low-interest or interest-free loans and 17% received low-cost or free insurance. Another 16% received subsidies for fixed costs or business costs and 14% were given priority access to foreign currency exchange services, while 7% received priority access to re-export quotas (see Fig. 23).

3.9 *Nearly Half of Surveyed Enterprises Optimistic About Economies in Target Countries*

According to the survey, 49% of the enterprises had a positive outlook on the economies in target countries. 23% of these said they were ready to expand their investment and 26% chose to continue to wait and see; 29% were still evaluating, while 9% were "not optimistic but not withdrawing" and 7% were "not optimistic and ready to withdraw"; 6% were "not sure" (see Fig. 24).

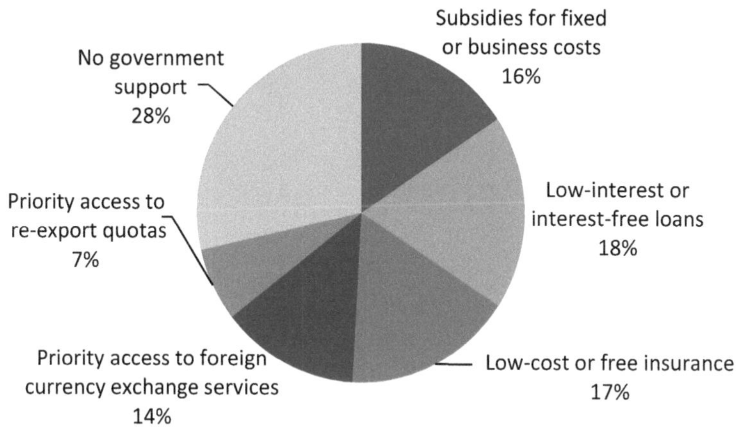

Fig. 23 National policy support received by surveyed companies

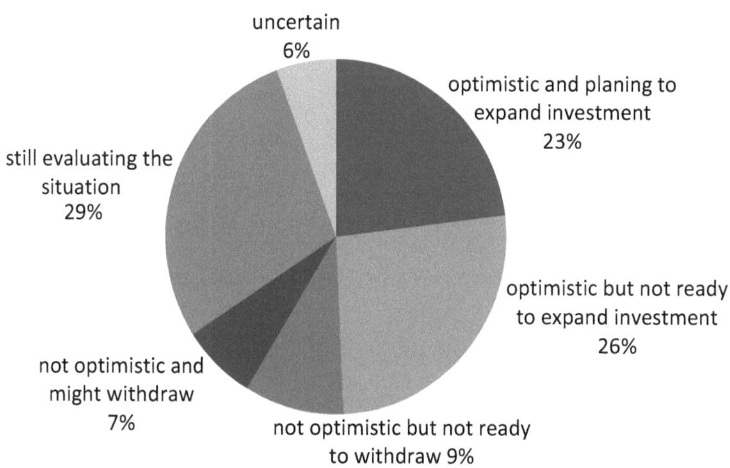

Fig. 24 Confidence in future investment in target countries

4 Evaluating the "Going Out" Policies of Chinese Enterprises

4.1 Nearly 70% of Enterprises Satisfied with Investment Management Policies

According to the survey, 47% of surveyed enterprises were "generally satisfied" with approval and filing processes for foreign investment. Meanwhile, 20% of the surveyed enterprises were "satisfied" and 33% were still "dissatisfied" (see Fig. 25).

Fig. 25 Satisfaction with investment management policies

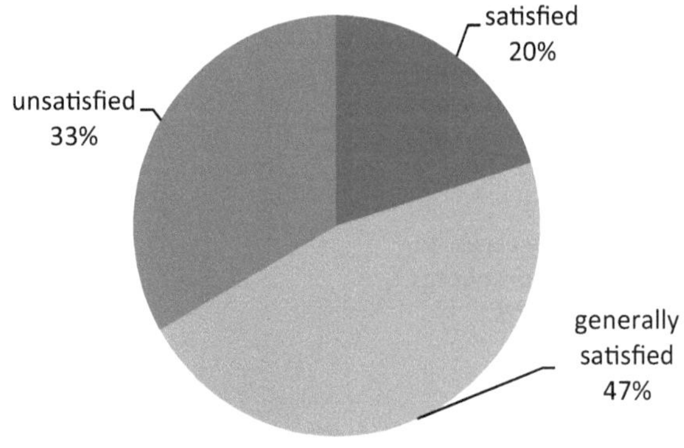

Fig. 26 Satisfaction with foreign currency exchange policy

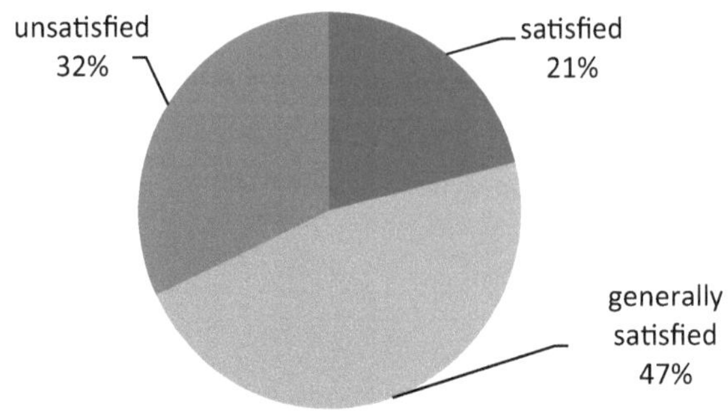

4.2 Nearly 70% of Enterprises Satisfied with Foreign Currency Exchange Policy

According to the survey, 47% of enterprises were "generally satisfied" with foreign exchange policies, while 21% were "satisfied" and 32% were "dissatisfied" (see Fig. 26).

4.3 Nearly Half of Enterprises Dissatisfied with Financial Policy

44% of the surveyed enterprises expressed dissatisfaction with financial policies, 48% were "generally satisfied", and only 8% were "satisfied" (see Fig. 27).

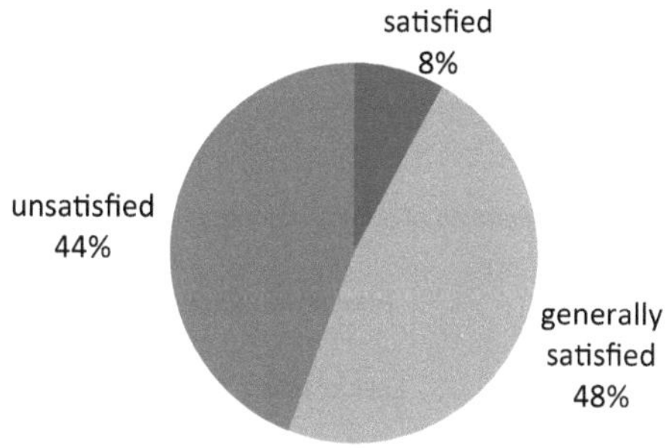

Fig. 27 Satisfaction with financial policy

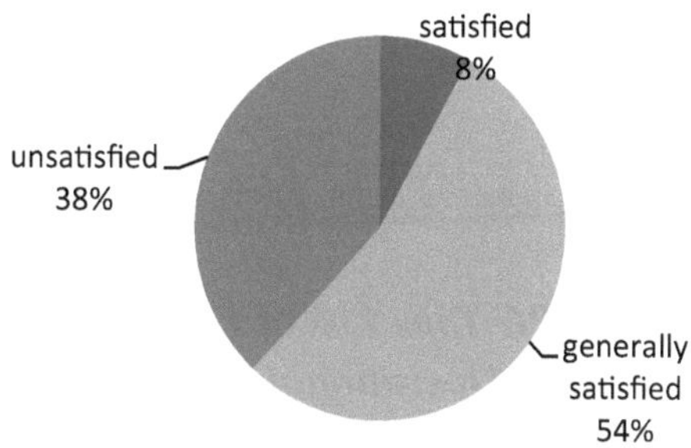

Fig. 28 Satisfaction with insurance policies and services

4.4 More Than Half of Enterprises Satisfied with Insurance Policies and Services

Survey data indicates that 54% of the surveyed enterprises were "generally satisfied" with insurance policies and services, while 8% were "satisfied" and 38% were "dissatisfied" (see Fig. 28).

5 Investment in BRI Countries by Chinese Enterprises and Influencing Factors

5.1 Political Risk a Constraining Factor in BRI Investment

According to the survey, 32% of enterprises investing in BRI countries considered political risk to be their biggest risk. This was followed by low levels of local social development (19%) as the most significant risk factor in constraining their development, while lack of the rule of law and poor governance accounted for 15% and 10% respectively. Lastly, 3% of the enterprises surveyed felt that insufficient financial resources were a limiting factor when investing in the BRI (see Fig. 29).

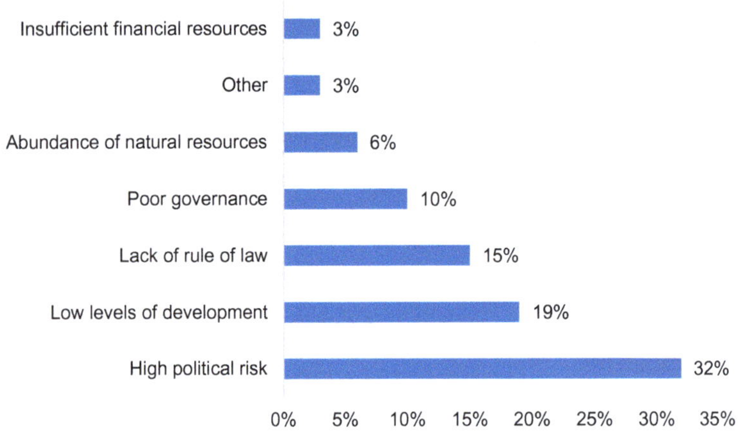

Fig. 29 Limitations on investment in BRI countries

5.2 EPC Tops List of Diverse BRI Investment and Operational Models

Investment and operation models used by Chinese enterprises investing in BRI countries were diverse. The most popular model was EPC (Engineering, Procurement, Construction) and accounted for 19%; product exports to local market represented 16%; joint ventures accounted for 15%; financial, consulting and intermediary services accounted for 9%; wholly-owned enterprises and industrial parks represented 8%; labor partnerships, M&A of local enterprises and authorizing overseas businesses all made up relatively small percentages (see Fig. 30).

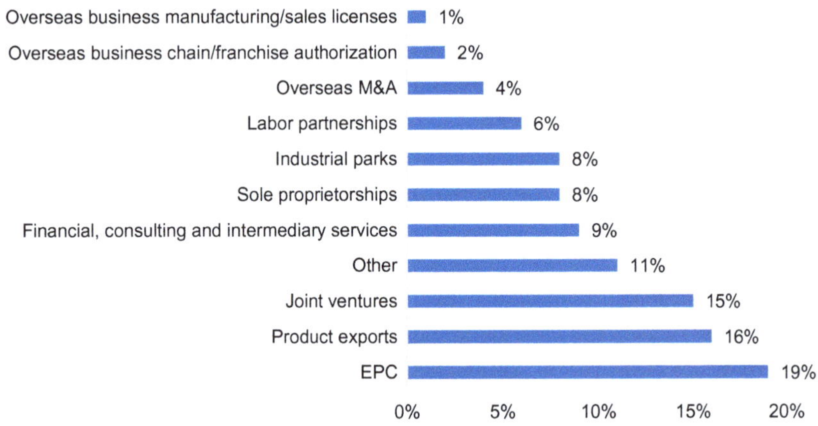

Fig. 30 Business models used by enterprises in BRI countries

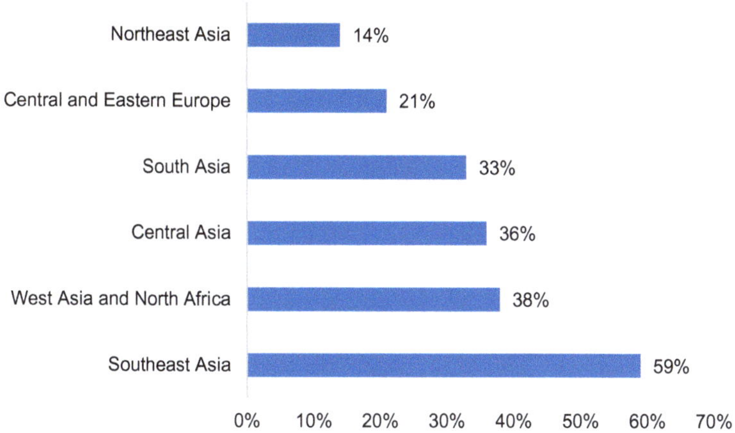

Fig. 31 Investment distribution within BRI

5.3 *BRI Investment Concentrated in Southeast Asia*

The survey shows that 59% of enterprises surveyed have invested in Southeast Asia followed by 38% of enterprises that invested in "West Asia and North Africa", 36% in "Central Asia", while 36%, and 33% invested in Central and South Asia respectively. Meanwhile, 21% of enterprises chose to invest in Central and Eastern European BRI member countries, while only 14% invested in Northeast Asia (see Fig. 31).

5.4 *BRI Investment Concentrated in Infrastructure and Transportation*

The survey shows that 41% of the enterprises investing in BRI countries preferred infrastructure, while investments in transportation, information technology, energy, and finance account for 27%, 21%, 21%, and 13% respectively (see Fig. 32).

5.5 *Political Instability Main Risk for Companies, Citing Canceled Contracts After Regime Changes*

This survey shows that "political instability" was the most critical risk faced by Chinese enterprises as regime changes could result in the cancellation of contracts. 31% of respondents expressed grave concern over this risk. This was followed by 26% of companies naming "legal risk" (i.e. incomplete legislation resulting in discrimination against foreign countries) as their biggest concern, followed by "financial risk",

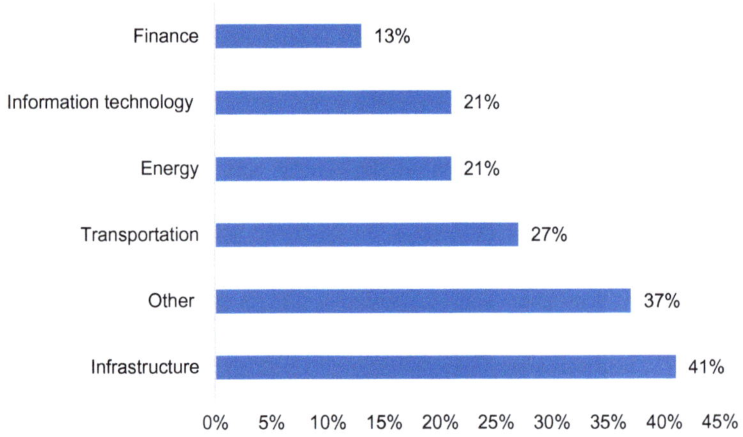

Fig. 32 Investment in BRI countries by industry/sector

which includes low sovereignty ratings, poor financial status and long-term debt in host countries. Financial risk (18%) was followed by "security risk" (i.e. extremism and terrorism), which accounted for 17% of responses (see Fig. 33).

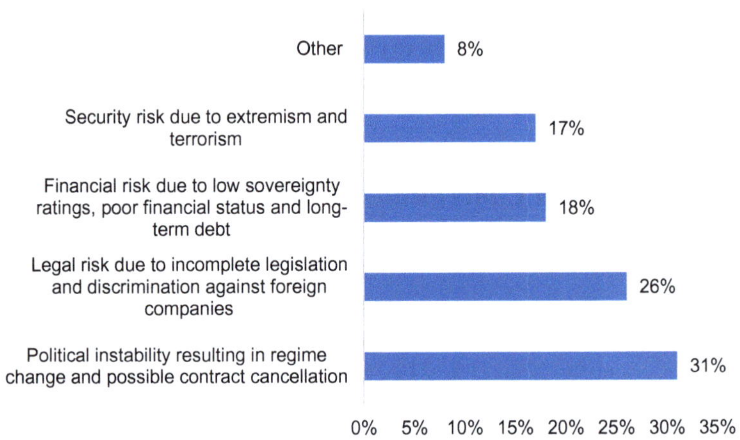

Fig. 33 Major risks faced by Chinese enterprises investing in BRI countries

6 Conclusion

Chinese enterprises have diversified overseas investments and private enterprises now play a major role in the process of "going global". Having been influenced by factors such as changes in overseas investment environments, large Chinese overseas investment declined in 2017 and foreign investment plans have become increasingly rational and steady. The most preferred destination for investment for Chinese enterprises remains Southeast Asia, while other regions vary widely. Industries that have attracted the most overseas investment from Chinese firms are construction and mining. More Chinese enterprises are now choosing to set up representative offices overseas. Many companies also feel that improvements could be made in areas of policy support such as bank loans.

Policy supports are the primary driving force for enterprises "going global". Chinese enterprises generally seek to expand industrial chains and explore overseas market opportunities due to intense domestic competition. However, the freedom of capital flow and legal approvals in host countries influence the decision of Chinese companies to engage in foreign investment. Competition from domestic counterparts overseas is also one of the biggest constraints to expanding overseas.

Other challenges that Chinese enterprises face overseas include poor local investment environments, high operating costs, and unskilled local labor. Risks faced by enterprises include legal issues, political unrest, war, and policy risk. To mitigate these concerns, enterprises must strengthen their contact with Chinese embassies, foreign commercial institutions, and Chinese organizations. Low local employment rates of Chinese enterprises "going global" also shows that Chinese enterprises must improve efforts to localize.

Chinese enterprises also face slow ROI when investing overseas and while awareness of corporate social responsibility (CSR) is gradually increasing, there is still room for companies to strengthen their CSR efforts. Access to information on overseas investment through service platforms can also be improved. While Chinese enterprises generally view China's policies positively, financing policies that support overseas investment by Chinese enterprises can also be promoted better. The survey also shows that nearly 70% of the companies surveyed were satisfied with the existing policies on approval and filing of overseas investment projects and investment management. Nearly 70% were also satisfied with foreign exchange policies, and more than half are satisfied with the insurance and service policy. This shows that China's policy environment for enterprises "going out" is friendly. However, there is still room for improvement.

Finally, topics on investment in BRI countries show that local political risks are the main factors limiting business activities of Chinese enterprises, but the ways in which Chinese enterprise engage BRI countries are diverse with EPC and commodities topping the list. Most Chinese companies invest in BRI countries in Southeast Asia, concentrating their investment in transportation. As the BRI enters its fifth year, China has increased policy support for Chinese enterprises investing in BRI countries while the overall economic environment has also improved and the awareness of Chinese enterprises doing business overseas has increased. It is expected that more Chinese enterprises will invest in BRI countries over the next five years as they search for better business opportunities.

New Opportunities and Challenges in the Globalization of Chinese Enterprises

CCG Enterprises Globalization Research Group

Abstract Economic globalization is an irreversible trend and China is a firm supporter of this. However, unilateralism, trade protectionism, and other "anti-globalization" trends have negatively influenced international trade. In this context, what opportunities and challenges will Chinese enterprises face as they "go global"? To answer this question, CCG invited experts from the political, business, and academic fields to discuss lessons learned from MNC investment in China as well as Chinese enterprises that have invested overseas during the past 40 years of reform and opening up. Other topics we will discuss include "Belt and Road Initiative" (BRI) development and bilateral China-US investment in the context of increased trade friction.

Keywords "going out" · China · Enterprise globalization

1 Forty Years of Reform and Opening Up: Inbound Investment and "Going Out"

Over the past 40 years of reform and opening up, China has adhered to the strategies of "bringing in" and "going out", with inbound and outbound investments having made great contributions to China's economic and social development. So, what then are the challenges, experiences, and lessons that have been learned by foreign and Chinese enterprises during this 40 year period?

Panelists *(in order of speaking)*:

Mats Harborn, President of the European Union Chamber of Commerce in China

HE Ning, former Director-General of the Department of American and Oceanic Affairs at the Ministry of Commerce of P.R.China; former Minister for Economic and Commercial Affairs at the PRC Embassy in Washington

CCG Enterprises Globalization Research Group (✉)
Center for China and Globalization, Beijing, China

H. H. Wang and M. L. Miao (eds.), *The Challenge of "Going Out"*, The Chinese Enterprise Globalization Series, https://doi.org/10.1007/978-981-99-3326-6_4

H.E. Nicholas Rosellini, UN Resident Coordinator in China, Representative of UNDP in China

LI Jiping, Executive Vice President of China Association for the Promotion of Development Financing, former Vice President of China Development Bank

LIU Zhiping, Vice President of SK Group China

HE Donghui, Co-Executive President of Fotile Group

Mats Harborn: Over the past four decades, if foreign companies wanted to succeed in China, the most important thing was to choose the right time, place, and field. Now, standing at this new point, foreign companies must be more innovative and bring new value to the Chinese market. At the same time, the Chinese government must clearly define its role, establish clear, strong rules, and undertake policy formulation and implementation. In the past few years, China has proposed many good initiatives, such as the Belt and Road Initiative to improve the infrastructures in Africa, the Middle East and Europe, which are major priorities in these regions. But these initiatives have caused some misunderstandings and anxiety among various countries. Therefore, attention must be paid to how information is communicated to others in foreign countries. It is also very important to be transparent about this information.

HE Ning: Over the past 40 years of reform and opening up, our country has made great achievements. While bringing tangible economic benefits to the Chinese people, it has also directly or indirectly brought numerous economic benefits to many other countries. It has also liberated our minds, reduced tariff barriers, and opened up the service market. The many achievements of reform and opening up have shown that it was the right way to achieve economic success. In the future, we should aim to continue undertaking reforms and we also need to establish a community of common interests so that everyone can enjoy the rewards of China's economic development. Only when this is achieved will we see a better situation in terms of business environment and foreign trade relations.

H. E. Nicholas Rosellini: The achievements of China's forty years of reform and opening up are a good demonstration of how economic success can be turned into success in terms of human-centered development. It is estimated that 800 million people have been lifted out of poverty over the past 40 years. The average life expectancy has been extended by ten years. This shows that China has reached a high level of socio-economic development. Three years ago, the 2030 Agenda for Sustainable Development was adopted. The Agenda set out 17 Sustainable Development Goals (SDGs). As a global agenda, it requires cooperation between countries and cooperation between governments and businesses. So far, China has done much and has played a leading role in both building a low-carbon society and developing a low-carbon economy. China has also established the Belt and Road Initiative (BRI), and I think China can work with countries along the BRI to ensure sustainable social, environmental, and economic development worldwide.

LI Jiping: In the next decade or so, there should be a profound change in China's financial system i.e., moving from the traditional bank credit mode to the stage of paying equal attention, or even giving priority, to the capital market. In terms of financing methods, there are mainly financial, credit, and securities financing, among which the latter two are mostly adopted by developed countries. The biggest problem in Asian countries like ours is that banks are dominant, that is to say, the issuance of loans is dominant. In contrast, European countries and the US dominate the capital market.

LIU Zhiping: An important result of reform and opening-up is the promotion of the Chinese market's opening up and rapid growth. At the beginning of reform and opening up, the enterprises investing in China were more cautious in capital registration because they did not know much about the Chinese market. However, along with the development of the Chinese economy and rapid market expansion, foreign enterprises have expanded their investments here. In the process of reform and opening up, every improvement made in the business environment can bring forth new investment rounds. I think foreign companies should have confidence that China remains the world's most essential and dynamic market region. I hope that China's business environment will continue to improve.

HE Donghui: In the past 40 years, China has become one of the world's biggest manufacturing countries. We definitely hope to become a manufacturing power in the next 40 years through continuous reform and further opening up. In our experience, enterprises must have a core set of values or a positive workplace culture. In 2008, Fotile introduced outstanding elements of Chinese traditional culture rooted in Confucianism to refine our management system. Our team now abounds with endless energy and potential while building a top-quality brand in China. Many private enterprises must look for internal driving forces and fully integrate these with enterprise management tools, so that the next 40 years will see not only a stronger and larger manufacturing industry, but also a competent team of well-trained industrial professionals that can play an important role in China's rejuvenation.

2 The Development of the "Belt and Road" and Its Future

Five years have passed since President Xi Jinping first proposed the Belt and Road Initiative (BRI) in 2013. Since then, the BRI has seen much progress and gained the support of many countries. However, some within the international community have many doubts regarding the BRI. To discuss this point, CCG has invited Chinese and foreign panelists to discuss and put forward their predictions on the BRI.

Panelists *(in order of speaking)*:

LONG Yongtu, former Vice Minister at the Ministry of Foreign Economic Cooperation and Trade of P.R.China, former Secretary-General of Boao Forum for Asia

CHEN Jian, former Vice Minister at the Ministry of Commerce of P.R.China, member of the 12th CPPCC National Committee

Alistair Michie, Secretary General of British East Asia Council (BEAC)

H.E. Stanley Loh, Ambassador of Singapore to China
Alidad Mafinezam, President of the West Asia Council
Pierre Dorbes, Head of Delegation at International Committee of the Red Cross(ICRC) for East Asia.
LI Xinhua, Vice Chairman of China National Building Material Group Co., Ltd.

LONG Yongtu: It is necessary to be both pragmatic and ideological when implementing the BRI. Although we need to build roads and undertake other infrastructure projects, we must explain the BRI clearly to people both at home and abroad. As a positive initiative for China's development, the initiative enables many less developed areas of China to participate in the process of opening up to the outside world. It also helps solve the problem of regional socioeconomic disparities between richer and poor areas while also driving the socioeconomic development of countries along the BRI. In this way, the BRI is a continuation of the reform and opening up process that China has been implementing for decades.

CHEN Jian: The "Belt and Road" is an initiative, not a plan. This means that extensive consultations and joint contributions are needed to achieve the goal of shared benefits. To promote the sustainable development of the Belt and Road Initiative, we need to focus on three points: Firstly, the Belt and Road is an idea. This means that we need to fully understand how it can be carried out to avoid any misunderstandings. Secondly, extensive consultation with foreign partners is necessary. This means that we need to respect their opinions and not impose our own opinions on them. Thirdly, we should divide up the interests of Chinese enterprises and foreign enterprises. This means, for instance, that we should pay attention to the interests of local parties in host countries and any third parties involved in this process. Only by doing this can the BRI be promoted more sustainably.

Alistair Michie: The "Belt and Road" initiative is currently promoted in the Chinese way. But, if you want foreign countries to participate, it must be publicized and communicated in different ways. If we do a good job in terms of publicity and communication, we can really promote its development. While governments often carry out international and domestic interactions, the Belt and Road can move away from this format by working together with foreign private enterprises along the lines of reform and opening up. In terms of finance, we can work with regions with rich experience and resources and integrate them to bring more potential and value to the Belt and Road.

H.E. Stanley Loh: I have four suggestions for the "Belt and Road" 2.0: Firstly, it should make the most of financial arrangements and market mechanisms, and increase access to the market and diversify investment risks. Secondly, the "Belt and Road" must be innovative in terms of thinking and implementation. For example, the New International Land-Sea Trade Corridor that was built under the China-Singapore (Chongqing) Demonstration Initiative on Strategic Connectivity is a new land-sea transportation channel spanning Chongqing, Beibu Gulf and Singapore, reducing transportation time from three weeks to one week, which also reduces the cost of transportation.This channel is also strategically important: it turns the two networks of the Belt and Road, that is, one to the east and one to the west, into a large network. Thirdly, the "Belt and Road" should be built according to the rule of law. This means that commercial disputes, if any arise, can be solved through mechanisms such as a "Belt and Road" court. Fourthly, the "Belt and Road" should develop smart infrastructure that will lead to the digitalization of cities.

Alidad Mafinezam: The message of the Belt and Road is that we can improve connectivity and move beyond some of the geopolitical differences. From a North American perspective, the Belt and Road must expand to take care of the needs of North America, that is, the basic needs of the United States and Canada. For example, when you go to Silicon Valley, you find that our subway has not been upgraded for decades and is getting worse and worse. We want to improve our urban transportation system, but we have a huge funding gap. From a humanitarian point of view, the Belt and Road should also focus more on the local community and show a better understanding the needs of the people in the community. By doing this, the Belt and Road will be sustainable.

Pierre Dorbes: The Belt and Road Initiative is a great opportunity to help people address some of their most basic demands, such as the increase of access to cleaner water and shelter. As investors, enterprises can play a very important role. We hope that they will not bring harm to the local community, will be able to engage in dialogue with the community, and also take social responsibility outside of business to better integrate into the local community.

LI Xinhua: Our investments abroad follow three principles: firstly, it aims to promote the harmonious development of the local economy and society. Secondly, it aims to work together with partners, including international partners and Chinese enterprises. Finally, our investment abroad aim to set up certification institutions in the local community and the establishment of international inspections,. This will help us improve the local management evaluation of product quality so that we can bring goods of the highest quality to the local community.

3 Bilateral Investment Between China and the US Under the Influence of the US-China Trade War

In 2018, total global foreign direct investment (FDI) experienced a significant decline due to US policies and other factors. FDI is a bellwether for globalization and is also a potential sign of growth in corporate supply chains and future trade relations. The escalating US-China trade conflict since the beginning of the year will have a profound impact on investment prospects, entrepreneurial confidence and industry chains as well as upstream and downstream industries. What challenges does the US-China trade conflict bring to China and global trade and investment?

Panelists *(in order of speaking)*:

ZHU Guangyao, former Vice Minister of Finance of P. R. China

William Zarit, President of the American Chamber of Commerce in China (AmCham China)

WANG Huiyao, Vice President of the China Association for International Economic Cooperation at the Ministry of Commerce of P.R.China

MENG Xiaosu, Chairman of China National Real Estate Development Group Corporation Limited, Chairman of HuiLi Fund

David Zweig, Director of the Center on China Transnational Relations of the Hong Kong University of Science and Technology

Jacob Parker, Vice President of the US-China Business Council

ZHU Guangyao: In 2019, we may encounter the following challenges: the first challenge is trade disputes. Aside from China, the US also has trade friction with the European Union and other countries. This is likely to affect the confidence of the market and the stability of the global economy. The second challenge is Brexit. If there is a 'hard Brexit', it will be seriously damaging to the British, the European, and even the global economies. Thirdly, the US Federal Reserve's interest rate trend will significantly impact the market. Fourthly, as some emerging market countries have capital outflows, they risk currency devaluation and even financial market turmoil.

Moreover, the final challenge is the impact of geopolitics. This may affect the price of bulk raw materials, especially oil products, and the global economy. Under US-China trade tensions, strengthening bilateral communication is crucial. The head of state diplomacy plays a leading role, and under its leadership, communications at all levels should be strengthened. Moreover, entrepreneurs, academia, and think tanks of the two countries should further communicate to provide policy advice to the governments. Enhanced mutual understanding and trust through non-governmental exchanges are crucial to developing stronger US-China relations.

William Zarit: The trade conflict between the US and China has brought harm to businesses in both countries. AmCham's survey in China shows that US tariffs are causing severe harm to US companies in China. Since the beginning of reform and opening up, the US has played a very active role in China's socio-economic development. Many of China's exports to the US have received its investment, making the Chinese economy achieve unprecedented growth. Furthermore, Americans have been able to buy more products, US companies have made more money from this, and American political leaders have gained more support. However, Americans often overlook that the Chinese market is not as open as the US market. Also, many problems, such as intellectual property issues, have always existed. Therefore, we now need to undertake further discussions. Both sides should open their markets to each other to be fair and so that both countries can benefit.

WANG Huiyao: The heads of the two states have recently released positive signals of reconciliation, and businesses in both countries are particularly looking forward to resolving the US-China trade friction. At the top level, there are no significant differences between the two sides. General Secretary Xi Jinping and Premier Li Keqiang have repeatedly stressed the need to strengthen intellectual property protection and indicated that China would actively cooperate with the WTO to ease market access for foreign companies. As the global value chain continues to develop, countries worldwide are seeing their economies mutually interlinked and integrated. If this value chain is cut off, it may bring substantial worldwide risks or even cause a financial crisis. I believe that China and the US have the wisdom and ability to solve the trade friction and can come to an agreement that suits both countries.

MENG Xiaosu: Since President Trump took office, real estate thinking has deeply influenced American politics, and economic interests have become his top priority. In addition to the competitive and trade relationship between China and the US, there is actually a layer of a teacher-student relationship. China's market economy, housing reform, and many financial products are learned from what America has done. I think there is still a solution to the friction between China and the US. China needs to follow its commitments to resolve its trade deficit and open up more, while the US needs to understand the difficulties of China's push for reform and also not be too sensitive regarding the "Made in China 2025" plan.

David Zweig: I think the US and China are caught in a strategic competition. On the one hand, the US is a global hegemonic power trying to keep its position, and on the other hand, China is a strong emerging power. Looking back at history, both countries have benefited from the integration that began with reform and opening up. However, the Americans now believe that they have opened up their technological, economic, and educational resources only for the Chinese to challenge the US after learning, so there has been little domestic support for US-China engagement in recent years. While I think the US may exaggerate the potential threat posed by China, China should indeed continue to open wider to the world and make real reforms. By doing this, the US can see China's determination to promote fair trade. Only in this way can the relationship between the two countries ease.

Jacob Parker: There are five problems in the current US-China relationship. The first problem is market access and fair competition, and the second one is state-owned enterprise reform. The US government and companies are very concerned about Chinese state-owned enterprises because they are not market-based and detrimental to foreign companies. The third problem is overcapacity. For example, overcapacity in aluminum, steel, glass has affected the global prices of these commodities and, as a result, is hurting US producers. The fourth problem is intellectual property rights, and the fifth problem is industrial policy subsidies. China's industrial policy mainly focuses on various strategic industries regarding the industrial policy. Some Chinese companies are involved in developing international standards; however, they sometimes do not choose the best technology or the best products, but instead, they choose the enterprises and standards that are beneficial to China.

4 Adopting Higher Standards for Opening-Up

As 2018 marks forty years of China's reform and opening up, there is a lot of thinking about how to continue to push for further opening up. The intricate and multifarious nature of the international scene has created a sense of urgency. At the same time, the current waves of counter-globalization and trade protectionism have urged us to find new paths to promote China's opening up to the outside world.

Panelists *(in order of speaking)*:

LONG Yongtu, former Vice Minister at the Ministry of Foreign Economic Cooperation and Trade of P.R.China, former Secretary-General of Boao Forum for Asia

ZHU Guangyao, former Vice Minister of Finance of P. R. China

CHEN Jian, former Vice Minister at the Ministry of Commerce of P.R.China, member of the 12th CPPCC National Committee

WANG Huiyao, Vice President of the China Association for International Economic Cooperation at the Ministry of Commerce of P.R.China

ZHANG Hongli, co-Chairman of HOPU Investment, former Senior Executive Vice President of the Industrial and Commercial Bank of China

ZHANG Huarong, founder and Chairman of Huajian Group

LONG Yongtu: The current international trends of anti-globalization, trade protectionism and unilateralism force us to find other ways to promote China's opening up to the outside world. The Chinese government has recently responded by adopting higher standards for opening-up, which requires more joint efforts from all sides. In addition to actively participating in the WTO reform, we also need to actively participate in negotiations on regional trade agreements and regional trade blocs. Looking ahead, creating a good business environment is important for opening wider to the outside world and also for fostering core competitiveness. In improving China's business environment, we need to pay special attention to two aspects: the first aspect is how to implement the WTO national treatment to truly achieve equal treatment for all kinds of enterprises, including state-owned enterprises, private enterprises, as well as foreign-funded enterprises; and the second aspect is how to solve the problem of opening up and investment threshold of various Chinese industries.

ZHU Guangyao: How China can promote higher-level reform and opening up under the new situation is an extremely important strategic issue related to its development and fate. Firstly, we should have strong confidence in China's economy being able to further develop and achieve a shift from high-speed growth to high-quality development. Over the past 40 years of reform and opening up, China's economy has made tremendous achievements and its overall national power has risen quickly. On the premise that our own economy is developing well, we must also actively participate in global economic governance. In terms of opening up, external pressure is often the driving force behind our internal structural reform. The key here is how fast we go ahead with further reforms. In terms of WTO reform, there are three points we should keep in mind: firstly, its efficiency needs to be improved; secondly the appeal dispute mechanism settlement also needs to be improved; finally, while proposing reform programs, our own reform (e.g. structural reforms) should be undertaken.

CHEN Jian: China has developed rapidly during the opening up and reform period, and it is impossible to continue to open up without further reforms. In the first forty years of reform and opening up, China mainly conducted opening up in the horizontal levels, such as geographical opening up of Shenzhen and Shanghai. Internationally, we joined the international governance system, such as the economic governance system. In the next forty years, we need to carry out further reforms. A rough prototype for this has already been constructed: free trade zones and ports. This requires giving more local autonomy and making the market plays the most important role in allocating resources. In addition, we need to participate more deeply in constructing the global economic governance system so that the economic order is more inclusive and balanced. We also need further to liberate our minds and learn to be tolerant.

WANG Huiyao: Looking back on history and looking ahead, China must be more involved in international multilateral mechanisms. Since the 18th National Congress, China has undertaken various measures at home, such as by promoting and supporting globalization. More specifically, we have promoted the establishment of the Asian Infrastructure Investment Bank, launched the "Belt and Road" Initiative, and actively promoted negotiations on the Regional Comprehensive Economic Partnership (RCEP). We should also explore joining the Trans-Pacific Partnership and proactively participate in the TPP negotiations. This will also be a huge boost to China's socio-economic development.

ZHANG Hongli: If we want to open further to the outside world, we must follow the laws of the market. Many industries have market rules, including banking and finance. We must strictly follow and respect the market laws. Only in this way can enterprises grow, and this has been the secret weapon behind the success of China's powerful economic take-off over the past four decades. In the next step, China's financial sector will work to transition from quantity to quality and make the most of its structure. The 19th National Congress proposed clear measures to strengthen and accelerate the construction of multi-level capital markets. This refers to the ratio of direct and indirect financing. Increasing the proportion of direct financing to promote the conversion of enterprises from fund to capital will also contribute to the healthy development of China's economy.

ZHANG Huarong: As an enterprise expanding in Africa under the Belt and Road Initiative, we'd like to propose an idea. How has China attracted an incredible investment over the past 40 years of reform and opening up? How has China developed its economy and shared the benefits with foreign enterprises? Growing up from a poor child 50 years ago to an international entrepreneur, I shared my personal growth experience and social responsibility with them. Then, developing from an entrepreneurial team of ten people with three sewing machines to today, I shared my experience of business and international trade services with them. Although it is clear that the Belt and Road Initiative can help the socio-economic development of African countries, our enterprises must remember to respect local cultures and local laws and seek to communicate well with the local governments. Could the author please further explain these sentences?

Financing Structure and Risk Response in Overseas Investment and M&A by Chinese Enterprises

Shiwei Zhang and Xuejing Zhu

Abstract With the frenzy of domestic enterprises "going out", financing models used in overseas M&A are becoming increasingly international. They range from self-financing to using overseas syndicated loans and issuing bonds abroad. By focusing on the financing structure of overseas investment and M&A, this paper explores domestic and overseas financing models. At the same time, it further analyzes financing risks in overseas M&A and countermeasures in the light of the current state of foreign exchange and capital outbound regulations by looking at recent cases. This paper also discusses strategies for dealing with foreign exchange and outbound capital risk for domestic financing. It also suggests that it is better to use an overseas special purpose vehicle (SVP), subsidiary financing or foreign loans under domestic guarantee before selecting a main domestic body to finance directly in China. This aims to assist domestic enterprises in implementing overseas M&A in a more standardized manner to reduce risks and uncertainties related to financing.

Keywords Financing models for overseas M&A · Domestic financing · Overseas financing · Financing risk · Countermeasures to foreign exchange and capital outbound risk

External financing is always a key issue for Chinese companies in the practical operations of overseas M&A. This is because they are usually required to pay a large cash sum to the target company, but it is often impossible or unnecessary for Chinese companies to pay this sum entirely with their own cash reserves. There have been multiple cases of overseas M&A activities that have been unsuccessful due to financing issues. In this paper, the authors seek to analyze existing overseas financing models used by domestic enterprises, discuss the risks and related responses

S. Zhang (✉) · X. Zhu
Zhonglun Law Firm, Beijing, China

H. H. Wang and M. L. Miao (eds.), *The Challenge of "Going Out"*, The Chinese Enterprise Globalization Series, https://doi.org/10.1007/978-981-99-3326-6_5

in overseas M&A financing under the current regulatory environment and provide recommendations for domestic enterprises.

1 Overview of Financing Models Used by Domestic Enterprises in Overseas M&A

1.1 Domestic Financing of Domestic Enterprises

Overseas M&A financing models used by domestic enterprises can be divided into two types: domestic financing and overseas financing. Domestic financing refers to direct domestic financing of domestic enterprises, including both debt financing and equity financing.

1.1.1 Debt Financing

The more common methods of debt financing include bank loans and the issuing of bonds.

Bank Loans

Bank loans enable domestic enterprises to use external funds with compensation to finance investments. The advantage of bank loans over equity financing is that creditors generally do not participate or interfere in the operations or management of domestic enterprises. However, bank loans can potentially increase the asset-liability ratio of domestic enterprises and have the added burden of paying back the loan with interest. Banks also set high thresholds for loans for domestic enterprises including proof of stable operation, good credit or sufficient qualified collateral.

The China Banking Regulatory Commission (CBRC) issued its *Commercial Bank M&A Loan Risk Management Guidelines* on February 10, 2015 in relation to M&A loans, which further relaxed control over M&A loans (CBRC [2008] No. 84).

Issuance of Bonds

Bond issuance refers to the issuing of bonds by domestic enterprises according to statutory procedures whereby they promise to pay interest and the principal to bondholders according to a pre-approved schedule. When issuing bonds, domestic enterprises need to receive approval from or file with the relevant authorities. Therefore, large domestic enterprises with good credit are able to issue more bonds.

A convertible bond is a kind of corporate bond that can be converted into common stock at a particular time based on certain conditions. This means that convertible bonds have the characteristics of both bonds and stocks. Investors can receive principal and interest when the bonds are due, and when the conversion conditions are met, bondholders can convert bonds into common stock within a certain time according to the conversion price. By doing so, bondholders can become shareholders of the company, participate in its business decisions, and receive dividend distributions. Due to its convertibility, the interest rates of convertible bonds are generally lower than those of straight bonds. For companies that issue convertible bonds, this can help reduce financing costs.

1.1.2 Equity Financing

Equity financing refers to introducing capital through a capital increase and share enlargement. The funds raised by equity financing have no maturity date, and the holders have no pressure to repay capital with interest. However, the new shareholders resulting from equity financing can participate in the operation and management of the enterprise and enjoy dividends according to their shareholdings. This dilutes the rights and interests of the original shareholders and can lead to the transfer of control of the enterprise.

Equity financing can be divided further into public and private placements depending on which financing channels are used. Public placement refers to raising funds by issuing shares of domestic enterprises to public investors through the stock market, including such specific forms such as listing and non-public offering of shares; private placement means that enterprises attract specific investors to inject funds in the form of a capital increase and share enlargement.

In the recent case of China Molybdenum's (CMOC) acquisition of Anglo American PLC's niobium and phosphorus business in Brazil through its overseas subsidiary, CMOC purchased 100% of the shareholders' equity of AAFB[1] and AANB for cash. CMOC also bought the niobium sales business of AAML as well as the debts of AANB and AAFB. CMOC firstly paid the M&A consideration with its own funds and bank loans, and then secondly paid the M&A consideration indirectly by replacing the previously paid self-financing funds through a private offering of shares. At present, CMOC's non-public offering of A shares has been approved by the Securities Regulatory Commission. Post-M&A, the shareholding structure of AAFB and AANB is as follows (see Fig. 1).

1.2 Major Models Used in Offshore Financing

1.2.1 Direct Cross-Border Financing for Domestic Enterprises

Cross-Border Loans for Domestic Enterprises

Cross-border loans for domestic enterprises are one of the main ways to raise funds abroad directly. Under the current policy guidance of "expanding inflows", it is

[1] These are all abbreviations of the names of foreign companies.

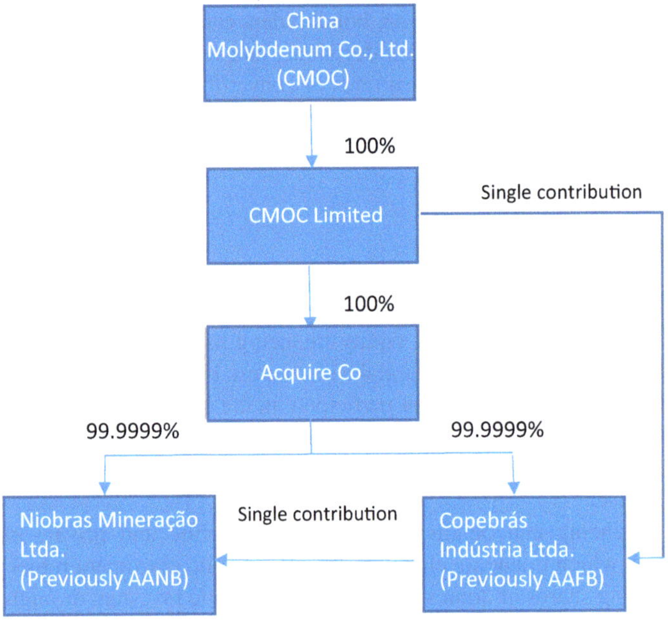

Fig. 1 Shareholding structure of AAFB and AANB. *Source* "*Report on the Implementation of Major Asset Purchase (Acquisition of Overseas Niobium and Phosphorus Business) by China Molybdenum Co., Ltd.'s (CMOC)*", October 2016

noted that the *Notice of the People's Bank of China on Full-coverage Macro-prudent Management of Cross-border Financing 2017 (2017 PBOC Cross-border Financing Notice)*, which came into effect on January 12, 2017, has expanded the upper limit of cross-border financing[2] by domestic non-amount enterprises. It has also replaced the pre-approval process with cross-border financing contract filing.

Of course, cross-border loans are not easy due to various factors such as limitations of collateral valuation and uncertainty in overseas M&A projects. This means that when taking out cross-border loans, domestic enterprises should consider factors such as the structure of overseas M&A transactions, regulatory processes, and the financing terms.

Cross-Border Bond Issuance by Domestic Enterprises

The National Development and Reform Commission (NDRC) issued *Implementation Opinions on Encouraging and Guiding Private Enterprises to Actively Conduct Overseas Investment* in July 2012. This aims to support key enterprises when issuing RMB and foreign currency bonds abroad. The *Notice of NDRC on Promoting the Reform of Managing the External Debt Issuance by Enterprises with a Record-filing*

[2] Cross-border financing refers to the act of domestic institutions integrating funds from non-residents in both domestic and foreign currencies.

and Registration System issues,[3] which came into effect on September 14, 2015, abolished the requirement for approvals of the issuance of foreign bonds of enterprises over a certain limit and also implemented management guidelines for record-filing and registration.

Before Document No. 2044 was issued, the threshold of direct issuance of bonds by domestic enterprises was relatively high. Generally, RMB bonds are issued by state-owned enterprises, which rarely directly issue bonds in currencies other than RMB. After the implementation of Document No. 2044, the NDRC brought the overseas issuance of RMB and other currencies under unified management, reducing the regulatory threshold for direct issuance. However, the choice of cross-border bond issuance should still be based on the structure of overseas M&A. Currently, overseas issuance of bonds by domestic enterprises is still not the main source of funds for overseas M&A.

1.2.2 Use of Offshore SPVs by Domestic Enterprises for Indirect Offshore Financing

There are further inconveniences in terms of financing procedures and other aspects for domestic enterprises when directly conducting cross-border financing. At the same time, the State Administration of Foreign Exchange (SAFE) issued its *Notice on Relevant Issues Concerning Foreign Exchange Administration for Domestic Residents to Engage in Overseas Financing and Round Trip Investment via Overseas Special Purpose Companies* on July 4, 2014. The Notice abolishes the mandatory return of funds provision and allows offshore financing and other related funds to be retained for overseas use. In this context, in recent years, most domestic enterprises have chosen to use overseas special purpose vehicles (SPVs) for financing and M&A.

Debt Financing

Currently, debt financing by domestic enterprises through SPVs includes M&A loans, domestic guarantees on foreign loans, and overseas debt issuance.

<u>M&A Loans</u>

Since the Chinese government tightened capital controls in late November 2016, about half of the dozen offshore M&A transactions recognized by foreign exchange regulators have utilized offshore debt financing. At present, it appears that SAFE has not yet restricted domestic companies from using offshore SPVs for offshore financing. As one of the mainstream methods of offshore financing, M&A loans refer to loans issued by a commercial bank to an acquirer (i.e., a subsidiary) to pay

[3] NDRC [2015] No. 2044. The foreign debt mentioned in the Notice refers to the debt instruments with a maturity of more than one year, which are borrowed from abroad by domestic enterprises and their controlled overseas enterprises or branches, priced in local or foreign currency, and need to repay the principal and interest as agreed, including overseas issuance of bonds, medium and long-term international commercial loans, etc.

M&A related costs. The recent acquisition of Syngenta by China National Chemical Corporation (ChemChina) was financed by an offshore SPV. Meanwhile, when CITIC Capital, Carlyle Group, and other consortia acquired McDonald's in China, they also used an SPV established by the consortium in Hong Kong to raise M&A funds through offshore loans. To guarantee repayment, the shares of the SPV were pledged to an offshore bank.

Domestic Guarantees on Foreign Loans

The most common practice regarding domestic guarantees on foreign loans is for the domestic bank to issue a bank guarantee to the offshore lending bank by having domestic enterprises apply for it. The offshore bank then provides a loan to the domestic enterprise's offshore SPV, which provides a counter-guarantee to the domestic bank. This can be conducted so that the domestic enterprise directly offers insurers backstops to the overseas bank, which provides loans to the overseas SPV of the domestic enterprise.

However, the Chinese regulator should register domestic guarantees on foreign loans. Furthermore, given the unpredictable timing of SAFE approvals, the authors suggest that domestic enterprises communicate with the Chinese regulator before filing for approval or creating a record to avoid any problems.

Overseas Bond Issuance

Domestic enterprises can also use overseas SPVs to issue bonds indirectly (i.e., the issuing body and act are entirely outside of China) to raise funds. Before Notice 2044 was implemented, most domestic enterprises issued bonds abroad indirectly. However, Notice 2044 expands the objects of foreign debt issuance supervised by the NDRC to include "foreign enterprises or branches controlled by domestic enterprises". Therefore, foreign enterprises controlled by domestic enterprises issuing foreign bonds abroad should also register and file as stipulated in Notice 2044.

Compared to bank loans, bonds are more flexible and can reduce the cost of M&A transactions by reasonably predicting market trends and setting issuance prices. For example, Hony Capital's[4] acquisition of Pizza Express, a British pizza chain, was financed by bonds in the form of a leveraged buyout (LBO). Of the £900 million deal between Hony Capital and Pizza Express, £610 million was financed by issuing high-yield bonds. The remaining £300 million was financed by a joint venture between Hony Capital's RMB and USD funds in the form of equity investment. The details are shown as follows (see Fig. 2).

Equity Financing

In addition to debt financing, many domestic enterprises also use equity financing when working through overseas SPVs. For example, equity financing and debt financing were both used in the acquisition of Syngenta by ChemChina. According to our sources, the M&A deal was made up of a three-tiered structure (i.e., the first

[4] As the specific information of the case cannot be obtained through public channels, it has not been determined whether the main body of Hony Capital's bond financing is from its overseas SPV.

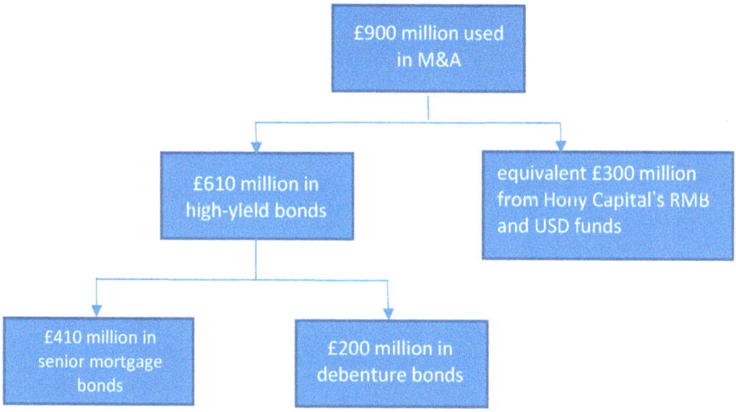

Fig. 2 Hony Capital's LBO acquisition of Pizza Express. *Source* Wang Yaya, Hony's Efforts in Cross-Border M&A, *China Foreign Exchange*, published on Jan. 15, 2015, No. 2

tier was China National Agrochemical Co., Ltd., a subsidiary of ChemChina; the second tier was based in Hong Kong; and the third tier was based in Europe) and six overseas SPVs. The transaction was completed by an all-cash offer and while the consideration was locked at US$43 billion, the overall actual capital required was as high as US$50.4 billion. This included equity financing in the amount of US$25 billion and debt financing of US$25.4 billion.

The US$25 billion in equity financing was arranged as follows: SPV1 was capitalized with a US$15 billion special fund, and then SPV2 was financed with that US$15 billion and other US$5 billion of senior capital raised by CITIC Bank. ChemChina indirectly held 75% of SPV2, and SPV2 issued US$5 billion of common stock on top of that and financed SPV3 with US$25 billion.

Of the US$25.4 billion in bond financing, CITIC Bank financed SPV3 with a US$12.5 billion loan, SPV4 and SPV5 remained unchanged, and the HSBC Syndicate financed SPV6[5] with a US$7.5 billion loan. Together with the US$5 billion debt restructuring loan provided by HSBC syndicate and the US$200 million liquidity provided by CITIC and HSBC syndicate respectively, the transaction could raise up to US$50.4 billion overseas using offshore SPVs. The financing structure of the transaction is shown below (see Fig. 3).

Meanwhile, the structure of actual transaction proceeded as follows (see Fig. 4).

The Combined use of Multiple Financing Methods

Domestic enterprises can also use multiple financing methods to conduct M&A when using overseas SPVs. The acquisition of Lexmark by Apexmic combined multiple financing methods including M&A loans, private investment, shareholder loans, and

[5] Sources show that ChemChina had subsequently updated its financing structure and part of the SPV6 loan was replaced by equity financing, which totaled $5 billion in size and was a senior tranche of the CITIC Trust-sponsored Fengxin Jianda Fund.

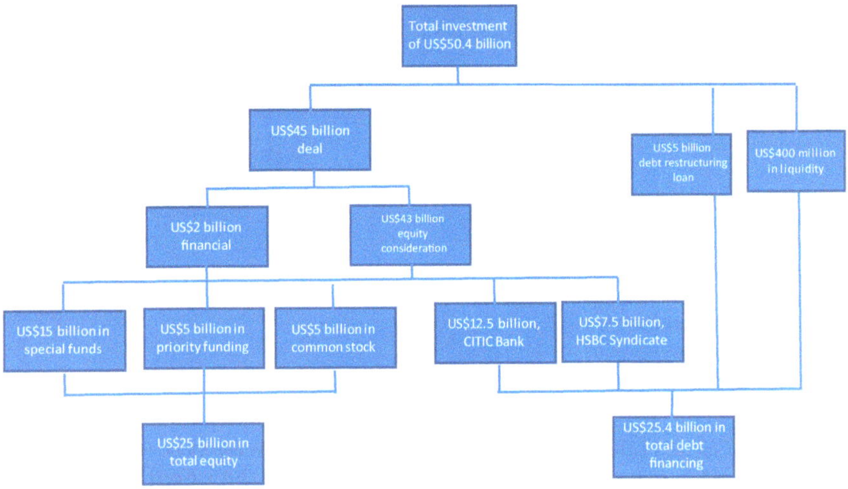

Fig. 3 Financing structure of ChemChina's acquisition of Syngenta. *Source* the Game of Syngenta M&A, *Caixin Weekly*, No. 39, 2016, October 10, 2016

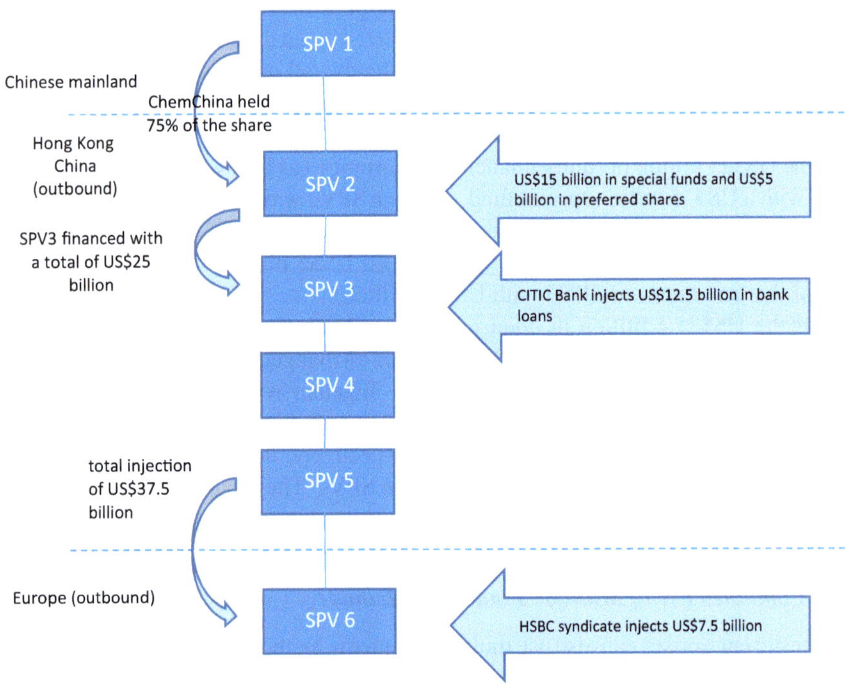

Fig. 4 Structure of the deal for the acquisition of Syngenta by ChemChina. *Source* the Game of Syngenta M&A, Caixin Weekly, No. 39, 2016, October 10, 2016

private convertible bonds. According to the *Draft Report on Major Asset Purchases* disclosed by Apexmic in May 2016, Apexmic planned to establish Subsidiary I and Subsidiary II in the Cayman Islands with two private offered funds; Subsidiary II would also establish a consolidated subsidiary in the US. The consolidated subsidiary and Lexmark would be merged, making Lexmark the sole entity after the merger. The share consideration for the transaction was estimated to be approximately US$2.7 billion, and the funds were raised by applying for M&A loans from the Syndicate (the Subsidiary II and the merged subsidiary applied for M&A loans from the Syndicate led by the state-owned banks), and cash contributions (Apexmic and two private offered funds will invest in Subsidiary I in cash respectively).

Apexmic's cash contribution came from its cash and loans from its controlling shareholder, CNEST, as follows: (1) Apexmic's funds of RMB 700 million; (2) RMB 1.9 billion in funds borrowed from CNEST, and (3) CNEST's financing through the issuance of exchangeable bonds.

However, it should be noted that, according to the *Report on the Implementation of Major Asset Purchases* released by Apexmic in November 2016, the transaction structure was adjusted with financing by Apexmic, Pacific Alliance Group and Shuoda Investment using their own funds. Of this amount, Apexmic contributed approximately US$777 million in cash while the remaining amount was obtained through an overseas SPV applying for medium and long-term M&A loans from the Syndicate. In December 2016, Apexmic completed the whaling of Lexmark, a NYSE-listed company with assets amounting to eight times its own.

In summary, in examining recent cases, we have found that it is a more common practice for domestic companies to use offshore SPVs as the main channel for financing and overseas M&A. The reason for this is that using offshore SPVs for financing avoids Chinese foreign exchange and capital outbound regulations (provided, of course, that domestic entities also provide no cross-border guarantee), which to a certain extent also avoids uncertainties caused by Chinese regulatory audits. Meanwhile, the entity carrying out the M&A can enjoy the tax benefits of an offshore SPV, which also facilitates indirect capital operation through the offshore superstructure.

2 Financing Risks of Overseas M&A and Responses

2.1 Risks and Problems of Overseas M&A Financing

2.1.1 General Risks

For complex overseas M&A projects, the difficulties and risks encountered in financing usually include the following:

Overseas Investment Approvals

When conducting direct overseas M&As, domestic enterprises must complete approval, registration or filing procedures required by the Development and Reform Commission (NDRC), Ministry of Commerce (MOFCOM), State Administration of Foreign Exchange (SAFE) and State-owned Assets Supervision, and Administration Commission (SASAC) (for state-owned enterprises). Obtaining approval or recording the transaction with the NDRC is key in the review of overseas M&A. Before that, overseas M&A transactions are, in principle, not allowed to sign any legally binding documents, which restricts the progress of overseas M&A.

Scheme Design of Financing Structure

In debt financing, when the actual results of an M&A transaction do not meet expectations, the actual profit generated through normal business transactions by the target company is less than the interest rate of its liabilities. This may lead to the risk of repaying the capital and paying interest on time. In equity financing, if too many new shares are issued, the original shareholders may lose control. Therefore, poor choices in terms financing options can cause significant stress on the finances and operations of domestic companies.

Debt Risk

Chinese companies are generally highly indebted and financially leveraged in overseas M&As. According to Zerohedge, a leading US financial blog site, Chinese companies invested US$250 billion in overseas acquisition deals in 2016. Various Chinese companies, such as Wanda, Fosun, HNA Group, Zoomlion, Anbang Insurance, and Rosenery are burdened with huge debts due to their highly leveraged overseas mergers and acquisitions.

Improper assessment of overseas M&A transactions and their value can lead to excessive debt-funded operation and deterioration of financial financing risks. This is particularly the case in offshore financing, where the financing entity SPV is often an empty shell without stable cash flow or financing capacity. This can affect the offshore SPV's ability to repay its debts if it becomes more desperate for outbound money or faces obstacles to the guarantee. Of course, under new strict control measures in overseas investment, the pressure of outbound domestic capital has moved from SAFE to MOFCOM and the NDRC. Suppose an enterprise wants to engage in overseas M&A. It would need to undergo a formal audit examining both compliance and its financial efficiency and solvency conducted by the NDRC and the Commerce Committee/Ministry of Commerce.

Exchange Rate Fluctuations and Policy Risks

Exchange rate policies can directly affect the cost of cross-border financing. For example, if the cost of cross-border M&A is in a foreign currency and the RMB depreciates against that foreign currency, the change in the exchange rate will result in a difference in the foreign currency-denominated loan and the currency of repayment, causing the financing costs of the investing enterprise to increase.

2.1.2 Foreign Exchange and Capital Exit Risks

With the tightening of regulations, relying entirely on domestic entities for financing will likely result in bottlenecks in foreign exchange and capital exit strategies. Since the second half of 2016, the Chinese government has taken a position of "expanding inflows, controlling outflows and reducing deficits", and has introduced a series of regulatory policies on foreign exchange and the capital exit of RMB. They have also conducted regulatory reviews of enterprises with large transaction volumes or large foreign exchange purchases (over RMB 5 million) to prevent the loss of large amounts of foreign exchange reserves. The author has taken the liberty to summarize recent regulatory policies (see Table 1).

In view of the current policy, given that domestic banks need to be audited by SAFE to remit more than US$5 million abroad, outbound capital (e.g. direct capital injection to offshore SPVs) will be severely restricted. This means that domestic enterprises cannot split remittances to circumvent the new regulations.

2.2 Response

Cross-border M&A transactions are very complex, and financing is the most important part of transactions. For these reasons, domestic enterprises should pay attention to the response of overseas M&A financing risks. The following are suggestions from the authors on this topic.

2.2.1 Response Strategies for General Risk

Choose the Appropriate Financing Structure and Method

Domestic enterprises should pay close attention to regulatory policies issued by supervisory authorities and adapt their financing structures and methods accordingly. In the case of Qihoo 360's privatization, publicly available information shows that the amount of equity financing of Qihoo 360 was twice the amount of debt financing. This is rare as equity financing will reduce the original shareholders' equity ratio, and creates more risk than debt financing. The high percentage of equity financing for Qihoo 360's privatization was based on its strong market presence. However, not all companies are that attractive and and risk tolerant. Therefore, domestic companies must have an in-depth understanding of their current situation and their market match before raising capital.

In addition to traditional financing methods, domestic enterprises can try other financing methods. These include issuing bonds abroad, issuing convertible bonds abroad, and stock swaps. However, care should be taken to ensure the appropriate ratio of own capital, debt capital, and equity capital in the financing structure.

Table 1 List of recent regulatory policies on foreign exchange and capital exit in overseas investment

Departments	Regulations as well as Q&A	Main contents
SAFE	*SAFE Circular on Policies for Reforming and Standardizing Management of Foreign Exchange Settlement of Capital Accounts* In effect from June 9, 2016	Discretionary foreign exchange settlement in the foreign debt sector and discretionary foreign exchange settlement of capital accounts
People's Bank of China (PBOC)	*Notice on Further Clarification of Issues Concerning Overseas RMB Lending by Enterprises in China* In effect from Nov. 26, 2016	Integrated macro-prudential management of domestic and foreign currency for domestic enterprise RMB offshore lending[a]
NDRC, MOFCOM, PBOC and SAFE	NDRC, MOFCOM, PBOC and SAFE Press Conference Nov. 28, 2016	Implementing filing system-based foreign investment management, and verifying foreign investment projects of some enterprises in accordance with relevant provisions
NDRC	*Notice of the General Office of the National Development and Reform Commission on the Adjustment of the Reporting Format of Information Reports on Overseas Acquisition or Bidding Projects* In effect from Dec. 5, 2016	Emphasized the necessity and authenticity of ODI; added audited financial statements as well as project due diligence reports
NDRC, MOFCOM, PBOC and SAFE	NDRC, MOFCOM, PBOC and SAFE Press Conference - answering questions on the strengthening of supervision of outbound investment by relevant Chinese governmental departments Dec. 6, 2016	Closer attention on certain irrational outbound investment trends in real estate, hotels, cinemas, the entertainment industry and sports clubs, as well as the potential risks in association with overseas investment projects involving (a) large investments in businesses unrelated to the core business of the Chinese investor, (b) outbound investment made by limited partnerships, (c) investment in offshore targets that have assets valued larger than the Chinese acquirers, and (d) projects with very short investment periods

(continued)

Table 1 (continued)

Departments	Regulations as well as Q&A	Main contents
SAFE	Interview with Officer in Charge from SAFE Dec. 8, 2016	Cracking down on false foreign investment, and encouraging real and compliant foreign investment. Identification of four categories of abnormalities in outbound investment[b]
SAFE	*Circular of the State Administration of Foreign Exchange on Further Advancing Foreign Exchange Administration Reform to Enhance Authenticity and Compliance Reviews* In effect from Jan. 26, 2017	Four points to enhance authenticity and compliance reviews for ODI
SAFE	SAFE Press Conference on *Circular of the State Administration of Foreign Exchange on Further Advancing Foreign Exchange Administration Reform to Enhance Authenticity and Compliance Reviews* Feb. 8, 2017	Under the macro-prudential management framework, domestic Chinese enterprises can borrow foreign debt within a certain percentage of their net assets
SAFE	*Circular of the State Administration of Foreign Exchange on Further Advancing Foreign Exchange Administration Reform to Enhance Authenticity and Compliance Reviews* Policy Q&A (second issue) May 2, 2017	If the funds of domestically guaranteed foreign loans are used for ODI, and the overseas financing under the domestic guarantee of foreign loans replaces the currency investment of domestic institutions, according to the current regulatory principles of foreign investment, if the overseas equity investment of domestic institutions is restricted, cross-border insurance shall be suspended When the funds of domestically guaranteed foreign loans are used in special industries such as real estate, hotels, cinemas, the entertainment industry and sports clubs, as well as (a) large investments in business unrelated to the core business of the Chinese investor, (b) outbound investment made by limited partnerships, (c) investment in offshore targets that have assets valued larger than the Chinese acquirers, and (d) projects that have a very short investment period, it is necessary to strengthen reviews in accordance with the current outbound investment regulatory principles

(continued)

Table 1 (continued)

Departments	Regulations as well as Q&A	Main contents
PBOC	*Measures for the Administration of Financial Institutions' Reporting of High-Value Transactions and Suspicious Transactions* July 1, 2017	Reduce the threshold requiring "Reports on High-Value Transactions" and clarify reporting requirements for transactions based on reasonable suspicion

Source Legal database of LexisNexis

[a] 1. The PRC lender and the overseas borrower should have shareholding relationship; 2. The PRC lender should not fund its overseas loan through debt financing or with investment from individuals; the size of the loan should commensurate with the overseas borrower's scale of operations, and the actual usage of the overseas RMB loan will be examined 3. The PRC lender should perform pre-registration of overseas RMB loans with the local in-charge State Administration of Foreign Exchange ("SAFE"); 4. The loan term should be between 6 months and 5 years. For a loan term more than 5 years, record-filing with the local PBOC branch is required

[b] First, some of the enterprises established in less than a few months are carrying out overseas investment activities without any entity operation; secondly, the scale of overseas investment of some enterprises is much larger than the registered capital of their domestic parent company, and the operating conditions reflected in their financial statements can hardly support the scale of their overseas investment; thirdly, the overseas investment projects of individual enterprises are far away from the main business of their domestic parent company; fourthly, the source of RMB investment of individual enterprises is abnormal, being suspected of illegal individual transfer of assets to overseas and illegal operation of covert money dealer

[c] 1. Enhancing authenticity and compliance reviews for ODI. Allowing funds for overseas loans under domestic guarantees to be transferred back for domestic use. 2. The domestic institution shall make up for the losses incurred in previous years before remitting the profits overseas. 3. In issuing overseas loans, a domestic institution shall make sure the sum of the outstanding overseas loans in the domestic currency and those in foreign currencies is no higher than 30% of its owner's equity in the audited financial statements for the previous year. 4. When going through ODI registration and outward remittance procedures, a domestic institution shall explain to the bank the sources and purposes (use plan) of the investment funds, and present to the bank authenticity evidencing materials

Financing Through International Syndicate

Domestic enterprises often use syndicated loans[6] to obtain financing for overseas M&A. The advantage of this method is that with the help of international capital market financing, it is possible to obtain large amounts of funds with long maturities that cannot be provided by a single bank. It is also makes it possible to reduce financing costs.

---

[6] A syndicated loan involves the participation of several financial institutions, and using the same loan agreement, a group of banks led by a bank authorized to operate a loan business and provide financing to the same borrower on agreed terms and conditions.

Rationally Determine the Value of Target Enterprises Through Intermediaries

Before financing, domestic enterprises should evaluate the value of the target enterprise. Domestic enterprises can hire professional investment banks and other intermediaries to provide in-depth and comprehensive services, including detailed investigation of the target enterprises' field of operation and financial situation. This will help domestic enterprises determine their actual value and provide a basis for the design of their financing plans.

Finding a Suitable Strategic Investor

In the case that the domestic enterprises are 'weak', they can cooperate with a third party that is stronger economically or is more professional to complete the overseas M&A together. This can solve any financing problems, ensure strategic management of the enterprises, reduce risk and guarantee a win–win situation.

2.2.2 Responses to Foreign Exchange and Capital Exit Risk

In light of the restrictions on foreign exchange and capital exit under current policies, domestic enterprises can consider the following risk response measures after carrying out comprehensive risk assessment.

Give Priority to Overseas Financing by Overseas Entities

When considering financing structures and main entities, it is likely that domestic enterprises will not pass foreign exchange and capital exit procedures if they use their main entity is domestic. Therefore, domestic enterprises should use overseas SPVs as main entities for financing M&A deals. Enterprises with overseas subsidiaries that are operating normally can establish financing and trading institutions to repay debts through the combined cash flows of the overseas target enterprise and overseas subsidiaries.

Regarding financing methods, it is recommended that domestic companies choose offshore options such as offshore M&A loans or foreign loans under domestic guarantee that do not require exit permissions. For example, CITIC Capital and Carlyle Group's acquisition of McDonald's in China utilized an offshore loan from a Hong Kong SPV to raise M&A funds. Several recent overseas M&A projects have also been completed using foreign loans under domestic guarantee, such as Tesiro's acquisition of 81% equity of Leysen and Aier Eye Hospital Group's acquisition of 75% equity of AW Healthcare Management. Of course, foreign loans under domestic guarantee must also be carefully approved. Therefore, it is suggested that domestic companies consider the current regulatory requirements and conditions, such as the relationship between the guarantor and the borrower and the use of the funds for foreign loans under domestic guarantee.

Outbound Exit of Funds Under Domestic Financing

Dual-Currency Bonds. When using dual-currency bonds, investors usually use their own USD funds or other foreign currency funds to invest in overseas projects while at the same time using RMB funds to invest in domestic projects. Therefore, dual-currency bonds can be used to circumvent regulations on the exit of domestic capital. After exiting, the funds can be transferred to SPV shares held by listed companies or other investors. In Forest Lighting's M&A of LEDVANCE in March 2017, Forest Lighting joined forces with International Data Group (IDG), a dual-currency bond, to complete the deal. IDG's Zhuhai Harmony Excellence acted as GP and listed Forest Lighting acted as LP to issue dual-currency bonds for Harmony Mingxin. The structure of the M&A transaction of LEDVANCE by Forest Lighting is as follows (see Fig. 5).

Two-Way Cross-Border RMB Fund Pooling. The principle of this method is that MNCs have equity affiliates both at home and abroad. MNCs can also designate domestic member enterprises or finance companies to open special RMB deposit accounts to deposit funds. The People's Bank of China currently imposes a cap on

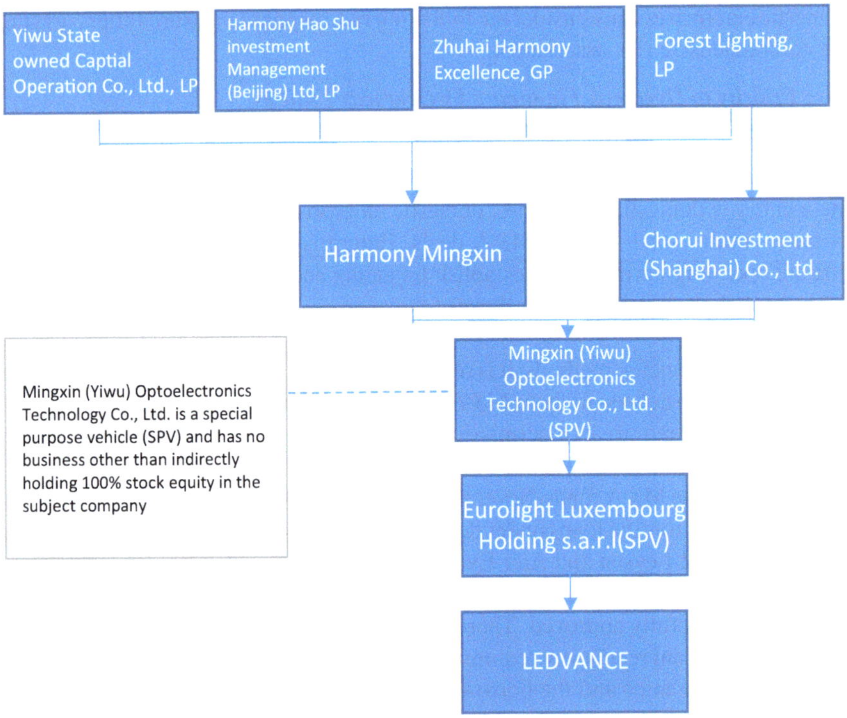

Fig. 5 Transaction structure of Forest Lighting's Acquisition of LEDVANCE. *Source Preliminary Plan for the Issue of Shares and Payment of Cash to Purchase Assets and Raise Matching Funds and Related Transactions by Forest Lighting (Revised)*, April 2017

two-way cross-border RMB pooling. This means that companies that pool funds must meet specific demands, such as business hours and revenues. In addition, offshore subsidiaries must be funded by their operating cash flows, not by borrowed RMB. However, in practice it is difficult for domestic banks to confirm the source of funds from abroad.

In terms of overseas lending, this method is also heavily regulated. For example, the *Notice on Further Clarification of Issues Concerning Overseas RMB Lending by Enterprises in China* issued on November 29, 2016 as well as the *Circular of the State Administration of Foreign Exchange on Further Advancing Foreign Exchange Administration Reform to Enhance Authenticity and Compliance Reviews* issued on January 26, 2017, impose strict requirements on the lending balance, lender qualifications, and the registration process. For these reasons, non-multinational conglomerates with insufficient capital or those involved in sensitive industries should not engage in overseas lending.

In summary, in the current restrictive regulatory environment, domestic enterprises create capital exit plans and offshore financing structures based on the nature of the transactions and their overall situation. In principle, in order to reduce the financial costs and risks of M&A deals, it is preferable to utilize an offshore SPV for offshore financing or foreign loans under domestic guarantee, and only then resorting to direct domestic financing by domestic entities.

Shiwei Zhang Partner at Zhong Lun Law Firm, focusing on securities issuance and listing, corporate M&A, private equity fund establishment and investment.

Legal and Compliance Concerns

Establishing a Compliance Management System to Manage the Risk of the World Bank Sanctions

Jihua Ding

Abstract When participating in projects funded by Multilateral Development Banks (MDBs) such as the World Bank (WB), enterprises may be sanctioned if they fail to comply with the relevant compliance requirements. If this happens, the enterprises then lose the opportunity to undertake further projects funded by these banks. Using the recent cases of the WB's sanctions against Chinese enterprises as an example, this paper analyzes the trends and reasons why the WB has sanctioned Chinese enterprises. This paper also explores the types of WB sanctions and the compliance programs requiring the establishment of enterprises. Finally, the author suggests that enterprises participating in WB projects should undertake targeted actions to avoid sanctions, improve their understanding of the sanctions system, strengthen their awareness of compliance risk, and make careful decisions. Furthermore, they should also accelerate the establishment of compliance management systems to ensure systematic and institution-wide self-monitoring and management to enhance their compliance.

Keywords Compliance management system · The World Bank (WB) · Sanctions risk

Since 2008, when Chinese enterprises began to go abroad and undertake overseas investment on a large scale, poor understanding of the common and uncommon international rules and regulations has resulted in non-compliant business practices. As a result, Chinese enterprises have been sanctioned by local governments and/or international organizations. This has caused enormous economic and reputational losses to the enterprises and led to a negative international image of Chinese enterprises.

As a major international MDB, the World Bank Group[1] (hereinafter referred to as the "WB" or "WBG") has established a system of internationally accepted

[1] The World Bank Group is a general term of five institutions: the International Bank for Reconstruction and Development (IBRD), the International Development Association (IDA), the International Finance Corporation (IFC), the Multilateral Investment Guarantee Agency (MIGA), and the International Centre for Settlement of Investment Disputes (ICSID). In the text, it is referred to as "the World Bank (WB)" or "the World Bank Group (WBG)".

J. Ding (✉)
Deputy Director of Beijing New Century, Academy on Transnational Companies, Beijing, China

H. H. Wang and M. L. Miao (eds.), *The Challenge of "Going Out"*, The Chinese Enterprise Globalization Series, https://doi.org/10.1007/978-981-99-3326-6_6

sanctions. If the WB identifies non-compliance in the bidding and operation of an enterprise participating in its funded project, the enterprise will be de-barred under its sanctions procedures. Once a company is sanctioned by the WB, it is prohibited from participating in any WB-funded projects and may even face sanctions from other MDBs, thereby restricting it from participating in MDB-funded projects.

It is worth noting that there is a high degree of geographical overlap between the distribution of WB-funded projects and the locations of "Belt and Road" projects; Chinese enterprises are involved in a large number of WB-funded projects in these regions. If these enterprises are de-barred by the WB for non-compliance, they will not be allowed to participate in projects funded by the WB or other MDBs. These enterprises may also become targets of other governments, enterprises and financial institutions, or face unfavorable cooperation. This will affect further access to projects and business opportunities, and will not be conducive to the smooth implementation of the Belt and Road Initiative. For these reasons, it is recommended that Chinese enterprises pay close attention to these concerns and avoid them.

1 Cases, Trends and Causes of World Bank Sanctions on Chinese Enterprises

At the beginning of the 21st century, a number of Chinese enterprises and individuals were debarred[2] by the WB. As Chinese companies undertook few WB-funded projects, and the influence of the companies and individuals involved held minimal influence at the time, they did not attract the business community's attention. However, this has changed. In recent years, the WB has debarred an increasing number of Chinese companies. Some of these enterprises are influential in the international arena, resulting in the WB's sanctions system attracting widespread attention from the business community.

[2] The word "debarment" used in the World Bank's sanctions regime means to "delist", "disqualify", and "blacklist". When a company is de-barred by the WB, it is neither eligible to receive or participate in the WB-funded contracts, nor to be designated as subcontractors, consultants, manufacturers or suppliers, or service providers for the WB-financed projects.

1.1 Recent Shocking Cases of Companies Sanctioned by the WB

On May 14, 2019, the World Bank announced its decision to impose debarment sanctions on Sieyuan Electric Co., Ltd., a company based in Shanghai.[3] The reason for this was that the enterprise falsified past contractual documents to meet the contract requirements when participating in the procurement process for a WB-funded power project contract in Ghana. The WB considered this action fraudulent and in violation of its procurement guidelines. The enterprise subsequently settled with the WB. The company and its 28 affiliated subsidiaries were disbarred for 15 months as part of the settlement agreement.

Moreover, if the WB sanctions an enterprise for more than one year, other MDBs can consider cross-debarment. This means that the enterprise and its subsidiaries would be ineligible to participate in any projects financed by the WB and other MDBs for the next 15 months. Suppose the firm commits to continue to cooperate fully with the WB's Integrity Vice Presidency, meets its required compliance conditions, and fully complies with the terms and conditions of the settlement agreement. In that case, the WB can remove the company from the debarment list and the international multilateral bank list at the end of the sanction period. The enterprises can also continue participating in projects funded by the WB and other multilateral banks.

It is worth noting that less than a month after the abovementioned company was sanctioned, on June 5, 2019, the WB announced that it had debarred the China Railway Construction Corporation Ltd (CRCC), which is a Chinese state-owned construction and engineering company. This debarment was also applied to its wholly-owned subsidiaries (i.e., China Railway 23rd Bureau Group Co., Ltd. (CR23) and China Railway Construction Corporation (International) Limited (CRCC International)) and the CRCC's 730 controlled affiliates[4] simultaneously. The sheer number of sanctioned subsidiaries within a single enterprise is shocking and broke the WB's previous record, which was set when it sanctioned SNC-Lavalin Group Inc. and its 133 subsidiaries in 2013. The company was sanctioned because of its misconduct during the prequalification and bidding process for the East-West Highway Corridor Improvement Project in Georgia (preparing and submitting information that misrepresented the personnel and equipment of CR23 and the experience of other entities in its group belonging to CRCC).

According to the WB's Administrative Sanctions System and the WB's Procurement Guidelines, these actions are considered fraudulent practices. After a long period of communication, the company cooperated with the WB and reached a settlement agreement, which shortened the disqualification period. After their nine-month

[3] World Bank, World Bank Group Debars Sieyuan Electric Co., Ltd., Accessed on June 16,2019. http://www.worldbank.org/en/news/press-release/2019/05/14/world-bank-group-debars-sieyuan-electric-co-ltd.

[4] The World Bank, World Bank Group Debars China Railway Construction Corporation Ltd. And two subsidiaries: http://www.worldbank.org/en/news/press-release/2019/06/05/world-bank-group-debars-china-rail way-construction-corporation-ltd-and-two-subsidiaries, June, 16, 2019.

Table 1 Number of Chinese companies and individuals sanctioned by the World Bank in recent years

Years	Enterprises	Individuals	Merged enterprises and individuals [5]
2004	1	2	3
2009	4	0	4
2011	3	1	4
2013	1	0	1
2014	1	0	1
2015	15	0	7
2016	4	0	2
2017	20	2	9
2018	50	3	21
2019 (Jan.-June)	815	0	10
Total	914	8	62

Source Author's compilation based on WB sanctions list

debarment, CRCC, CR23, CRCC International, and its 730 controlled affiliates were conditionally non-debarred for 24 months. As a condition for the release of sanctions, the companies and their affiliates had to commit to enhancing their integrity compliance programs to be consistent with the principles set out in the World Bank Group Integrity Compliance Guidelines. The company also had to commit to fully cooperating with the World Bank Group Integrity Vice Presidency. They would again be eligible to participate in WB-financed projects during this period as long as they complied with their obligations under the settlement agreement. If they did not, the conditional non-debarment would revert to debarment with conditional release.

1.2 *Overall Situation of World Bank Sanctions on Chinese Enterprises*

As of June 12, 2019, there were 54 Chinese companies sanctioned by the WB. In some cases where an enterprise directly or indirectly controls multiple enterprises, which are also affected, this number would increase to 914 if all were included. In addition, the WB has also sanctioned eight individuals, as detailed in Table 1. 18 enterprises and four individuals on the sanctions list were cross-debarred by the WB for being sanctioned by other international development banks. Two enterprises were sanctioned by the African Development Bank; 15 enterprises and two individuals were sanctioned by the Asian Development Bank; and the Inter-American Development Bank sanctioned one enterprise and one individual.

[5] The number of merged enterprises refers to the number of enterprises directly or indirectly controlled by one enterprise that are sanctioned as one.

Of course, the above statistics were obtained solely based on the WB's publicly sanctioned list and it should be noted that the WB has also notified the Chinese government of violations by some Chinese companies for misconduct that are currently under investigation. The list of these companies, however, is not publicly available. Some companies have reached settlements with the WB on their own initiative or participated in its voluntary disclosure program before initiating investigations. [6]The exact number of enterprises involved in these two groups is not available to the public, but it should be within the single digits when combined with relevant information disclosed in previous years.

More than 99% of the sanctioned enterprises are engaged in infrastructure and engineering projects. The WB often sanctions these enterprises for bidding non-compliance, which includes providing incorrect information or falsifying documents, both of which violate the anti-fraud provisions of the WB's procurement guidelines.

1.3 Why Chinese Enterprises were sanctioned by the WB?

Since 2015, the number of Chinese enterprises sanctioned by the WB has continuously increased. As more Chinese enterprises are "going out", this trend is likely to continue. There are several reasons why Chinese companies are sanctioned by the WB:

WB projects are generally in countries with a high risk of corruption. Studies have shown that the countries that receive the most funding from the WB (underdeveloped and developing countries in the world) are also considered to be at higher risk for corruption. Transparency International's (TI) annual Corruption Perceptions Index (CPI) monitors global corruption risks, scoring more than one hundred countries and territories from 0 to 100, and countries that score below 50 are considered to have serious corruption problems. In FY2014, the Integrity Vice Presidency of the WB surveyed and reported on 32 countries, 19 of which ranked 110th or lower in TI's 2013 Corruption Perceptions Index (177 countries), and more than 60% of the complaints were suspected to be related to corruption and embezzlement.

The International Development Association (IDA) provided the most funds in FY2015 to 10 countries, including Bangladesh, Ethiopia, Ghana, India, Kenya, Myanmar, Pakistan, Nigeria, Tanzania, and Vietnam, where the average CPI was only 30 points. In 2015, the analysis of the International Bank for Reconstruction and Development (IBRD) on ten countries that once received its aid (i.e., Argentina, Colombia, Egypt, India, Indonesia, Morocco, Poland, Turkey, Ukraine) was slightly better, with an average corruption index of 38.3. From 2005 to 2015, these countries were penalized in more than 280 Foreign Corrupt Practices Act (FCPA) enforcement cases in the US. Clearly, the local business environment has an essential influence

[6] The World Bank. https://www.worldbank.org/en/projects-operations/procurement/debarred-firms, 26, June, 2019.

on corporate noncompliance when Chinese companies participate in WB projects in these countries or regions.

Companies do not know enough about the WB sanctions system, the design of which is based on the US legal system. This system acts as an institutional guarantee to ensure that its procurement policies are undertaken correctly.

In procurement contracts for WB projects, the companies involved in bidding and providing services are required by contract to comply with its procurement policies. Generally speaking, only companies that participate in WB projects will take the time to understand the relevant policies, and those that do not participate in WB projects will not. However, based on past cases and the actions of Chinese companies that the WB has sanctioned, these enterprises did not take enough time to understand the sanctions system. Instead, they simply decided to not undertake said projects after being sanctioned.

Government, media, and society also fail to pay enough attention to such cases, which is also an important reason why domestic enterprises do not attach enough importance to the sanctions system. In recent years, as China's enterprises have begun to go global, many of them have participated in WB-financed projects. However, most failed to thoroughly understand or pay enough attention to the sanctions system, resulting in unknowingly breaking the rules. There are also cases where cultural differences have led to different understandings of procurement policies, resulting in misconduct and consequent sanctions. Such companies can significantly mitigate the impct of sanctions if they seek professional legal advice.

Corporate compliance awareness is generally weak. When participating in WB projects, some enterprises may not realise that behavior considered acceptable in their home country is not necessarily appropriate when operating in other countries. In looking at companies previously sanctioned by the WB, some seem to have made simple mistakes (e.g., forging bid documents, signatures, official seals) or overlooked conflicts of interest (using qualifications or performance of the parent or sister company as their own) and other forms of non-compliance. As a result, the WB has sanctioned companies for not complying with the WB's contractual requirements during the construction phase or project completion.

State-owned enterprises face greater compliance risks. In 2014, the WB became concerned that state-owned enterprises (SOEs) were already taking on a growing proportion of its funded projects and becoming involved in many social development projects. In several countries, SOEs are the targets of a relatively high proportion of complaints and investigations requests received by the Integrity Vice Presidency of WB, making up a third of the WB's sanctions list. Some SOEs involved in projects have conflicts of interest when parent and subsidiary companies bid for the same contract or commit fraud by using each other's experience and qualifications. The integrity and compliance survey results show that SOEs engage in tacit collusion in domestic projects, lack clear rules, standards and transparency, have non-transparent management and supervision structures, resulting in corruption and project losses. In recent years, the WB has focused on proposing solutions to the risks of SOE participation in projects, not only by working with SOEs, but also by discussing with relevant government departments and adjusting the World Bank Group Integrity Compliance Guidelines based on the unique characteristics of SOEs.

2 Types of World Bank Sanctions and Corporate Integrity Compliance Programs

The World Bank sanctions regime[7] defines five types of "sanctionable conduct" and proposes five types of sanctions. When enterprises are subject to sanctions, they must implement a compliance program that meets the requirements of the WB in order to be de-barred.

2.1 Basic Information on "Sanctionable Conduct"

The World Bank Group may sanction companies and individuals found by the Integrity Vice Presidency to have committed: (1) corrupt practices; (2) fraudulent practices; (3) coercive practices; (4) collusive practices; and (5) obstructive practices. With respect to specific "sanctionable conduct," Table 2 indicates that of the 416 cases, which include sanctions notices, temporary suspensions and reconciliation handled by the WB from 2007 to 2017, there were 339 cases of fraud. These included 163 cases of falsification of third-party documents, 46 cases of falsification of bank guarantees or warranty documents, 32 cases of falsification of manufacturer authorization documents, 64 cases of forged performance and experience documents, and 23 other types of document forgery. Moreover, there are also 43 cases of conspiracy, 83 cases of corruption, 19 cases of obstruction of investigation, and 2 cases of coercion.[8]

2.2 Binding Targets and Sectors Involved

The *Procurement Guidelines*[9] issued by the WB makes it clear that projects financed in whole or in part by loans provided by the IBRD, credits or contributions and project preparation advances provided by IDA, WB grants, or trust funds administered by the WB and implemented by beneficiaries, shall comply with the guidelines. The Guidelines require borrowers (including beneficiaries of the WB loans), bidders, suppliers,

---

[7] Jihua Ding, "How to defuse the growing risk of the World Bank sanctions", *Finance and Economics*, July 2019.

[8] The World Bank,World Bank Group Sanctions System Annual Report FY18, 2018.

[9] World Bank Group, Guidelines Procurement of Good, Work, and Non-Consulting Services Under IBRD Loans and IDA Credits & Grants by World Bank Borrowers, 2014.

Table 2 Statistical analysis of various types of "sanctionable conduct" from 2007 to 2017

Numbers	Types	Fraud									Conspiracy	Corruption	Obstruction	Coercion
		Falsification of third-party documents				Other types of fraud								
		Falsification of bank guarantees or warranty documents	Falsification of manufacturer authorization documents	Falsification of performance and experience documents	Other types of document falsification	False invoices or payment certifications	Misrepresentations or concealment of conflicts of interest and representation	Misrepresentations of past performance or experience	Misrepresentations of future performance	Other types of fraud				
320	Notice of sanction hearing	44	29	57	18	26	41	46	18	53	34	69	19	2
96	Reconciliation	2	3	7	5	20	21	18	12	20	9	14	0	0
Total		46	32	64	23	46	62	64	30	73				
Quantity of forgery and other fraud		163				219								
Number of sanctionable conduct		339									43	83	19	2
There are a number of sanctionable conduct in one case						59								

Source Department, data and lessons of the World Bank on suspension and debarment: 2007–2015, Second Edition

contractors and their agents (whether publicly stated or not), subcontractors, subcontractors of consulting services, service providers, and any of their employees to adhere to the highest ethical standards in the procurement and execution of contracts for WB loans.

In the WB's bidding contracts or tender documents, some specify that they have the right to audit relevant projects, some have explicit clauses stating that there must be no misconduct, and some have compliance requirements in the proxy disclosure. This means that bidders who have participated in relevant projects (whether they win the bids or not), or successful bidders who have signed contracts, are subject to the WB's sanctions system.

Around 50% of the WB's funds are spent on infrastructure projects in the energy, transportation, water, and IT sectors. These sectors are often high compliance risk areas, which the WB monitors. In 2008, a WB investigation found that companies had produced false qualifications to build infrastructure projects in East Asia and pharmaceutical companies in South Asia. The investigation found evidence of large-scale corporate cartel bidding in contracts of WB projects. In 2009, WB projects had the highest number of newly established cases with the health, transport and water sectors. A Transparency International poll rated construction as the most corruption-prone sector, and a survey of international companies showed that companies in the construction sector were more likely to lose contracts to bribery than companies in any other sector. In 2010, global road projects received an all-time high of US$9 billion in WB loans, accounting for 15% of WB's total lending for the year. The Integrity Vice Presidency's 2011 analysis of past sanctioned and pending sanctioned cases in the road sector found that WB-funded projects were not immune.[10] The WB has accused approximately 25% of the companies involved in 500-odd WB-financed projects of one or more allegations of fraud, corruption or both.

As seen in Table 3, which contains historical data on a total of 1,119[11] cases opened by the WB involving sanctionable conduct from 2007 to 2017, the top five sectors at high risk of WB project non-compliance include Transportation; Health, Nutrition and Population; Water; Agriculture and Rural Areas; and Energy and Mining.

---

[10] Curbing Fraud, Corruption, and Collusion in the Roads Sector, The World Bank Integrity Vice Presidency, 2011.

[11] In FY2014, the World Bank launched a new strategy and developed a global practice (GP) theme to replace industry classification by promoting knowledge flow across sectors, regions and the World Bank. Due to the access of data, the author makes statistics according to the industry classification standards before 2014, but the trend reflected does not affect the overall judgment. Due to the addition of new industries after 2014, the sum of the sub data is not equal to the overall data. In 2014, the statistics of social development industry included rural, urban and residential projects.

Table 3 Data Analysis for industries registered a case by the World Bank, 2007–2017

Sectors	Numbers	Percent(%)
Agriculture and rural areas	107	10
Economic policy	1	0
Education	76	7
Energy and mining	91	8
Environment	29	3
Finance and private sector	41	3
Global information and communications technology	7	1
Health, nutrition and population	200	18
Public sector management	72	6
Social protection	38	3
Transportation	208	19
Urban development	32	3
Social development	33	3
Water	142	13
Projects that do not belong to any sector	36	3
Total	1,119	100

Source Compiled by the author based on the annual reports of the WB's Integrity Vice Presidency in previous years

2.3 *Types of Sanctions as Well as Aggravating and Mitigating Factors*

There are five possible types of sanctions in the World Bank's sanctions guidelines.[12]

2.3.1 Debarment with Conditional Release

This type was set as a benchmark sanction category by the WB in 2010. The minimum period is three years, during which the target will not be eligible for WB-financed projects. If the target meets certain conditions after three years, it may be removed from the sanctions list. The WB may also require individuals to attend compliance training and education to ensure compliance awareness. The WB maintains a zero-tolerance attitude toward such misconduct as fraud and corruption.

[12] The World Bank,world bank sanction guidelines.

2.3.2 Debarment

This type of sanction is imposed for a relatively short time (one year or less) for deterrence, where the defendant company has a strong compliance program in place, and the sanctionable conduct is an isolated incident created by an employee or employees who have been since released from their contracts. The opposite extreme, where there are no reasonable grounds to believe that the defendant can be rehabilitated through compliance or other conditions, requires indefinite debarment. This sanction often applies to natural persons, privately held companies, and shell companies.

2.3.3 Conditional Non-Debarment

In this case, the company must meet the compliance conditions set by the WB within a specific time. If the company does not meet the conditions within the specified period, it is subject to de-barring. This type of sanction applies when the respondent has taken comprehensive and voluntary corrective measures, indicating that the sanction is already unnecessary. It is also applicable when the respondent's parent company and its affiliates did not directly engage in misconduct, but its lack of systematic oversight caused the misconduct to occur, for which it is liable.

2.3.4 Letter of Reprimand

When the misconduct is minor or the company is only a peripheral participant, the penalty of debarment or conditional non-debarment is too severe. In such cases, the WB will issue a letter of reprimand to the respondent, either publicly or privately. For example, the affiliate of an accused company can be held jointly liable for misconduct due to an incident of oversight deficiency even if the affiliate did not participate in any misconduct.

2.3.5 Restitution

In some cases, the WB requires the indicted enterprise to provide compensation or appropriate remedies to the borrower or other entities to make up for the loss caused by the misconduct. In the case of fraud in executing a contract, a quantifiable amount may be required to return to the client's country or project. This is applicable in cases where the error resulted in clear and quantifiable damages. Adopting restitution is often tricky, mainly due to the lack of clear criteria for calculating the amount to be restored and the poor identification of the right person to be compensated.

The WB adopts a cumulative misconduct calculation approach in sentencing. When making a sanction recommendation, it does so for other misconducts (corruption and conspiracy occurring in the same bid) or misconduct in different circumstances (misconduct in different projects or the same project occurring in different periods). Each sanctionable act is considered separately after it occurs and cumulatively as the basis for the sanction. If the WB has previously charged the subject with misconduct, the WB will consider increasing the sanction. Sanctions are also considered to be mitigated if they are not significant participants or if they cooperate with the WB's investigation. See Table 4 for specific considerations.

2.4 *Implementing Effective Integrity Compliance Programs to Lift Sanctions*

The WB draws on the "carrot and stick" policy to impose compliance requirements on sanctioned companies to promote companies participating in WB projects to curb corruption and take responsibility for corrupt practices. By establishing a compliance program, companies demonstrate their efforts to establish self-corrective mechanisms for misconduct. Whether for conditional non-debarment or settling with the WB, companies must establish a compliance program as required by the Integrity Compliance Office (ICO). Companies are encouraged to invest resources (budget and human resources) to prevent misconduct, and to take the initiative to identify, monitor and remedy misconduct.

To guide companies in developing compliance programs, the WB has issued its *Integrity Compliance Guidelines,* which state that effective compliance programs prevent, monitor, investigate and remedy corrupt, collusive, coercive and fraudulent practices. Companies should integrate integrity and compliance efforts and responsibilities into their daily operations. The document covers 11 goals: (1) clearly prohibit misconduct; (2) assign compliance responsibilities to management, employees, and compliance departments; (3) initiate compliance programs beginning with risk assessment and review; (4) develop internal policies for employee due diligence; restrictions on public officials' arrangements, gifts and hospitality as well as entertainment and travel reimbursements; political contributions; charitable contributions and sponsorships; facilitation payments; record keeping; fraud; collusive and coercive practices; (5) conduct compliance management of business partners, including due diligence, letting the other party to make a commitment to integrity and compliance and make a formal and informal notification of their own commitment, proper documentation, appropriate compensation costs, and oversight; (6) improve internal control systems and strengthen controls in the financial, contractual responsibility, and decision-making processes; (7) ongoing training and communication; (8) develop incentive systems, including positive encouragement and disciplinary action; (9) establish reporting channels, clear responsibility for reporting, provide consultation and advice, set up internal hotline, and conduct regular certification through review; (10) remedy misconduct, establish investigation processes, and take responsive action; and (11) carry out joint actions to promote integrity compliance programs.

Table 4 Aggravating and mitigating factors considered in sanctions

Considerations	Specific factors	Aggravating circumstance
Severity of the violations	Repeated patterns of illegal behavior; The defendant's use of complex means (degree of sophistication of planning, diversity of techniques applied, degree of concealment) to commit the offense, the number and type of persons or organizations involved, the continuous development or duration of the scheme over a long period of time, the involvement of multiple jurisdictions; Two or more organizers, management and planners play a key role in the illegal act; The role of the management in the violation: senior management in the organization is involved, condones or is deliberately unaware of the misconduct; Public officials or the WB staff involved in the conspiracy or are implicated	Considering one or more factors, sanctions can be increased by one to five years
Actual damage caused by the violations	Damage to public welfare or projects: misconduct will obviously lead to or involve the risk of death or personal injury, and public health or safety is threatened by misconduct; Extent of damage to the project: poor contract performance (e.g., quality or quantity of products and services not in accordance with the terms of the contract) results in delays	Considering one or more factors, sanctions can be increased by one to five years
Interference with the Integrity Vice Presidency's investigations	Interference with the investigative process: deliberately destroy, forge, modify or hide the evidence or make false statements to the investigators in order to seriously impede Integrity Vice Presidency's investigation; and threaten, harass or intimidate any party to prevent it from disclosing the information related to the investigation, and seriously hinder the World Bank's right to audit the contract or obtain information; Intimidate or bribe the witness: the defendant intimidates or injures the witness's property, work, reputation, family members or significant others, and the defendant bribes the witness, resulting in the witness's failure to cooperate with the World Bank	Considering one or more factors, sanctions can be increased by one to three years

(continued)

Table 4 (continued)

Considerations	Specific factors	Aggravating circumstance
Past history of violations	In the past, there were debarment or other penalties: the past history must involve misconduct other than debarment of the defendant for misconduct. Prior history may include debarment from other multilateral banks	Considering one or more factors, sanctions can be increased by ten years
Considerations	Specific factors	Mitigating punishment
Play a backseat role in misconduct	The defendant is a minor, highly insignificant or peripheral participant. Individuals participation without decision-making power; and condone, or intentionally ignore misconduct	Up to 25% reduction
Voluntary corrective measures	Cessation of misconduct: the timetable for action indicates the extent to which it reflects genuine regret and reform intentions, or the severity of the anticipated steps to mitigate the sanction. Internal action against those responsible: the management takes all appropriate measures to address misconduct, including taking appropriate disciplinary actions and/or remedial measures against the relevant employees, agents or representatives; Effective compliance plan: establish, improve and implement the company's compliance plan; Restitution or financial remedy: when the defendant voluntarily resolves any deficiencies in the enforcement of the contract or returns funds obtained through misconduct	Up to 50% reduction, and in exceptional cases a more substantial reduction may be required

(continued)

The WB is concerned with the effectiveness of integrity compliance programs developed by enterprises. While an effective compliance program does not necessarily guarantee that misconduct will not occur, it should at least include appropriate measures that: (1) strive to prevent misconduct from occurring; (2) enable the detection of possible misconduct; (3) allow for investigation of suspected misconduct; and (4) remedy well-documented misconduct.

Therefore, an effective corporate compliance program must address the risks it faces. The Integrity Compliance Office works with all parties to jointly oversee the enterprises' implementation of an integrity compliance program benchmarked against the WB's *Integrity Compliance Guidelines.* Based on this, the Integrity

Table 4 (continued)

Considerations	Specific factors	Aggravating circumstance
Cooperate with the investigation of the Integrity Vice Presidency	Defendant's assistance and/or continuous cooperation with the Integrity Vice Presidency: according to the Integrity Vice Presidency's statement, the defendant provides substantial assistance in the investigation, including voluntary disclosure; the authenticity, completeness and reliability of any information or testimony provided; the nature and scope of assistance and the timeliness of assistance; Internal investigation: the defendant conducts an effective internal investigation into the misconduct and relevant facts about it, and also imposes sanctions on it, and shared the results with the Integrity Vice Presidency. Instruct the defendant to conduct internal investigation on the behaviors and facts related to the misconduct beyond the scope of sanctions, and share the results with the Integrity Vice Presidency; Admission or acceptance of guilt or acceptance of responsibility: admission of guilt or responsibility for misconduct prior to an investigation is more important than investigation or subsequent procedures. Voluntary restraint: voluntary restraint of World Bank funded tenders prior to the outcome of the investigation can also be considered as a form of assistance and/or cooperation	Up to 33% reduction, with more significant reductions in special cases

Source World Bank Sanctioning Guidelines

Compliance Office reviews the enterprises' conduct of compliance management. They also review whether companies allocate resources and tailor compliance policies and controls to these risks based on their size, industry characteristics, geographic location, and specific risks.

To improve the effectiveness of an integrity compliance program, companies may consider the following steps and processes: (1) When establishing a compliance department, companies can set up compliance functions at both the headquarters and the worksite. Some companies may choose to have regional compliance officers and local integrity focal points between organizations to serve as resource providers and supporters of integrity compliance initiatives; (2) When conducting integrity compliance due diligence, companies should refuse to hire and work with potential employees or business partners with integrity compliance issues; (3) Document and archive decision records and processes; (4) Use reporting mechanisms to receive integrity recommendations and report integrity concerns, which should serve to increase employees trust in reporting mechanisms as they can report incidents confidentially without fear of retaliation; (5) Companies should take appropriate action against misconduct. Appropriate action against misconduct includes investigations, disciplinary actions, other remedial measures, and continuously revising and optimizing integrity compliance programs; (6) Companies should actively promote the concept of integrity compliance, either internally by holding ethics days, conducting competitions, discussing compliance issues, or externally by engaging business partners in integrity commitments and compliance training and taking collective action on compliance; (7) When the World Bank Integrity Compliance Office determines whether a sanctioned business is eligible for its sanctions to be lifted, it wants to see that the business has allocated resources according to the risks it faces, complies with the principles of the code of integrity, and has a solid track record of implementing compliance programs. The Integrity Compliance Office will also seek assurances that the firm will continue to advance its integrity compliance program after being released from sanctions, for example, through management commitment or the development of a forward-looking action plan.

3 Suggestions for Enterprises to Manage the Risk of World Bank Sanctions

Given the global trend of strengthening corporate compliance, the compliance program advocated by both the WB and countries to prevent and combat corruption is becoming a global standard. The integrity compliance program promoted by the WB may become a prerequisite for enterprises of a particular scale to participate in its projects in the future. Enterprises undertaking projects financed by the WB and MDBs should take the initiative to establish compliance management systems to hedge against compliance risks and enhance their competitiveness through increased compliance.

3.1 Targeted Prevention of Compliance Risks

The World Bank Integrity Vice Presidency assesses reports of fraud and corruption in WB-financed projects through a detailed review system. It examines the effectiveness of the WB's anti-corruption control mechanisms in preventing, detecting, and responding to fraud and corruption. Based on more than ten years of experience, the Integrity Vice Presidency issues red flags for common fraud and corruption in the procurement of Bank-financed projects. The following situations in a bid may be considered red flags by the WB and companies should be aware of them: (1) Complaints from bidders and other parties (including WB staff, competitors, contractors or other bidders, government officials, employees of NGOs, and other MDBs); (2) Numerous contracts with values just under procurement thresholds (tailoring a contract to fall just under the procurement threshold or seemingly arbitrarily splitting a contract into several more minor contracts to avoid higher-level review or competitive bidding); (3) Unusual bid patterns such as bid-rigging and quotation exception; (4) Seemingly inflated fees from agents or prices of goods to intermediaries or suppliers; (5) Suspicious bidder; (6) Lowest bidder not selected; (7) Unjustified and/or repeated sole source awards; (8) Unjustified changes in contract terms and value; (9) After the contract has been signed and during implementation, contractors often propose different orders; (10) Goods/services are of low quality or not delivered.

In addition, enterprises that are participating in or have participated in WB projects in recent years and will continue to participate in similar projects in the future should strengthen their ability to identify of existing compliance risks in relevant projects. If there are compliance risks in current projects, enterprises should take particular efforts in identifying, rectifying and responding to them and may even participate in the WB's voluntary information disclosure program. If a company has been involved in projects with high compliance risks in the past (within ten years), it should also take appropriate risk control measures to significantly develop effective compliance programs to prevent compliance risks in current or future projects.

3.2 Improving Understanding of the WB Sanctions System

Enterprises participating in WB projects must strengthen their understanding of its sanctions system. Based on the feedback from enterprises participating in WB projects, it is clear that many do not understand the sanctions system. As a result, they ignore notices of sanctions proceedings and are de-barred by the WB. This has resulted in missed opportunities to communicate and reconcile with the WB at an earlier stage.

It is worth noting that while an effective response can help companies mitigate fact-specific allegations and disputes, responding to WB documents also poses practical challenges for companies. On the one hand, WB documents issued to companies may not fully disclose evidence related to allegations, and respondent companies and lawyers may respond inappropriately. On the other hand, the absence of a factual basis for some allegations may limit the defendant's flexibility to defend itself later in the sanctions process. It is more likely, that the sanctions committee may use a reasoned defense response letter as a basis for admitting the facts. It is also important to note that some enterprises may believe that the Integrity Vice Presidency does not have compulsory investigative powers over enterprises, which lead to confrontation with the WB's investigation. Senior US experts designed the WB's investigation and sanction procedures and investigation methods, which means that approaches are based on the experience of the US Department of Justice and European Union law enforcement agencies, providing the WB with a diverse range of investigation methods. Furthermore, the WB can collect relevant information from multiple channels by establishing a global information network through long-term cooperation with government departments and financial institutions of countries.

In addition, the investigative team is highly experienced, staffed not only by former government investigators but also by lawyers and other intelligence experts. Therefore, whenever the Integrity Vice Presidency initiates an investigation, and a company receives corresponding notification documents, it must be taken seriously. While professionally responding to the investigation, a comprehensive self-examination should also be undertaken. If found guilty of non-compliance, it is best to quickly settle with the WB to ensure the most favourable outcome for the company.

3.3 Strengthen Compliance Risk Awareness and Make Prudent Decisions

From a broader perspective, the current era of globalization is changing and leading to new business rules. This means that compliance will likely become a prerequisite for all enterprises to carry out business cooperation. Compliance must be part of the strategic decision-making level of enterprises, not only for domestic operations but also for "going out" and international operations. When the domestic market is affected by the international market, if there is no compliance behavior in the domestic market, there will be no compliance behavior in the international market either. Enterprises should put the awareness of compliance before the awareness of competition and globalization, considering it as the primary consideration for business decisions.

When undertaking projects supported by the WB or other MDBs, all enterprises must assess the compliance risk of the project location in detail and make prudent decisions. If they are unaware of compliance risks, or if they prepare to follow domestic business habits or usual practices to participate in the bidding. Suppose they do not comprehensively assess the compliance risks exposed by the project. In that case, enterprises must strengthen their compliance training as soon as possible and engage experienced compliance experts or lawyers who are well versed in compliance to participate in related projects and provide advice and opinions. In this way, enterprises can make correct decisions and protect their business results in the complex, changing, and strongly regulated international business environment.

3.4 Promoting the Creation of Enterprise Compliance Management Systems

What should enterprises do to strengthen compliance awareness? What is the most feasible way? Most international enterprises choose to establish an effective compliance management system and apply systematic and institutionalized management tools to meet the challenges of compliance risk. Enterprises should do two things in creating a compliance management system.

Establish a compliance management system.[13] This includes establishing a compliance management organization, formulating various compliance management policies that respond to external laws and regulations and internationally accepted rules in the course of business, and institutionalizing compliance training, compliance performance assessment, and self-monitoring systems. Senior management should also lead by example in developing and adhering to a culture of compliance. If the company has business with the World Bank or other international multilateral development financial institutions, then the company's compliance management system should cover all sanctionable behaviour.

Ensure the effectiveness of compliance management systems. To ensure that the compliance management system is well designed and can be effectively implemented, the following steps are crucial: make decisions based on compliance risk; provide sufficient and appropriate resources; ensure that the compliance management department reports to the board of directors independently; integrate compliance function into other departments; internally evaluate the independence of compliance; monitor compliance in high-risk areas such as third parties and high-risk ares such as bidding, and provide training to business partners with high compliance risk; establish effective reporting and monitoring channels, and carry out targeted compliance training and communication for all staff. It is worth noting that the initiatives mentioned above are also important indicators for the World Bank Integrity Compliance Office to assess the effectiveness of enterprise compliance programs.

4 Conclusion

When participating in WB-funded projects, enterprises need to comply with international rules. Strengthening compliance awareness can help companies proactively prevent, monitor, and respond to compliance risk. With the ability to control the compliance risk when taking part in WB projects, enterprises will be able to participate in more projects funded or procured by other multilateral development banks and governments of developed countries, providing them with more business opportunities in the international market. Therefore, enterprises committed to globalization

---

[13] Jihua Ding, "Six steps to create an effective enterprise compliance management system", *China Foreign Exchange*, July 2019.

should speed up the process of establishing compliance management systems and strengthen their compliance management capabilities.

Jihua Ding Ph.D., Deputy Director of Beijing New-century Academy on Transnational Corporations (NATC), Expert of National Enterprise Compliance Committee. Research fields: MNC strategy, cross-border M&A and corporate compliance management.

How Can Chinese Enterprises Cope with Increasingly Stringent Global Compliance Challenges and Government Investigations—From the Perspective of Anti-Monopoly Work and Data Protection

Zhisong Deng and Jianmin Dai

Abstract In recent years, the global regulatory environment has been treacherous. In the areas of anti-monopoly work and data protection, regulators have frequently imposed heavy fines on non-compliant enterprises; anti-monopoly law enforcement techniques have constantly changed, and new laws related to data protection have been implemented. Against this background, compliance challenges and legal risks faced by Chinese enterprises expanding abroad have intensified and have resulted in delays, blocks, or even the shelving of transactions that require massive compensation packages and even changes to business models. Executives may also face personal criminal liability. To effectively address these risks, Chinese companies should pay close attention to trends in legislation and law enforcement worldwide, strengthen risk identification capabilities, ensure that they have adequate response plans and carry out multi-jurisdictional coordination during the process, and undertake targeted remedial and improvement measures afterwards to ensure sustainable overseas expansion.

Keywords Chinese enterprises · Anti-monopoly · Data protection · Legal risks · Compliance

The year 2018 saw the start of the "China-US trade war", which, as of September 2021, still has not yet been resolved. In 2018, the term "trade protectionism" became a buzzword. Following in the footsteps of the Trump administration, the European

Z. Deng (✉)
Dentons China Competition and Antitrust Practice, Beijing, China

J. Dai
Dentons China Competition and Antitrust Practice, Shanghai, China

H. H. Wang and M. L. Miao (eds.), *The Challenge of "Going Out"*, The Chinese Enterprise Globalization Series, https://doi.org/10.1007/978-981-99-3326-6_7

Union has also passed legislation specifically to review Chinese investments.[1] India and various South American countries such as Brazil, Argentina and Chile, have also launched anti-China policies.[2] Such behaviour and policies demonstrate the ever-changing nature of the geopolitical and regulatory environment.

Despite the turbulent economic and political situation around the world, after more than a decade of "going out", the development and growth of China's enterprises cannot deviate from their current track of globalization. For Chinese enterprises, participating in a globalized world is not only a reflection of a company's strength, but also a necessary part of China's economic restructuring efforts and industrial transformation. Therefore, Chinese enterprises should embrace the opportunities and challenges this brings rather than thinking of it as their 'Achilles' Heel'.

Although the difficulties in compliance continue to grow, there is a silver lining. Regulators have imposed heavy fines on companies in recent global legal debates and discussions on antitrust and data protection. However, understanding overseas regulatory trends and enforcement priorities, conducting thorough due diligence on transactions, and identifying various risks beforehand are all precautions that companies can take to better protect themselves. Chinese companies should also stay abreast of the latest trends in major global jurisdictions, sort out regulatory and compliance requirements, and establish sound response plans so that they are prepared before anything happens. Compliance has become a significant risk for Chinese companies, which must understand fully the risks involved when expanding into overseas markets.

1 Treacherous Global Regulatory Waters

Despite rising trade protectionism, Chinese enterprises' overseas investments have continued to increase. After a temporary decline in 2017, China's foreign trade levels generally recovered in 2018.[3] Despite trade friction, the US, Europe, and Asia remain highly sought after by Chinese investors.[4] Since President Xi proposed the "Belt and Road Initiative (BRI)" in 2013, countries and regions along the route have also provided overseas investment opportunities. In terms of the overall trend, China's foreign investment represents a new era in which foreign and private enterprises go

[1] China Council for the Promotion of International Trade, "15 European countries will legislate to review Chinese investment", http://www.ccpit.org/Contents/Channel_3673/2018/0522/1006130/content_1006130.htm.

[2] Minister of Commerce:Statistics of trade friction cases, http://trb.mofcom.gov.cn/article/cx/.

[3] The Ministry of Commerce:*China Foreign Trade Situation Report* (Spring 2018).

[4] CCG, *Report on Chinese Enterprises Globalization (2018)*, quoted from www.cssn.cn, http://news.cssn.cn/zx/bwyc/201812/t20181203_4787501.shtml.

hand in hand. However, it also has brought with it a significant shift from traditional projects such as infrastructure and manufacturing to high-tech, intelligent manufacturing and other fields.[5]

However, while the "going out" of high-end manufacturing projects, services, and technology will likely result in minor changes, the regulatory environment around the world is changing rapidly. There are breakthroughs and innovations in traditional anti-monopoly law enforcement techniques, while new laws related to data protection are also coming into effect worldwide. There is a tendency for the two to complement each other and integrate. In particular, as Chinese companies move up the industrial ladder, acquire advanced technologies overseas and respond to mid- and high-end consumer demand, the TMT industry has become increasingly active in overseas M&A transactions. This means that the regulation of emerging industries continues to challenge the forefront of the legal field.

1.1 Anti-monopoly and Competition Law Regulation

Although anti-monopoly law is not a newly emerging area of law, national or regional competition enforcement agencies have made frequent moves in recent years, making antitrust compliance an important issue in new times and new industries. The most well-known case is Google, which has been fined repeatedly in the EU for monopolistic practices with fines totaling more than 8 billion euros. As a major foreign player in Europe, Google has a significant market share in online search and advertising, and it owns the Android operating system. The European Commission's Competition Commissioner Margrethe Vestager, known for her tough style, has investigated or fined many non-European companies aside from Google, including Amazon, as well as Hollywood studios Disney and Warner. More recently, Apple has also been receiving increased attention.[6]

The increased cooperation between enforcement agencies also poses new challenges to the global compliance of multinational companies. This year, for example, after the establishment of China's new antitrust enforcement agency, the State Administration for Market Regulation, Director Zhang Mao led a delegation to visit the European Union and sign a cooperation agreement with Vestager in the area of competition.[7] This signifies that cooperation and coordination in the field of antitrust

[5] CCG, *Report on Chinese Enterprises Globalization (2018)*, quoted from www.cssn.cn, http://news.cssn.cn/zx/bwyc/201812/t20181203_4787501.shtml.

[6] www.huanqiu.com, "EU Charges Apple With App Store Antitrust Violations in Spotify Case", https://www.msn.cn/zh-cn/news/technology/%E6%AC%A7%E7%9B%9F%E5%B0%86%E5%B0%B1spotify%E6%8C%87%E6%8E%A7%E5%AF%B9%E8%8B%B9%E6%9E%9C%E5%B1%95%E5%BC%80%E5%8F%8D%E5%9E%84%E6%96%AD%E8%B0%83%E6%9F%A5/ar-AAAXjLt.

[7] The State Administration for Market Regulation: "Zhang Mao Visited EU with Delegation, Signing a Competition Agreement and Successfully Holding China-EU Competition Dialogue

enforcement will continue to advance and strengthen among different countries, while also presenting multifaceted risks for companies.

In addition to Europe and the US where the anti-monopoly enforcement is traditionally active, countries along the Belt and Road have also accelerated their own anti-monopoly legislative processes. These anti-monopoly laws include the *Law of the Russian Soviet Federative Socialist Republic on Competition and Restriction of Monopoly Activity on Commodity Markets*, *Indian Competition Law*, *Vietnam Competition Law*, and Turkey's *Act on the Protection of Competition*. At the same time, the anti-monopoly enforcement efforts of BRI countries have been intensified, with countries like Singapore and Russia frequently issuing high anti-monopoly fines. The fines are generally targeting foreign-invested enterprises.

1.2 Personal Information and Data Protection Regulation

Data security and privacy protection have become a topic of concern in recent years. According to the *Breach Level Index* released by Gemalto, 974 data breaches were observed worldwide in the first half of 2016, which led to the successful theft or loss of data records exceeding 554 million. In response, significant jurisdictions worldwide have improved their laws and legal systems in this area. In Europe, in April 2016, the European Parliament formally adopted the most stringent regulations in its history - *General Data Protection Regulation* (GDPR)—to replace the *EU Data Protection Directive* issued in 1995. Although the GDPR only came into effect in May 2018, it has already been utilized against American Internet giants.[8] In the US, in May 2017, President Trump signed an executive order titled "Strengthening the Cybersecurity of Federal Networks and Critical Infrastructure". The US Department of Homeland Security (DHS) is currently implementing this law. Companies face significant legal risks for data and privacy protection in these countries.

In February 2019, the US Federal Trade Commission (FTC) announced that TikTok, owned by ByteDance, agreed to pay a US$5.7 million settlement to resolve charges for violating the *US Children's Online Privacy Protection Act (COPPA)*. The investigation reportedly began in 2016 when Musical.ly, a short music video platform, illegally collected names, emails and other personal information from users under the age of 13 without parental consent. However, Musical.ly was acquired by Douyin's parent company ByteDance in November 2017, and later merged with TikTok in August 2018, continuing under the name TikTok. As a result, Douyin had to pay the fine.[9]

---

under Witness of Both Sides Leaders", http://home.saic.gov.cn/xw/zj/201904/t20190410_292706.html.

[8] "French Highest Administrative Court Upholds 50 Million Euro Fine against Google for Alleged GDPR Violations", www.news.cn.

[9] "TikTok, owned by ByteDance agreed to pay a $5.7 million settlement to resolve charges for violating the US Children's Online Privacy Protection Act", http://www.sohu.com/a/298367918_260616.

In February 2017, Vizio, a subsidiary of Letv, was also charged jointly by the FTC and the State of New Jersey with collecting TV users' viewing data without their knowledge. Vizio was also charged for sharing this data with third parties without the knowledge or consent of the TV users. Ultimately, as part of a settlement agreement in the case, Vizio agreed to delete all data collected prior to March 1, 2016. In addition, Vizio agreed to implement a data privacy program as required, undergo an evaluation review every two years thereafter, and pay US$2.2 million in compensation.[10]

In another example, in July–August 2014, consumers in Singapore and Taiwan respectively complained to local regulators that Xiaomi phones were uploading users' personal data to servers located in mainland China without their consent. On August 10, 2014, Xiaomi issued a statement, acknowledging that its phones would automatically upload users' phone numbers, IMSI (International Mobile Subscriber Identity) and IMEI (International Mobile Equipment Identity) codes back to Xiaomi's servers in Beijing without their consent. Xiaomi apologized for this and stated that it would improve its products to protect the privacy of its users.

1.3 Cross-Regulation of Anti-Monopoly and Data Protection

Antitrust regulatory enforcement is increasingly directed at Internet giants. This means that the old antitrust laws are being challenged by new concerns. For instance, cutting-edge issues such as the sharing economy and the handling of data are no longer covered by traditional antitrust protection laws, leading to overlap in antitrust and data protection laws. Around the world, enforcement agencies have already made attempts to enforce antitrust regulatory laws.

Facebook, for example, was penalized by the German Federal Cartel Office on February 7, 2019, for dominating the social networking market and, in turn, abusing its dominant market position. Specifically, Facebook was able to access data at will after users logged into their accounts on its third-party platforms, including such apps like WhatsApp and Instagram, track the websites users visited, and also link that data to their Facebook accounts.[11] This is a clear case of competing or cross-regulation between antitrust and data protection, where the laws violated are not antitrust laws, but the specific abuses incorporated the EU code of conduct on data protection.

Shortly after this, on February 13, 2019, foreign media reported that the Japanese government planned to set up a new antitrust regulatory body, the purpose of which would be to monitor large technology companies, such as Facebook and Google, and ensure the protection of personal data. The agency would likely also draft new

[10] "Vizio was charged with collecting user data illegally and fined $2.2 million", http://www.sohu.com/a/125687359_114877.

[11] *Facebook is ruled by The German Federal Cartel Office of abusing its market position to collect information.* https://wallstreetcn.com/articles/3479106.

guidelines to assess whether M&As could lead to a monopoly of communications data or personal data.[12]

2 Challenges and Opportunities—Inseparable Legal Risks

The increasing legal risks for companies mean that they face more difficulties, from delayed deals to hefty fines or even barriers that make them unable to enter specific overseas markets due to forced divestment. Executives of companies also face significant risks. As in the case of Huawei's Meng Wanzhou, individuals can be subject to severe consequences of corporate expansion and even become embroiled in intergovernmental confrontation. Companies that have not yet "gone out" are eager to try, while companies that have "gone out" are skating on thin ice. It is essential for all companies and executives to have an excellent understanding of the legal risks of overseas government regulation before "going out" or going global. The following information lists the significant legal risks Chinese enterprises face when "going out".

2.1 Criminal Risks for Individual Executives

For companies going abroad, the potential criminal liability of executives is perhaps the most important concern. If the criminal risk is triggered, it may also spread to other countries that have extradition treaties with the country involved. Unlike China, many countries have criminal liability for some of the most severe monopoly violations, most notably the US, from the perspective of antitrust law. For example, China's National Development and Reform Commission (NDRC) imposed sky-high fines on the 12 Japanese parts and bearing manufacturers involved in the case of a Japanese auto parts company in 2014. However, this Japanese company had faced similar issues in the US, resulting in Japanese executives going to jail. In 2013, two Japanese executives from Denso were sentenced to 15 to 16 months in prison and fined US$20,000 for their involvement in the price-fixing of auto parts in the US.[13]

---

[12] The Japanese government plans to set up a new anti-monopoly agency, focusing on large technology companies such as Google and FB. http://tech.qq.com/a/20190213/009489.htm.

[13] Two executives of Denso were jailed for auto parts price fixing in the US. http://news.sina.com.cn/w/2013-05-22/110427194009.shtml.

2.2 Investment Setbacks

Antitrust reviews have traditionally been the reason why overseas M&A has been blocked or put on hold. The form of review is often in the name of competitive analysis, but in essence, it may impact the economic lifeline of the host country. For example, in the case of the China International Marine Containers (CIMC) acquisition of Borg Industries B.V., after the European Commission conducted a substantive review of the transaction, the acquisition proposal had to be adjusted. It was eventually approved on the condition that its tank business be stripped.[14]

Although the transaction was completed, there was a gap with the initial acquisition target. This is similar to the merger plan of European railroad giant Siemens and Alstom. In early 2019, France and Germany claimed that the transaction could help Europe resist the threat of competition from China's CRRC Corporation Limited (CRRC). However, the European Commission rejected the merger on the grounds that it would hinder market competition.[15] Although the deal did not directly involve Chinese investors, it serves as an example of how an anti-monopoly review can be used in the greater game of economic power.

In addition to the risk of centralized antitrust reviews, data security is also becoming a reason for the failire of certain deals. In March 2019, the Committee on Foreign Investment in the United States (CFIUS) asked Chinese mobile gaming company Kunlun Tech to sell its wholly-owned stake in the social networking software Grindr. As the world's most significant social networking software for sexual minorities, Grindr was founded in the US in 2009, with Kunlun Tech buying its shares in the company in 2016 and 2018. CFIUS's reviews of transactions have always focused on national security risks, including infrastructure and technology restrictions, and more recently, data security concerns.[16] CFIUS's request for divestment on the grounds of personal information security is not a case in point, with many Chinese companies suffering setbacks in investments in the pharmaceutical and health sectors.[17]

[14] CIMC reaches indirect holding of Burg Industries B.V.with EUR 48 million. http://finance.sina.com.cn/stock/s/20061208/11423147767.shtml.

[15] European railroad giants' merger plan falls through, making CRRC avoid rivals for now. http://www.nbd.com.cn/articles/2019-02-07/1298111.html.

[16] Social software endangers national security? It is reported that the US government asked Kunlun Tech to sell Grindr. https://m.21jingji.com/article/20190327/herald/691a0df26316002918ef81d8e5c2a929.html.

[17] CFIUS pressures a Chinese company to exit its investment in the US, raising concerns. http://www.ccpit.org/Contents/Channel_3673/2019/0415/1153460/content_1153460.htm.

2.3 Forced Delays in Transactions

Even if a transaction is not ultimately blocked, unnecessary delays can also have a significant impact on the parties involved. This requires companies to consider the timing and scope of government reviews during the initial stages of the transaction and take compliance into account. One example is the acquisition of the Swiss agrochemical seed giant Syngenta Group by ChemChina, which was expected to be completed by 2016. However, the offer deadline had to be extended several times due to national approvals involving nearly 20 jurisdictions. The deal was finally closed in mid-2017.[18]

2.4 Lengthy Civil Litigation and Huge Settlements

Costs related to weak compliance also include lengthy civil litigation, which often results in having to pay out substantial financial compensation. In January 2005, five Chinese vitamin-C manufacturers (China's Hebei Welcome Pharmaceutical Co. Ltd. (Welcome), North China Pharmaceutical Group Corp. (NCPC), Jiangshan Pharmaceutical (Jiangsu) Co., Ltd, Northeast Pharmaceutical Group Co., Ltd., and CSPC Weisheng Pharmaceutical Co., Ltd.,) were involved in a well-known legal case. These companies were sued by US enterprises in a local court for jointly negotiating to reduce the supply of vitamin-C products exported to the US. In 2013, the United States District Court for the Eastern District of New York, Brooklyn, ruled against Welcome and NCPC and awarded the plaintiffs approximately US$162 million in damages. The other three Chinese companies involved in the case settled out of court with the plaintiffs and paid a total of US$33 million in the settlement. However, Welcome's persistence took the case to the United States Court of Appeals for the Second Circuit and ultimately the Supreme Court of the United States. The case was finally settled in June 2018, ending in defeat after more than a decade. Regardless of the damages or settlement awarded by the court, the legal fees and efforts expended during that ten-year period alone are a painful lesson.

With improved laws and increased awareness of personal privacy, there have been frequent lawsuits over inadequate data protection. In November 2018, the customer reservation database for Starwood Hotels, a subsidiary of Marriott International, was hacked, resulting in a possible leak of about 500 million customers' personal information. In early December, a lawyer filed a class-action lawsuit against Marriott International in the US, seeking damages as much as US$12.5 billion.[19]

---

[18] Antitrust review was approved by the US and Europe, and ChemChina's acquisition of Syngenta made key progress, http://www.ce.cn/cysc/ny/gdxw/201704/07/t20170407_21779540.shtml.

[19] Marriott Hotel was hit with a class action lawsuit over database breach, up to $12.5 billion, https://tech.sina.com.cn/i/2018-12-03/doc-ihprknvs8439051.shtml.

2.5 *Adaptation of Business Models*

For some emerging Internet companies that use a "sharing economy" concept in their operations, it is the challenges to their operating models that are the most daunting, rather than financial fines or liability. At the end of 2018, for example, Germany's data protection regulator said it would investigate Mobike's data and privacy policies, citing violations of EU data protection laws. As a bike-sharing platform, Mobike collects a large amount of data from users through its mobile apps, including their exact location.[20] For non-European service providers like Mobike, the GDPR poses additional challenges due to its restrictions on transferring data outside the EU. Compliance in this area will likely change Mobike's approach to managing its user data, which will in turn impact its business model.

3 How Can Enterprises Better Handle Compliance Challenges

These cases prove that the journey of Chinese enterprises "going out" is far from easy thanks to an increasingly stringent regulatory and legal environment worldwide. However, in the face of risks, enterprises still can take advantage of overseas investment opportunities if they take the right preventive measures. Enterprises should manage compliance risks that may lead to investigations, while at the same time minimizing losses with the help of professional lawyers and a systematic response plan in the event of government investigations.

3.1 *Ex-Ante Prevention: Risk Identification and Multiple Control*

Understanding overseas regulatory trends and enforcement priorities are the prerequisites for effective compliance. Before making overseas investments, enterprises should conduct comprehensive and targeted due diligence, identify risks in advance, understand specific regulation and compliance requirements, and establish response plans. Meanwhile, enterprises also need to keep abreast of the latest legislative developments and regulatory trends in major jurisdictions worldwide to guide business decisions.

In addition to suitable risk identification, Chinese companies must also establish a comprehensive global compliance system. With the increasing awareness of the importance of compliance, many Chinese enterprises have initially established

[20] German data regulator investigates whether Mobike violates EU Data Protection Law. http://www.ccpit.org/Contents/Channel_3673/2018/1220/1103590/content_1103590.htm.

compliance systems based on domestic regulations, but it is evident that existing compliance measures are far from enough to deal with new issues and challenges that arise in the process of "going out". In order to adapt to the legal environments of host countries and reduce the risk of investigation, compliance systems must be developed in line with local situations. However, it is neither economical nor necessary for companies to develop separate compliance programs for each investment location. Therefore, large international firms and lawyers who work closely with foreign firms can establish compliance systems for Chinese companies going abroad that suit the legal environment of both domestic and foreign jurisdictions. This will enable companies to carry out unified top-down compliance management for their overseas branches while controlling compliance costs.

3.2 Response in the Midst of the Investigation: Cooperate with the Investigation and Conduct Multi-jurisdictional Coordination

A well-developed compliance system can prevent risks and help companies respond if investigated. Typical cooperation with government investigations includes establishing a response team, handling documents, internal self-examination, employee interviews, and attorney-client privilege. The primary response decisions include surrendering, settling, or submitting an undertaking.

Apart from proactively and effectively responding to individual foreign government investigations, companies must also consider how to respond to simultaneous or sequential investigations in multiple jurisdictions worldwide. Such investigations have become commonplace, and in antitrust jurisdictions, for example, LCD panels, auto parts, and roll-on/roll-off shipping have been subject to scrutiny by national antitrust agencies. Coordinating multiple jurisdictions is not an easy task. In addition to the different substantive and procedural legal systems, language barrieres, culture differences, and different ways of thinking can cause challenges in communication between regions. Therefore, in unfamiliar environments of different countries, it is essential to engage lawyers with the appropriate knowledge and skills who understand the demands and concerns of Chinese enterprises.

3.3 Post-event Summary: Adjustment and Improvement of the Compliance System

After problems are identified during a specific response, lessons learned can be applied in a timely manner to improve the compliance system. In the example of an anti-money laundering case involving the Agricultural Bank of China, as early as September 2014, the then-chief compliance officer of the bank's New York branch discovered a series of suspicious dollar transactions. The officer promptly contacted regulators and asked for advice. However, when the compliance department reported the risk to senior management at the New York Branch, it was not given immediate attention and failed to comply with the recommendations of the regulatory authorities. This resulted in the Agricultural Bank of China being penalized by the New York State Department of Financial Services in 2016, ending in a hefty settlement totaling US$215 million.[21] This is a typical example of failing to completely understand local regulations.

As more and more Chinese companies "go global" and become active in the global business arena, the risk of government investigations is bound to increase. In particular, as more Chinese companies invest in the EU and the US, local regulators have begun to watch Chinese companies even more closely. Overseas government investigations are often sudden, lengthy and time-consuming. Fines can also be enormous, resulting in a significant, negative impact on business operations. Chinese companies should work to increase their knowledge of development trends and the procedures of investigations carried out by other governments, strengthen compliance and internal control, take effective countermeasures, and implement targeted improvement measures after an investigation. This will ensure sustainable overseas expansion.

Zhisong Deng Senior Partner of Dentons, co-Chair of Dentons China Competition and Antitrust Practice.

Jianmin Dai Partner of Dentons, co-Chair of Dentons China Competition and Antitrust Practice.

[21] Yin Yunxia, Zhao Hexuan & Zhou Mengyuan: The Reasons for Overseas Violations by Chinese Companies from Beijing's Skyline. http://www.360doc.com/content/17/1214/19/22551567_713108568.shtml.

Risks and Opportunities in Investment

Investment and Cooperation Opportunities in Japan

Jinghao Jin

Abstract This paper provides an overview of investment by Chinese companies in Japan, assessing the total number of companies, direct investment flows, direct investment stock, and a partial list of investing companies. It also highlights the appeal of Japan as an investment destination as well as the hidden business opportunities in Japan. At the end of the paper, readers are reminded of the opportunities for Sino-Japanese cooperation in innovation. In this paper, the author suggests that Chinese companies should pay more attention to individual regions in Japan as many century-old companies are local businesses, as are most of Japan's 100 leading global companies. Various regions in Japan has also been actively working to attract foreign investment in recent years by providing grants and tailored services for foreign companies, which helps companies overcome issues in labor force reduction and efficiency. This is a rare opportunity for Chinese companies to "go out" and expand their presence in Japan.

Keywords Investment in Japan · Going out · Japan External Trade Organization (JETRO) · Regions of Japan · Innovation sector

With China's economy exceeding US$10 trillion, more than 40,000 Chinese companies have expanded their business overseas. As many Chinese companies are reforming to meet complicated international and domestic changes, more and more are looking to Japan. One of the most obvious trends is the increasing number of business tours to Japan. However, there is little research available on Chinese investment in Japan within the existing corpus of research.

Important guides for Chinese enterprises interested in investing in Japan include the *Guidelines to Countries (Regions) for Foreign Investment Cooperation (Japan), Report on Development of China's Outbound Investment*, and *Statistical Bulletin of China's Outward Foreign Direct Investment* all released by China's Ministry of Commerce. Other sources of information include books on investment in Japan published by Chinese and Japanese law firms and accounting firms, the website of

J. Jin (✉)
JETRO, Beijing, China

H. H. Wang and M. L. Miao (eds.), *The Challenge of "Going Out"*, The Chinese Enterprise Globalization Series, https://doi.org/10.1007/978-981-99-3326-6_8

the Economic and Commercial Office of the Embassy of the People's Republic of China in Japan, and official Japanese websites as the Embassy of Japan in China and the Japan External Trade Organization (JETRO). However, the information provided by these organizations is insufficient to counteract the "information asymmetry" on the considerable demand for investment cooperation in Japan from mainland Chinese businesses.

Using Chinese and Japanese language sources and the author's own experience assisting Chinese companies investing in Japan, the author attempts to provide a rough overview of the state of Chinese companies in Japan.

Due to the limited space and resources mean that this paper places more emphasis on opportunities for investment and cooperation available to Chinese enterprises in Japan.

1 How Many Chinese Companies Are Registered in Japan?

According to the *Report on Development of China's Outbound Investment (2018)* released by the Ministry of Commerce at the end of 2017, there were already 39,200 Chinese enterprises with OFDI status in 189 countries (regions), or over 80% of the countries in the world. Over 22,000 outbound enterprises were established in in Asia, accounting for 56.3% of the total number of enterprises engaging in outbound investment (Fig. 1).

But how many of these enterprises are located in Japan? At present, it is impossible to provide an accurate picture of the number of investment filings in Japan due to the limited data made public by the Ministry of Commerce's foreign investment filing system. The author has collected the data of 1,354 registered companies (based on the name of the enterprises in Japan), but believes that the actual number of filings and the number of Chinese enterprises in Japan is certainly greater.

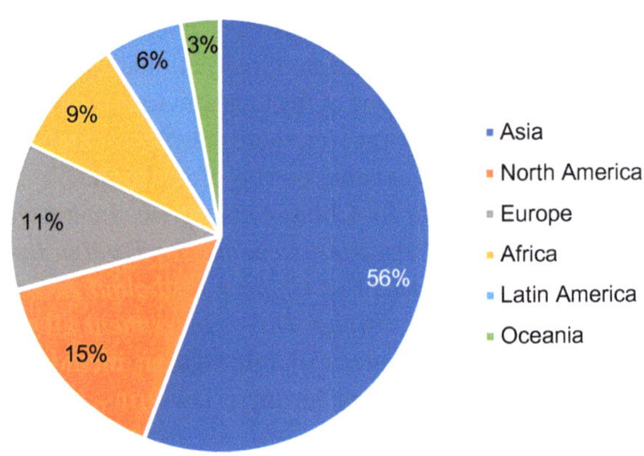

Fig. 1 Regional distribution of overseas enterprises established by Chinese enterprises. *Source* Ministry of Commerce of P.R.China, National Bureau of Statistics and State Administration of Foreign Exchange, *2017 Statistical Bulletin of China's Outward Foreign Direct Investment*

Direct investment flows by China to Asia in 2017 totaled approximately US$110.4 billion, accounting for 69.5% of all OFDI in that year (Fig. 2).

These direct investments mainly went to Hong Kong (SAR, China), Singapore, Kazakhstan, Malaysia, Indonesia, Laos, Thailand, Vietnam, Cambodia, Pakistan, the United Arab Emirates, South Korea, Cyprus, Japan, Myanmar and India, among others (Fig. 3).

According to the Ministry of Finance of Japan, direct investment flows to Japan in 2017 reached 2.1179 trillion yen (1 US dollar was worth 112.19 yen, the same

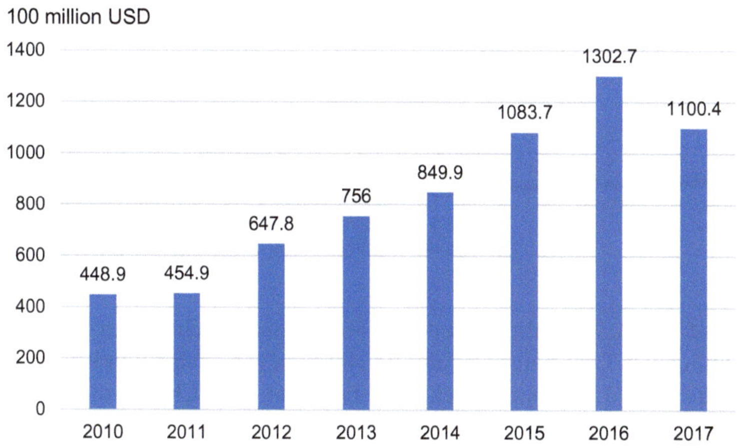

Fig. 2 Chinese direct investment in Asia, 2010–2017. *Source* Ministry of Commerce of P.R.China, National Bureau of Statistics and State Administration of Foreign Exchange, *2017 Statistical Bulletin of China's Outward Foreign Direct Investment*

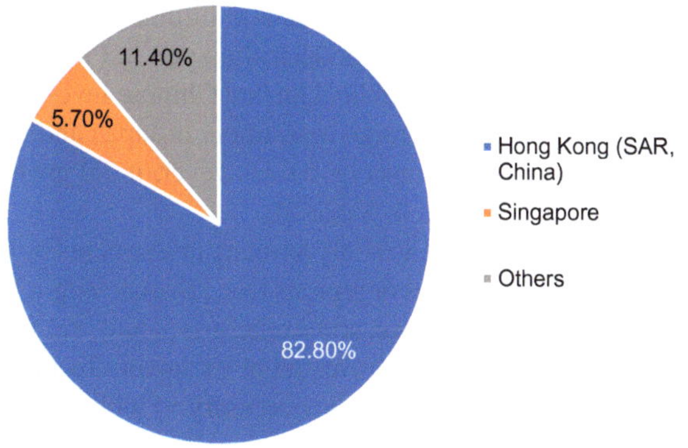

Fig. 3 Country and regional distribution of Chinese direct investment flows to Asia in 2017. *Source* Ministry of Commerce of P.R.China, National Bureau of Statistics and State Administration of Foreign Exchange, 2017 Statistical Bulletin of China's Outward Foreign Direct Investment. *Note* Others 11.4% (Kazakhstan 1.9%; Malaysia 1.6%; Indonesia 1.5%; Laos 1.1%; Thailand 1.0%; Vietnam 0.7%; Cambodia 0.7%; Pakistan 0.6%; Others 2.4%)

Table 1 China's direct investment stock in developed countries/regions at the end of 2017

Countries/Economies	Stock (100 million USD)	Percent (%)
European Union	860.15	37.5
United States	673.81	29.4
Australia	361.75	15.8
Canada	109.37	4.8
Bermuda	85.88	3.8
Switzerland	81.12	3.5
Israel	41.49	1.8
Japan	31.97	1.4
New Zealand	24.92	1.1
Norway	20.83	0.9
Total	2291.29	100.0

Source Ministry of Commerce of P.R.China, National Bureau of Statistics and State Administration of Foreign Exchange, 2017 Statistical Bulletin of China's Outward Foreign Direct Investment

below), of which 108 billion yen came from China, which ranked 8th (following 384.7 billion yen from Singapore and 109.4 billion yen from South Korea).

In terms of total investment stock, as of the end of 2017, Chinese investment stock in Asia totaled US$1,139.32 billion. This accounted for 63% of China's OFDI stock and made Asia by far China's largest market in terms of total OFDI stock. Of this amount, total direct investment in Japan was US$3.197 billion, accounting for 1.4% of China's total OFDI (Table 1).

According to public information on the official website of the Japan External Trade Organization (JETRO), Chinese direct investment stock in Japan reached 286.6 billion yen by the end of 2017 (it was below 200 billion yen at the end of 2016), accounting for only about 1% of the 28.5545 trillion yen in FDI stock in Japan.

It is also clear from the JETRO's public data that Chinese investment stock makes up a small share ($\leq$1%) of overall foreign investment in Japan and is only 1/30th the size of Japanese investment in China (Fig. 5). However, it did grow more than five times between 2010 and 2016 (Fig. 4, Table 2).

The above statistics are for reference only as many investments by Chinese companies are made through third countries or regions (e.g., British Virgin Islands, Cayman Islands, Hong Kong, etc.). Furthermore, some enterprises have not filed with Chinese commercial authorities or completed investment in Japan. To understand the full picture of Chinese investment in Japan, it is necessary to look at specific investment cases.

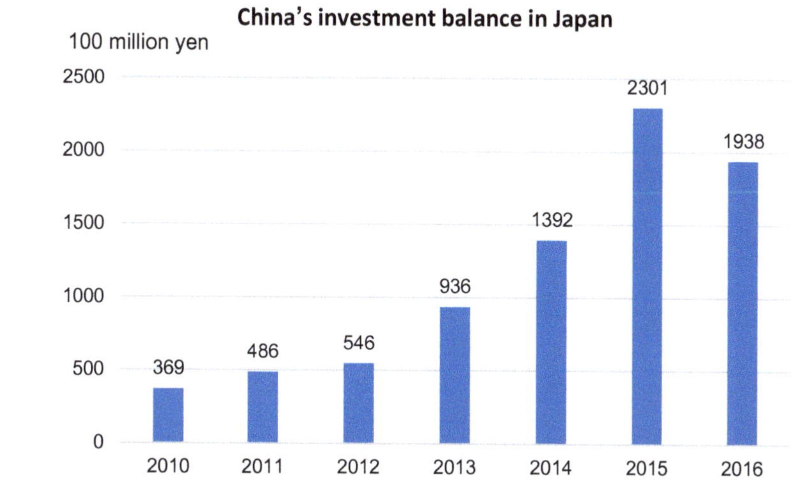

Fig. 4 Changes in the investment stock (balance) of Chinese investment in Japan. *Source* Based on the external balance of assets and liabilities (Ministry of Finance, Bank of Japan). Due to changes in the statistical standard of balance of payments, data prior to 2013 are for reference only

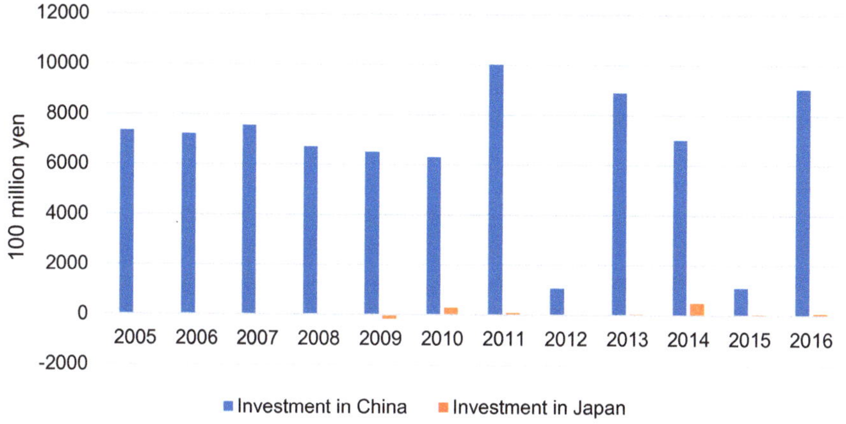

Fig. 5 Comparison of investment flows to China and to Japan in recent years. *Source* Ministry of Economy, Trade and Industry of Japan website

2 Which Chinese Companies Have Set up Companies in Japan?

Chinese companies frequently ask which Chinese companies have expanded into Japan and the sectors they invest in. The Japan External Trade Organization (JETRO) under Japan's Ministry of Economy, Trade and Industry, is responsible for promoting two-way trade and investment and has assisted thousands of Chinese companies to

Table 2 Investment balance ranking in Japan (at the end of 2016)

Ranking	Country/region	Balance (100 million yen)	Percent (%)
1	United States	70,101	25.18
2	Netherlands	38,003	13.65
3	France	33,511	12.04
4	United Kingdom	22,623	8.13
5	Singapore	22,104	7.94
6	Switzerland	12,944	4.65
7	Cayman Islands	11,993	4.31
8	Hong Kong, China	10,992	3.95
9	Luxembourg	8679	3.12
10	Germany	8499	3.05
…	…	…	…
16	the Chinese Mainland	1938	0.70

Source Based on the external balance of assets and liabilities (Ministry of Finance, Bank of Japan) Due to changes in the statistical standard of balance of payments, data prior to 2013 are for reference only

invest in Japan. According to its official website and public information, JETRO has assisted a wide range of Chinese companies to invest in Japan.

These companies[1] operate in Japan in a wide range of fields, including travel, e-commerce, automotive, pharmaceuticals, gaming, payment, 3D-VR, AI, driverless technology, robotics, energy, precision instruments, communications, financial services, environmental equipment, and merchandise outlets.

The reasons that these Chinese companies set up operations in Japan include obtaining stable procurement channels; strengthening customer relationships to

[1] Ctrip, Jingdong, Vipshop, Kaola, Alibaba, Spring Airlines, Juneyao Airlines, Hainan Airlines, Sichuan Airlines, Tongcheng International Travel, Great Wall Motor, Hengrui Medicine, Longrich, Sina Comic, Snail Games, Shanda Group, Himalaya FM, SF Express, UnionPay, Ningbo Fotile, 3dnest, Makeblock Co., Ltd., InferVision, Tusimple, CSJBOT, Dalian Hi-Think Computer Technology Corp. (DHC), Changzhou Haoda Science & Technology Co,. Ltd, Gotion High-Tech, Yang Sheng Tang, Dalian Lufei Optoelectronics Technology, Shenzhen Kaizhong Precision Technology Co., Ltd., Bei Jing JingYi Automation Equipment Co., Ltd., Hangzhou Dare Trade, Gpixel, Suzhou Changtu Network Technology Co.,Ltd., CASSTAR, Hisense Financial Information Service, Xingle Magazine, Dalian HengLi International Trade Co., Ltd, Akcome, Selen Technology, Baibao New Media, Ningbo Gintian Copper, MJStyle, Nanhai Haixing Electronics, Shanghai XuHe Environmental Equipment Co., Ltd., Xinjiang Joinworld Company Limited, Suzhou Tianmai Thermal Technology Co.Ltd., Contemporary Amperex Technology Co. Limited, Daddy's Choice, Zhejiang Haihua Pharmaceutical Co., Ltd., Trina Solar Co., Ltd., and Yiwu Commodity City Group Co., Ltd.

expand sales in Japan; promoting after-sales and logistics services; expanding high-end product R&D; manufacturing in Japan or conduct Original Equipment Manufacturer (OEM) production to increase the added value of their products by leveraging the "Made in Japan" label; and cooperate with Japanese companies on innovation.

Members of the China Enterprises Association in Japan include: Baosteel, Minmetals, China National Petroleum Corporation, Bank of China, Agricultural Bank of China, Construction Bank, Industrial and Commercial Bank, Bank of Communications, China Ocean Shipping (Group) Company, COSCO, Air China, Huawei, Shanghai Electric Power Co. Ltd., UnionPay International, Sinochem Holdings, China Pacific Insurance (Group) Co., Ltd., CITIC and other large Chinese enterprises' representative offices in Japan, which are involved in sectors including trade, manufacturing, finance, insurance, logistics, transportation, tourism, labor, cultural exchange and other fields. As of May 2018, the organization had a total of over 130 member companies.

Foreign investment filings on the website of the Ministry of Commerce of the People's Republic of China also showed that 1,354 companies[2] made outbound investment in Japan.

Chinese companies with a range of different advantages have 'landed' or are 'landing' in Japan. There are also many strong startups as well as business incubators and accelerators that are also entering Japan or exploring the possibility of

[2] The following is a list of the most representative of these companies. Anhui Jianghuai Automobile Group Corp., Ltd., Ansteel, Aux, Baosteel, Beijing Urban Construction Group Co., Ltd., Capital Airline, Crowne Plaza Beijing, Beijing Zhangguang 101 Science & Technology Development Co., Ltd., Foton, BYD, Smartisan, Hisense, DHC, Dalian Lufei Optoelectronics Technology Co., Ltd., Dong Feng Motor Corporation, Neusoft, Founder Group, Fuyao Glass Industry Group Co., Ltd., Galanz, State Grid Corporation of China, Haier, HLA, ShangHai Hyron Software Co., Ltd., Hisense, Ruijie Networks, Sound Group, Xiamen Airlines, Shandong RuYi Group, Shanghai Electric Power Co. Ltd., SAIC Motor Corporation Limited, Shanghai RuiXiang Intelligent Technology, Shanghai Silk Group Co., Ltd., BGI, Ubox, Saint Lucia Consulting, NavInfo Co.,Ltd., Tianjin Airlines, Tianjin Foreign Enterprises & Experts Service Co. Ltd., Suntech Power, Hiking Group, Shine Wing, Yada, BROAD Air Conditioning Co. Ltd., Lucky Air, Zhejiang Publishing & Media Co. Ltd., Zhejiang Tea Group, Yiwu Commodity City Group Co., Ltd., China Publishing Group Corp., Henan 863 Software Incubator Co., Ltd, Hopenoah, Himin Solar Co.,Ltd., Jiangsu LONGLIQI Bio-Science Co., Ltd (Longrich), Trina Solar Limited, JA Solar Holdings Co., Ltd., Ningbo Joyson Electronic Corp., Ecovacs Robotics, Quicktron Intelligent Technology Co., Ltd., Leyard Optoelectronic Co., Ltd., LONGi Green Energy Technology, Greenland Holdings Corporation Limited, China Southern Airlines, Inner Mongolia Eerduosi Resourses Company Limited, Inner Mongolia Little Sheep Restaurant Chain, Fotile, Pinjun express, Haier, Gamewave Group, People.cn Co., Ltd., CITS, iSoftStone, China International Travel Services Limited, Head Office, China Overseas Engineering Group Co., Ltd., China SHIPPING (Group) Company, China National Chemica,l Engineering Group Corporation Ltd., China National Machinery Foreign Economic and Technical Cooperation Co., Ltd. (CMIC), China Machinery Engineering Corporation, China Certification & Inspection (Group) Co., Ltd. (CCIC), CTIEC, China Petroleum & Chemical Corporation, PetroChina International Co., Ltd., China Silk Corporation, China General Technology (Group) Holding Co Ltd, Sinotrans Limited, China Mobile Communications Group Co.,Ltd., China Coal Energy Group Co., Ltd., China National Cereals, Oils and Foodstuffs Corporation, China Silk Corporation, Zhongtuxu Assets Management Corporation, CITIC Press Corporation, Zhongxing Telecommunication Equipment Corporation.

Table 3 Attractive aspects of the Japanese market

Ranking	Options	Ballots			Scores
		First	Second	Third	
1	Japanese market	158	20	20	534
2	Excellent partners (Japanese companies and universities)	25	50	29	204
3	Social/governmental stability	16	43	60	194
4	High quality R&D	19	38	15	148
5	World class global companies	24	26	24	148
6	Well-established infrastructure (transportation, logistics, information and communication, energy, etc.)	4	39	30	120
7	Availability of skilled talent	4	14	19	59
8	Comprehensive living environment	4	7	23	49
9	Most suitable as a gateway to Asia and a regional headquarters	3	12	14	47
10	Expected increase in demand/sales during 2020 Tokyo Olympics/Paralympics	3	9	20	47
11	Mature IP law	2	6	5	23
12	Other	4	2	7	23

Note Point values for responses 1, 2 and 3 are 3, 2 and 1 respectively. Options are sorted according to the total score
Attractiveness of conducting business in Japan (Choose up to Three)

investing in Japan. This will not be discussed in detail here because it involves sensitive information about companies.[3]

3 What Are the Advantages of Japan as an Investment Destination?

Many companies and investors ask about what advantages Japan provides as a destination for investment.

According to the JETRO Invest Japan Report 2018, the three major reasons foreign companies invest in Japan are the Japanese market, a large number of potential partners, and national and social stability (Table 3; Figs. 6, 7 and 8).

[3] For more cases of foreign enterprises investing in Japan, please browse the following websites.
https://www.meti.go.jp/policy/investment/pdf/tokuteibunya.pdf, https://www.meti.go.jp/policy/investment/pdf/H29FYtoushimiryokudohoukokusho.pdf, https://www.meti.go.jp/policy/investment/pdf/retoshiteikei.pdf, https://www.meti.go.jp/policy/investment/pdf/2017kanshindochosa.pdf, https://www.meti.go.jp/statistics/tyo/gaisikei/index.html, https://www.meti.go.jp/statistics/tyo/gaisikei/result/result_52/pdf/2018gaikyo-k.pdf.

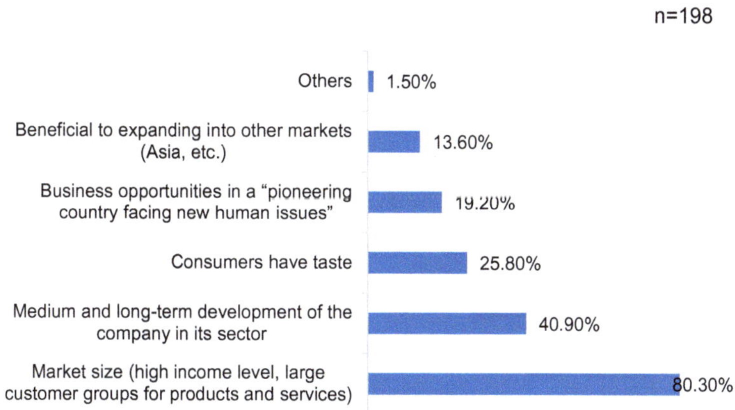

Fig. 6 Most attractive aspect of the Japanese market is its market size. *Note* Unique attractiveness of the Japanese market (Choose up to Two)

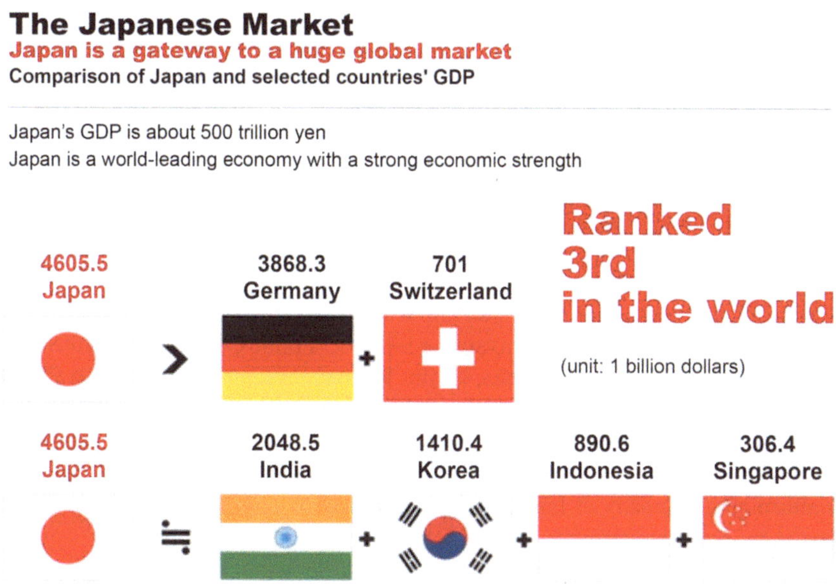

Fig. 7 Comparison of GDP of Japan and selected countries. *Source* Statistics Bureau of the Ministry of Internal Affairs and Communications, "World Statistics 2016"; IMF, "World Economic Outlook Database"; Economic and Social Research Institute of the Cabinet Office, "Prefectural Economic Yearbook 2014"

Fig. 8 Japan is a gateway (springboard) to international markets. *Source* Edited by the Japan External Trade Organization (JETRO) based on data from the Ministry of Economy, Trade and Industry of Japan

Of course, the size of Japan's market can't compare with the size of China's. After all, Japan's population is only one-tenth of China's, and its population is getting older by the day. However, despite this, why do many foreign companies still choose to set up companies in Japan?

One of the key reasons is that Japan can be used as a gateway (springboard) to international markets. Indeed, Japan has signed EPA (Economic Cooperation Agreement) with Singapore, Mexico, Malaysia, Chile, Thailand, Indonesia, Brunei, ASEAN, Philippines, Switzerland, Vietnam, India, Peru, Australia, Mongolia, EU, 11 TPP members, and is working with the US, China, Korea, Turkey, Colombia, and other countries to promote EPA and FTA (Free Trade Agreement) negotiations. Therefore, establishing a company in Japan can be conducive to entering markets with which Japan has signed agreements.

In addition, according to JETRO's analysis of the annual "Survey on the Trend of Foreign Funded Enterprises" (Ministry of Economy, Trade and Industry), there is a clear trend among Asian companies to see Japan as an ideal location for R&D investment. In fact, the number of companies with "R&D functions" among foreign companies in Japan has nearly doubled compared to 2005.

According to public information from JETRO, as of 2017, Japan ranked 8th out of 138 countries in terms of global competitiveness and 2nd in terms of business development, which is certainly an attractive factor for foreign companies to invest in Japan (Fig. 9).

In terms of ROI or direct investment, Japan surpassed Hong Kong (China), as well as the United Kingdom, Germany, France and the US (Fig. 10).

Global Competitiveness Indicators

8th out of 138 countries

Information source: World Economic Forum, "Global Competitiveness Report 2016-2017"
Note: Assessment based on economic growth, government efficiency, business efficiency, and basic design

Comprehensiveness of Business Development Environment

2nd out of 138 countries

Information source: World Economic Forum, "Global Competitiveness Report 2016-2017"
Note: Assessment based on the quality of business networks and company operations/strategies.

Fig. 9 Japan's competitiveness and business development environment

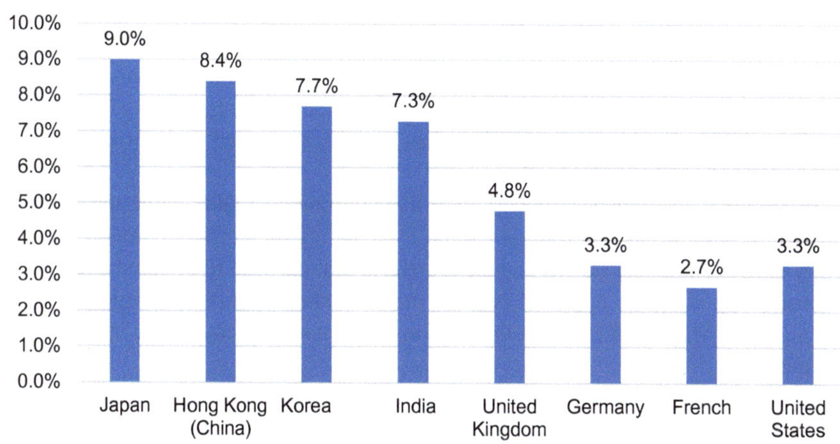

Fig. 10 International Comparison of Returns on Inbound Direct Investment (2008–2017, Average). *Source* Compiled from "IMF Data Warehouse" (IMF) (as of June 22, 2018) and "Our stock of foreign assets and liabilities" (Ministry of Finance, Bank of Japan). *Note* ROI on inward direct investment = amount of current direct investment income paid/opening and closing stock of inward direct investment × 100 (%)

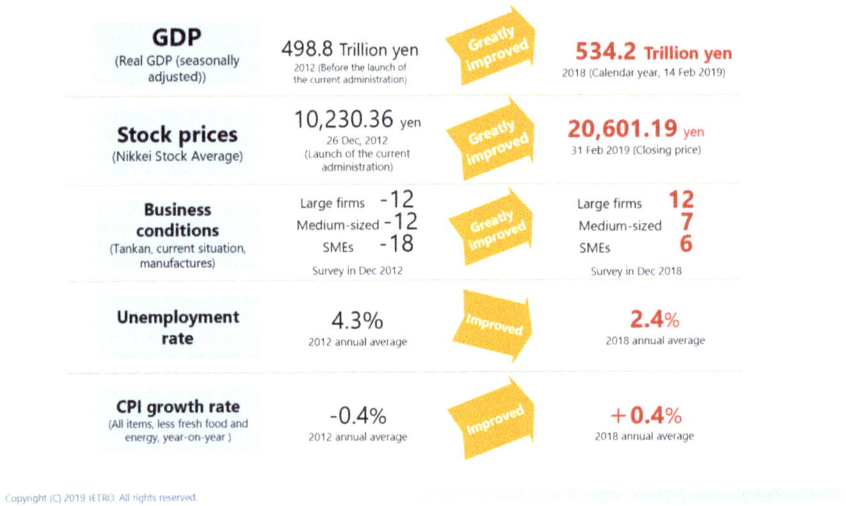

Fig. 11 Japan's economic indicators for fiscal year 2018

Considerable analysis has been conducted on recovery and general trends in Japan's economy, so no further details will be given here. Generally speaking, after more than 20 years of economic downturn, Japan's economy has improved significantly in terms of GDP, stock prices, its boom forecast, unemployment rate, and Consumer Price Index (CPI) (Fig. 11).

Does this mean that the cost of running a business in Japan very high? As the following data shows, the cost of doing business in Japan is lower than what most foreign companies would think. The cost of office space and salaries for mid- to high-level employees in some cities in China has actually surpassed the average levels in Japan (Figs. 12, 13, 14; Table 4).

In addition, the Japanese government has continued to take active measures to attract foreign tourists and foreign capital by reducing the corporate tax rate (effectively to 29.74% in 2018). The Japanese government has also liberalized energy and electricity, sped up the approval process in the medical and pharmaceutical fields, enacted the "Minshuku Law" in the tourism field, and implemented a special zone system.

The Japanese government also plans to improve its World Bank "Doing Business" ranking from 39th in 2019 to the top three among Organization for Economic Cooperation and Development (OECD) countries by 2020 (Fig. 15). To this end, it plans to ensure online company registrations are completed within 24 hours and one-stop services for foreign companies (Fig. 15).

At the same time, under the joint mechanism of the "Promotion Conference on Foreign Direct Investment in Japan" involving relevant government departments (Cabinet Office, Ministry of Economy, Trade and Industry, Ministry of Foreign Affairs), major banks, and JETRO, the Japanese government plans to implement reforms in nine key areas. These areas include company registration, social security,

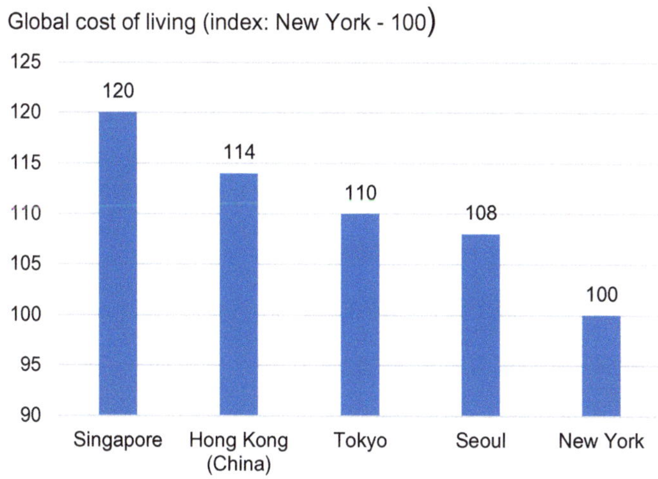

Fig. 12 A comparison of business costs. *Source* Edited by the Japan External Trade Organization (JETRO) based on the Economist Intelligence Unit's "Worldwide Cost of Living 2017". *Note* The cost of doing business in Japan is lower than you might think

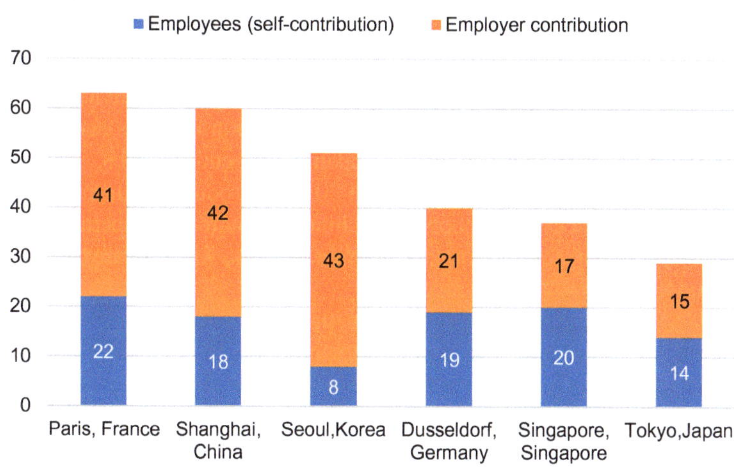

Fig. 13 Comparison of the contribution of employers to social security in different countries. *Source* Compiled by the Japan External Trade Cooperation Organization (JETRO) based on its "Investment-related Cost Survey (2016)". *Note* Figures are rounded to the nearest whole number. When there is a range of values, the maximum value is taken

national taxation, local taxation, subsidies, research and statistics, employee labor management, business registration, and the issuance of various documents through IT-orientation in various businesses, the one-time provision of the same material, as well as the unification of document formats by March 2020. The government further plans to reduce the cost of administrative procedures (operating time) by 22.3%.

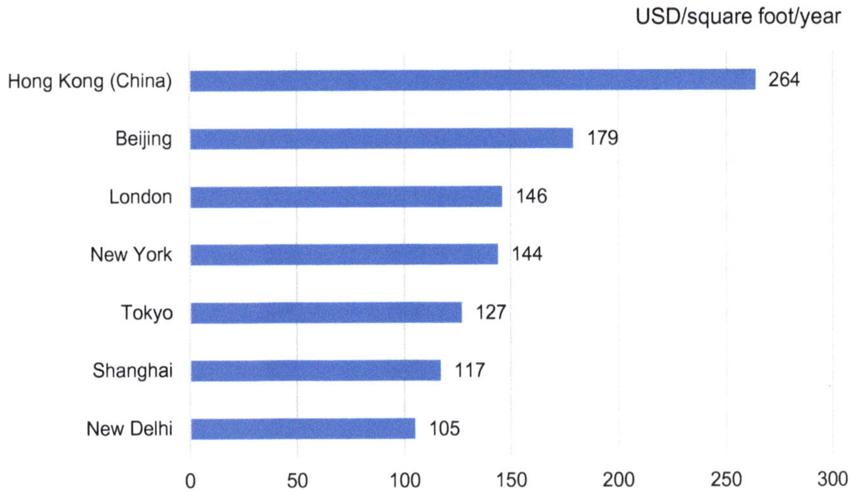

Fig. 14 Comparison of real estate costs in major cities around the world (As of the fourth quarter of 2016). *Source* CBRE, "Global Prime Office Occupancy Costs, March 2017". *Note* New Delhi (Connaught Place—Central Business District), Shanghai (Pudong), Tokyo (Otemachi/Marunouchi), New York (Midtown Manhattan), London (West End), Beijing (Financial Street), Hong Kong (Central District)

To attract more foreign high-level human resources and promote M&A between companies, the Japanese government is revising taxation methods and rates (there were 15,386 high-level professionals in Japan at the end of 2018, with plans to increase this number to 20,000 by the end of 2022); introducing information collection equipment (e.g., sensors.), robots or machinery for automatic operation based on data analysis, systems required for data analysis (servers, AI, software), and network security supplies, and giving tax incentives.

In addition, to promote foreign entrepreneurs to start businesses in Japan, a one year "Startup Visa" will be introduced, allowing foreign companies approved by JETRO to apply for an operation management visa after registering a company in a shared space. The Japanese government will also expand the scope of the "Sandbox" system, which will help companies in the financial, medical, and technology sectors to validate their business models, ideas, and R&D results in Japan as soon as possible.

Driven by these factors, Japan's FDI stock reached 30.7 trillion yen in 2018, setting a new record for the fifth consecutive year (Fig. 16).

The number of companies successfully attracting foreign investment continued to grow in recent years. By the end of 2018, JETRO alone has supported 19,447 foreign-invested projects in Japan, of which 2,013 have been successfully implemented (Fig. 17).

Table 4 Business cost comparison

Comparison of office space costs by city Unit: USD (sqm/year)			Average annual salary of IT professionals by city (2017) Unit: USD	
	Cities	Average monthly rent	Cities	Average annual salary
1	Hong Kong (Central)	3229.9	San Francisco	142,000
2	London (West end)	2529.6	Seattle	132,000
3	Beijing (Financial Street)	2162.6	New York	129,000
4	Hong Kong (Kowloon)	2040.4	Los Angeles	129,000
5	Beijing (CBD)	2039.1	New York	129,000
6	New York (Midtown)	1978.2	Los Angeles	129,000
7	New York (Midtown South)	1846.7	Austin	118,000
8	Tokyo (Marunouchi/ Otemachi)	1845.9	London	78,000
9	New Delhi (Connaught Place)	1649.7	Toronto	73,000
10	London (City)	1560.2	Japan	49,000

Note Rents are for the first quarter of 2018
Source 「June 2018 Global Prime Office Occupancy Costs」 (CBRE)
Note Data for Japan are for 2015
Source Japan's "comparative survey of IT talents in different countries" (Ministry of Economy, Trade and Industry); and the data of other cities come from 「State of Salaries Report 2018」 (Hired)
*The exchange rate of yen is converted by referring to the annual average of the Bank of Japan's mid-price data

4 Business Opportunities Throughout Japan

As the capital of Japan, Tokyo has a large number of industrial clusters and is home to about 75% of the headquarters of large Japanese companies and foreign enterprises. In addition to being a city where new popular cultures are born, Tokyo is also a city where traditional businesses and cutting-edge technology mix. Tokyo also has a highly developed network of firms, universities and research institutes and is rich in various R&D resources. In particular, foreign companies in IoT and AI, asset management, and fin-tech gather in large numbers. As a result, Tokyo is the top destination for foreign companies to invest in Japan. According to JETRO, more than 60% of the foreign companies it has assisted so far have made Tokyo their first stop when investing in Japan.[4] (Fig. 18).

[4] For information on the investment environment and policies in Tokyo, please refer to the following Chinese website. http://www.senryaku.metro.tokyo.jp/tokku/chinese/index.html.

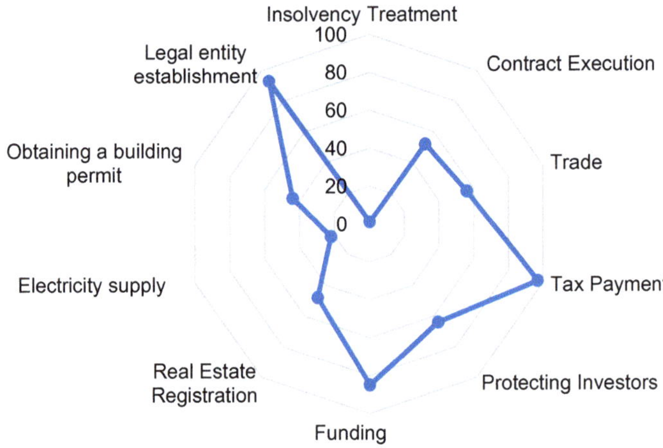

Ranking	2019
1	New Zealand
2	Singapore
3	Denmark
4	Hong Kong, China
5	Korea
6	Georgia
7	Norway
8	United States
32	French
33	Poland
34	Portugal
35	Czech Republic
36	Netherlands Belarus
37	Belarus
38	Switzerland
39	**Japan**

Fig. 15 Japan's overall and sub-rankings in the World Bank's "Doing Business" index. *Source* World Bank,"Doing Business 2019". *Note* The outer edge is the first, and the center is the 190th

However, in the next part of this paper, we will mainly focus on localities outside of Tokyo. The reason for this is that there are many companies in these regions with unique technologies (potential partners), distinctive industrial clusters, local resources such as agriculture, forestry, aquatic products and tourism resources, that

- Japan's inward FDI stock in 2018 renewed record at 30.7 trillion yen (approximately 278.2 billion US dollars).
- Record high achieved five years in a row

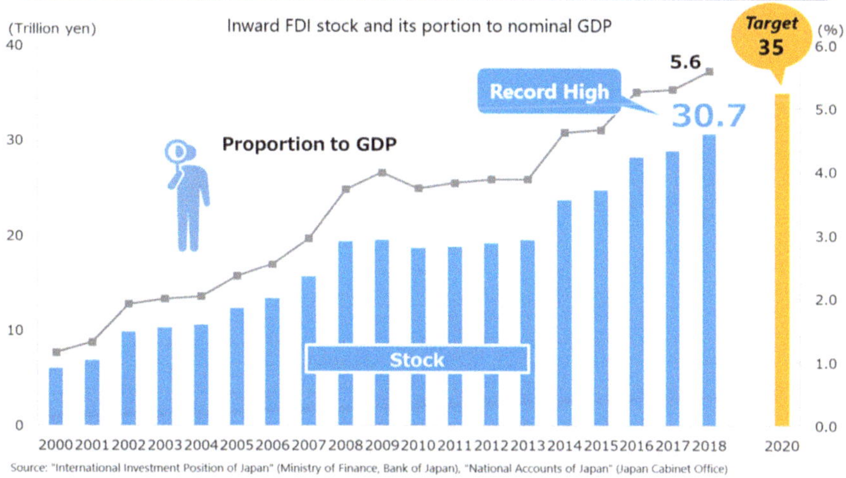

Fig. 16 Japan's inbound investment stock rose for 5 consecutive years

- JETRO has supported 19,447 projects (cumulative total in FY2003-2018).
- Achieved success in 2,013 projects in establishing business operation or expanding businesses in Japan (cumulative total in FY2003-2018)
- Asia ranked 1st (cumulative total since 2003)

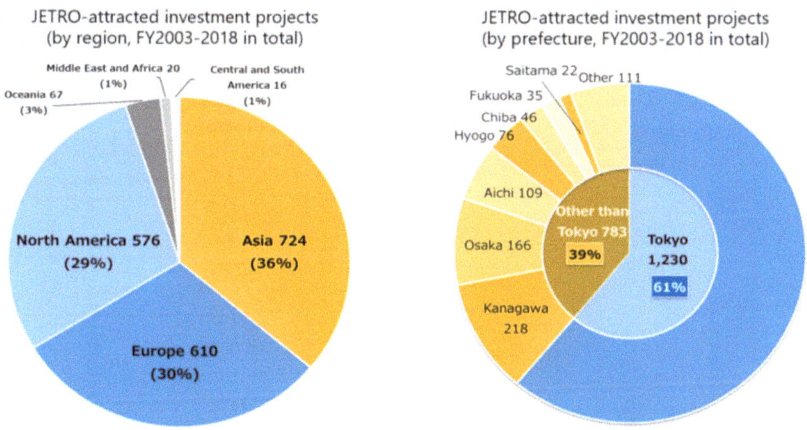

Fig. 17 The JETRO has successfully attracted 2,013 projects in recent years

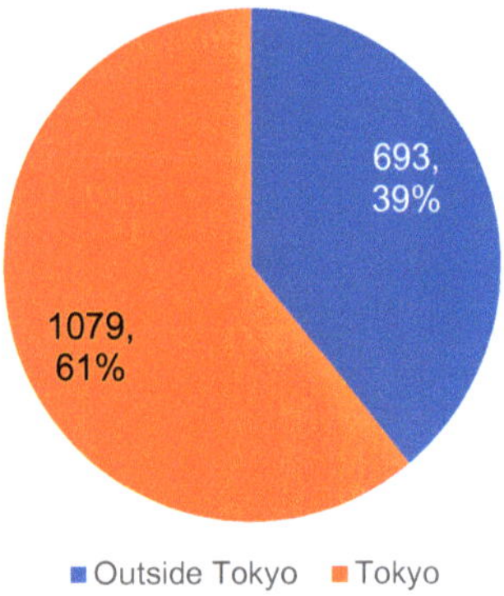

No.	Prefecture	Quantity
1	**Tokyo**	1079
2	Kanagawa	194
3	Osaka	138
4	Aichi	102
5	Hyogo	68
6	Chiba	41
7	Fukuoka	35
8	Saitama	22
9	Kyoto	12
10	Mie	11
11	Hokkaido	9
12	Hiroshima	6
13	Miyagi	5
14	Shizuoka	5
15	Niigata	4
16	Nagano	4
17	Gifu	4
18	Okinawa	4
19	Gunma	3
20	Shiga	3

Fig. 18 More than 60% of foreign companies assisted by JETRO choose to register in Tokyo

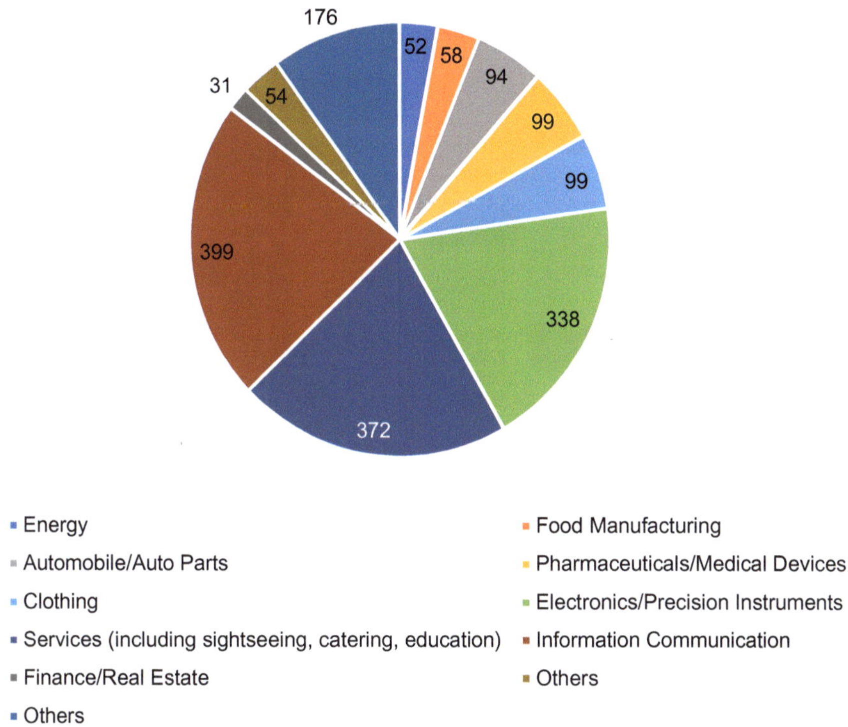

Fig. 18 (continued)

are relatively low in terms of cost and have excellent labor resources as well as business environments that are conducive to business development and R&D.

As the population ages and moves to large cities, there is an urgent need to improve regional productivity in Japan using robots and AI in high value-added tourism (more repeat visitors, longer stays, more tourist routes), in agricultural production in rural areas, and in the promotion and sale of local Japanese products and tourism resources overseas, all of which offer many business opportunities for Chinese enterprises.

If these can be integrated with Chinese sales channels, technology, talent, and industry experience, it could create new demand and innovation, which will promote the sustainable development in local Japanese economies, making them more active and thus helping Chinese companies transform and upgrade for better development (Fig. 19).

Here, we should pay special attention to the advantages of individual localities in Japan. First, the economic scale and market size of many parts in Japan is larger than that of many countries. For example, the GDP of Hokkaido + Tohoku Region exceeds that of Sweden. The GDP of Kanto Region exceeds that of Italy; the GDP of Chubu and Kinki Region exceeds that of the Netherlands and Switzerland; the GDP

Fig. 19 47 prefectures of Japan

of Chugoku Region exceeds that of Finland; while the GDP of Kyushu exceeds that of Belgium; and the GDP of Shikoku exceeds that of Hungary (Fig. 20).

Second, there are many outstanding "hidden champion" companies in Japan that Chinese companies should pay more attention to. In 2014, Japan's Ministry of Economy, Trade and Industry selected 100 companies as benchmarks and called them "Global Niche Top Companies". Despite being located in regional cities, they dominate the global market with their technology and ingenuity (Fig. 21). Below are brief introductions of some of the companies listed above.

BBS Kinmei: Founded in 1956, BBS Kinmei's main offices are in Hakusan City, Ishikawa Prefecture, mainly producing material grinding machines used in semiconductors, solar energy and machine tools. The company's main product is an edge polishing machine for 300 mm silicon wafers, giving it more than 80% of the global market share in this field. In 2007 and 2014, the company was selected as one of Japan's most vibrant 300 artisanal small and medium enterprises and was included in a list of the "Top 100 Global Niche Companies" by the Ministry of Economy,

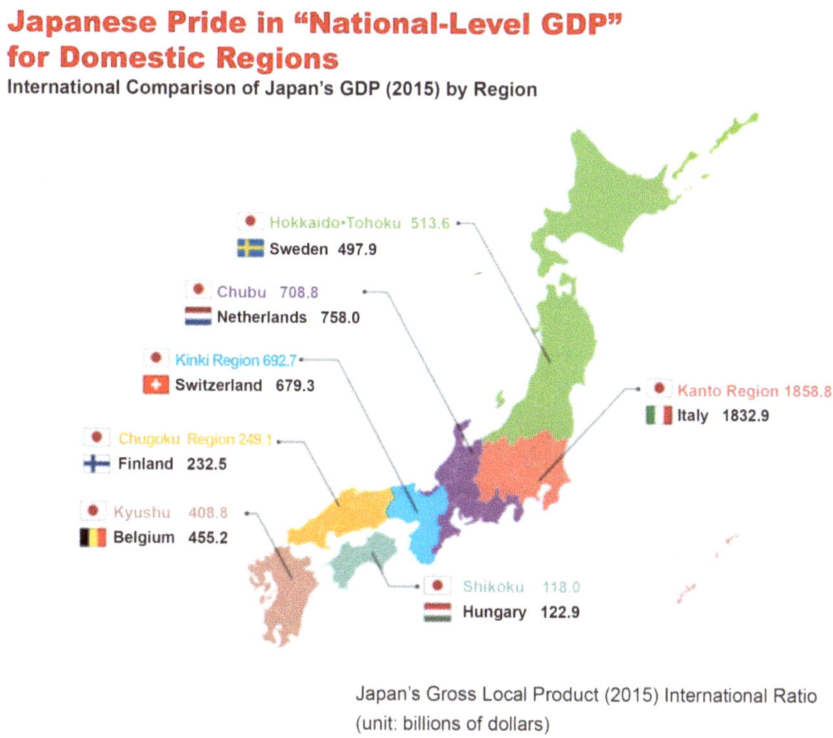

Fig. 20 Regional GDP in Japan often exceeds other countries' national GDP. *Source* Cabinet Office, "About the 2015 Prefectural People's Economic Calculation" (released in 2018)

Trade and Industry. The company has established service locations in many countries around the world, mainly in Southeast Asia, to provide accurate and rapid service according to the needs of their customers.

HORIBA: Founded in 1945 and incorporated in 1953, HORIBA is headquartered in Minami-ku, Kyoto. Its primary business is the manufacture and sale of automotive testers, environmental monitors, scientific/medical testers, and semiconductor testers. Its star product is the "MEXA", an engine emission testing device that measures emissions restricted by environmental regulations. HORIBA has about 80% of the global market share. It also has offices worldwide, including in Brazil, Canada, and Singapore.

SIGMA Corporation: Founded in 1937 and headquartered in Kure City, Hiroshima, SIGMA is a Japanese manufacturer of precision parts. It produces automotive precision parts, safety prevention products, and laser flaw detection devices. SIGMA's laser flaw detection technology has an exclusive global patent and holds 100% of the global market share. The technology uses lasers to inspect precision parts with a diameter of only 4 mm. The semiconductor laser can effectively avoid the interference of external light, conduct screen processing through the device's

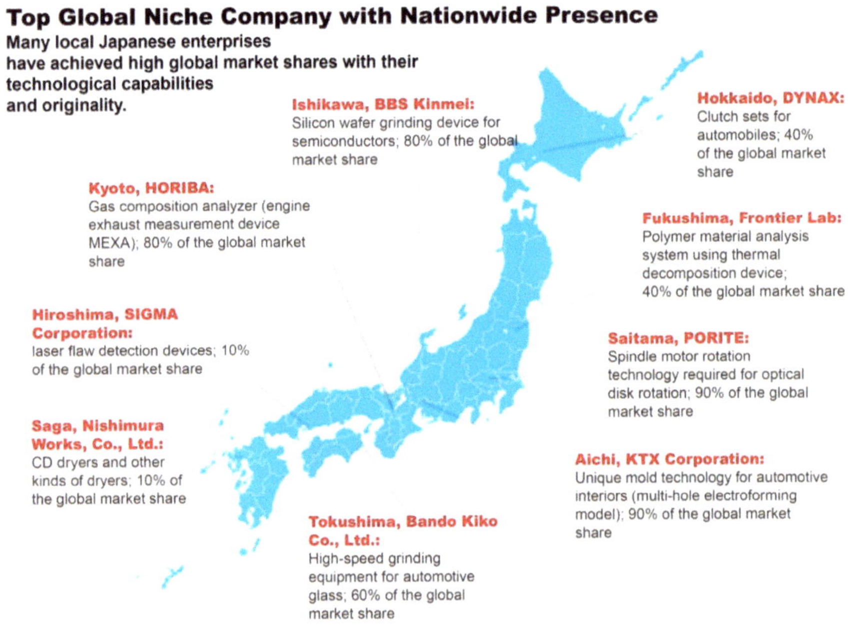

Fig. 21 There are many "hidden champion" companies throughout Japan. *Source* "Japan–China Venture Capital" official account, slightly edited by the author

algorithm, and then determine the quality of the product. As a result, the device has improved the efficiency and accuracy of the final inspection stage in industries like auto and machinery manufacutring, thereby attracting a large number of customers. The company also has a subsidiary in Jiangsu, China - SIGMA Precise Machinery Co.

Nishimura Works, Co., Ltd.: Founded in 1920 and headquartered in Saga, Nishimura Works is a research and development company, which has continued to develop new products since it was founded. Its main products are IB conveyors, CD dryers, and other dryers.

Bando Kiko Co., Ltd.: Established in 1968, Bando Kiko produces processing equipment for automotive glass.

KTX Corporation: Founded in January 1965 and headquartered in Konan-shi, Aichi-ken, KTX's primary business is the production and sale of mold-making equipment for automobiles, aircraft, medical devices, and housing equipment as well as various machines. KTX has branches in the US, Korea and Thailand, and a representative office in Shanghai, China.

PORITE: Founded in 1952 and headquartered in Saitama Prefecture, PORITE's core technology is powder metallurgy, and its main business is oilless bearings and mechanical components. From the company's beginning, it received numerous awards for its contributions to the field of powder metallurgy. As the company expanded, it continued its research on durability, miniaturization and labor-saving manufacturing of oilless bearings and eventually became the "hidden champion" in this field. Since 1990, it has set up subsidiaries or joint ventures in countries including Malaysia, China, France, Thailand, and India.

Frontier Lab: Established in 1991 and headquartered in Koriyama, Fukushima, Frontier Lab is an SME specializing in the research, manufacture and production of multifunctional pyrolyzers, peripheral accessories and metal capillary columns.

Dynax: Founded in 1973 and headquartered in Chitose, Hokkaido, Dynax's main business is the development, design, manufacture, and sales of wet-type friction plates and reaction plates for passenger cars, heavy-duty vehicles, and ships.

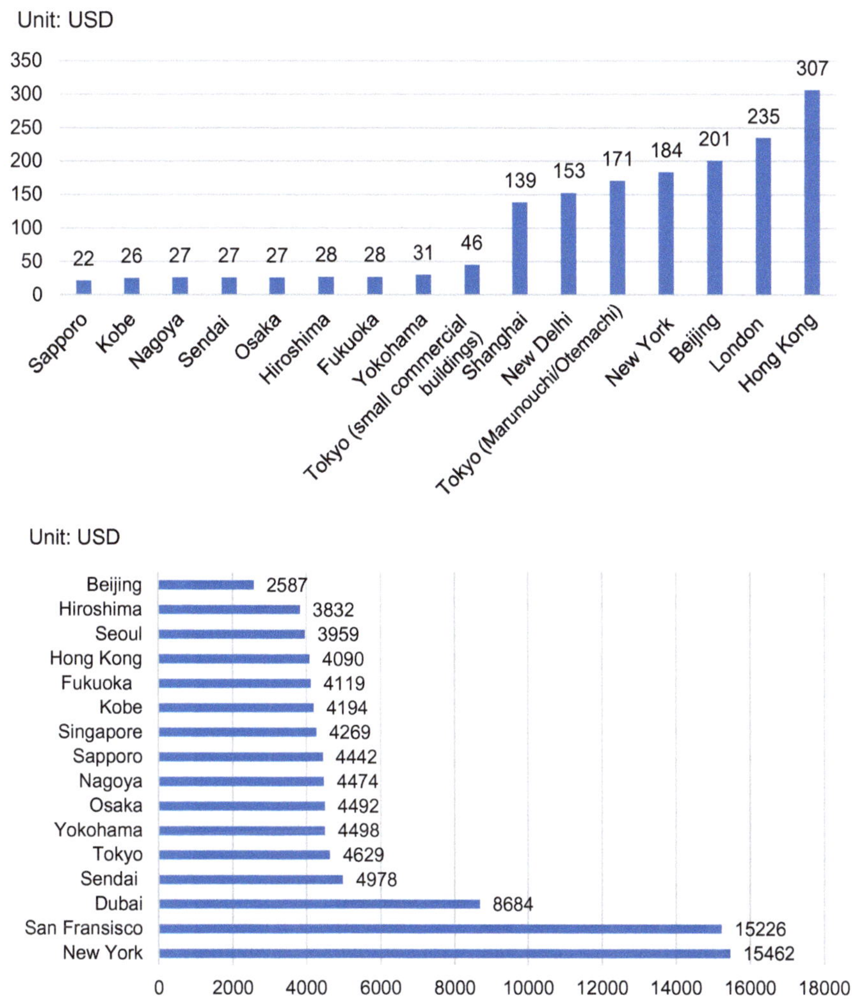

Fig. 22 Comparison of business costs across Japan. *Source* JETRO "Investment Cost Comparison" (July 2018)

(1) Office rent lower in major domestic cities compared to Hong Kong and Beijing.

Comparison of office rents in major world cities and Japan (Comparison of average annual cost per 1 sqft).

Note 1: World metropolitan areas are as follows: New Delhi: Connaught Place; Shanghai: Pudong; Tokyo (small commercial buildings): average rent for small commercial buildings in the 5 main districts; New York: Midtown Manhattan; London: West End; Beijing: Financial Street; Hong Kong: Central District.

Note 2: Costs for domestic metropolitans outside of Tokyo are calculated by JETRO based on average rents in commercial areas (as of July 2018).

Source: CBRE Global Prime Office Occupancy Cost, July 2018, market data on Sanko Estate's homepage (as of June 2018).

(2) Yokohama and Osaka have lower labor costs than San Fransisco and Dubai.

Comparison of salaries for managers in non-manufacturing industries in different cities (monthly) (Fig. 22).

To help local governments better attract foreign investment, the Japanese government (Ministry of Economy, Trade and Industry) and JETRO began holding RBC (Regional Business Conference) forums in 2018. The first implementation units were Fukushima-ken, Ibaraki-ken, Fukuoka, and Osaka. The RBC Fukushima Session, held in October 2018, welcomed 11 medical device manufacturers from Germany, Thailand, and other countries. In addition to gaining an understanding of how the local government in Fukushima was promoting investment, visits and exchanges with local R&D institutions and foreign-funded service organizations "Matchmaking" events with local enterprises were also arranged, directly resulting in a Thai company and a local (Japanese) local establishing a joint venture agreement to develop new products.

In April 2019, the Japanese government announced a second batch of RBC Forum host cities, where the Japanese government (Ministry of Economy, Trade and Industry), JETRO, along with relevant local governments, would work together to develop and implement investment strategies. This specifically included helping them hold RBC forums, inviting foreign enterprises interested in investment to attend meetings, visit the region, listen to local high-level speeches, and engage in business talks with local enterprises. The purpose of the RBC Forum is to help foreign companies understand the investment environment and attractiveness of different regions in Japan, while the various topics covered also reflect the needs of relevant localities. Key examples:

Fukushima-ken is keen to cooperate with medical device related companies and R&D companies.

Ibaraki-ken is home to about 1/3 of all R&D institutions in Japan, Tsukuba-shi has a R&D environment conducive to innovation, so it welcomes R&D companies.

Fukuoka-ken hopes to cooperate with companies outstanding in IoT and other areas, and seeks to attract cutting-edge growth companies from Asia, Europe and the US.

Osaka-shi has an ecosystem and environment suited to startups. It also hosted Hack Osaka 2019, an international innovation forum and hopes to cooperate with foreign enterprises focusing on business accelerators and (Venture Capital) VC.

Hokkaido is looking for Asian investors as well as European and American travel professionals to develop tourism products such as "adventure tours" by making full use of its rich natural resources and such unique tourism resources as Ainu culture.

Sendai-shi, taking lessons from the 2011 Tōhoku earthquake, hopes to attract creative tech companies focusing on disaster prevention and mitigation through a platform jointly built with Nokia, and to find partners who can cooperate in disaster prevention ICT technology (drones, etc.) being developed locally.

Yokohama-shi hopes to cooperate with large corporate open innovation platforms and foreign business accelerators to find innovative companies in life sciences. Yokohama boasts the Minato Mirai 21 area (with a large number of R&D facilities of multinational companies) and Shisheido's "S/Park" as well as the IoT platform "I Top" and and LIP, a life sciences platform with more than 230 companies and related groups. It is also looking to gather more R&D and innovation companies and form a startup ecosystem through cooperation with incubators such as WeWork.

GNI (Nagoya Economic Circle), including Aichi-ken, Mie-ken, Gifu-ken, and Nagoya-shi, has the advantage of having Japan's largest domestic manufacturing cluster, including the world's leading automobile-related manufacturing companies, GNI hopes to cooperate with AI and IoT companies in Europe, America, and Asia to help transform and upgrade the local manufacturing industry and improve efficiency.

Kyoto-shi is building on the strengths of having multiple research institutions like Kyoto University and a concentration of cutting-edge clinical research and high-end manufacturing. The city aims to build an innovation hub city in the life sciences sector through cooperation with pharmaceutical, medical device, and biomedical startups.

In addition, the Japanese government (Ministry of Economy, Trade and Industry) and JETRO have supported local governments (including public organizations) to encourage foreign investment through events like "Sapo-pro" in 2018.

The following are 25 places that are actively attracting foreign investment. Readers are encouraged to search for business opportunities in each of these places.

[Prefecture] 10 prefectures of Hokkaido, Miyagi, Fukushima, Ibaraki, Chiba, Aichi, Mie, Wakayama, Fukuoka, Kumamoto.

[shi-chō-son] Hokkaido Asahikawa Regional Industrial Activation Council, Sendai City, Miyagi Prefecture, Tsukuba City, Ibaraki Prefecture, Yokohama City, Kanagawa Prefecture, Komoro City, Nagano Prefecture, Nagoya City, Aichi Prefecture, Matsusaka City, Mie Prefecture, Iga City, Kyoto Prefecture, Kyoto City, Osaka City, Osaka Prefecture, Kobe City, Hyogo Prefecture, Fukuoka City, Kitakyushu City, Kurume City, Karatsu City, Saga Prefecture, 15 cities in total.

Hokkaido Asahikawa Regional Industrial Activation Council (Asahikawa City, Takasu Town, Higashikagura Town, Higashikawa Town)

This area is rich in agricultural and forestry resources and has many food and design companies, while the area focuses on attracting logistics, machinery and metal as well as IT-related industries.

Miyagi Prefecture

With a focus on automotive industries, the semiconductor industry cluster, and R&D resources at Tohoku University, the prefecture is looking to bring in foreign companies that will help drive employment or bring new management methods and technologies that will make local companies more international and dynamic.

Sendai City, Miyagi Prefecture

With the outstanding talent of Tohoku University, and the rich industrial clusters in the surrounding area, Sendai encourages IT and R&D companies to set up in the city. Having signed a cooperation agreement with a sister city in Finland in 2005, Sendai actively promotes mutual investment between enterprises of both sides. According to the "Sendai Economic Growth Strategy 2023", the city will provide support for the cultivation of international start-ups, start-up mentoring, testing of problem-solving ICT products, integration of local companies with IT companies and resources of large companies, Tohoku University's Joint Research and Development Center for Government, Civil and Academic Affairs, CareTech (integration of nursing care and technology), and HealthTech (health technology that integrates medical care and IT), with an investment of about 157 million yen in their development.

Fukushima Prefecture

This prefecture is home to one of the few medical device industry clusters in Japan, with many outstanding manufacturers that supply leading medical device companies and large corporations both inside and outside of Japan. Since the establishment of the Fukushima Medical Device Development Support Center in November 2016, it has become a one-stop support system from medical device development to production. The strength of the prefecture lies in its medical device supply chain technology and R&D support system.

Ibaraki Prefecture

About 1/3 of Japan's national R&D institutions are located in the prefecture's Tsukuba Scientific City, home to more than 20,000 researchers. The 2019 G20 Trade and Digital Economy Ministerial Meeting was also held in Ibaraki and the city hopes to attract more talented people and technologies from overseas to promote local employment and innovation.

Tsukuba City, Ibaraki Prefecture

This city is truly international with a large number of national and private R&D institutions, including the University of Tsukuba and the Tsukuba Center of National Institute of Advanced Industrial Science and Technology. It boasts over 9,000 foreign residents from 136 countries and regions. With its strong R&D institution and global talent resources, the city hopes to attract start-up companies and overseas entrepreneurs with new business models.

Chiba Prefecture

This prefecture has strong infrastructure with easy access to Narita Airport and Chiba Port, as well as a number of research and development facilities such as Kazusa Akademia Park. Makuhari Shintoshin, located midway between central Tokyo and Narita Airport, it also offers a convenient business environment with facilities like the Chiba Investment Support Center (CISC) and the Foreign Business Venture Center that provide low-cost offices for foreign companies.

Yokohama City, Kanagawa Prefecture

Yokohama City is actively working to attract foreign companies in life sciences and innovation through its Incentive Program, promoting incubators for foreign companies, and investment attraction activities by overseas offices, leveraging the city's advantages in transportation, a number of international schools, and medical facilities that can handle multilingual patients.

Komoro City, Nagano Prefecture

This city is home to many IT companies, electronic parts manufacturing, and production equipment manufacturing thanks to its geographical proximity to the metropolitan area, and such tourist attractions as Karuizawa. Its abundant sunshine and soil suitable for viticulture, (wine for Komoro was served when President Trump visited Japan) are also advantages in attracting foreign companies in IT and wine making.

Aichi Prefecture

Aichi Prefecture is known as an industrial region in Japan, with the largest domestic automotive industry, including Toyota Motor, and aerospace-related industries, and has been number one in Japan for 40 consecutive years in terms of product sales. In the future, it hopes to attract high-tech companies that will contribute to the upgrading of local industrial clusters and promote innovation in areas such as AI and IoT. It particularly welcomes innovations or new business models that can increase added value.

Nagoya City, Aichi Prefecture

Located in the center of Japan, Nagoya is a production base for automobiles and machine tools, as well as a cluster for next-generation technologies such as aerospace and environmental energy. Its business and service sectors are well-developed, and its convenient transportation links also attract many foreign companies. In the future, with the development of technologies such as IoT, big data, and AI, electric vehicles will replace vehicles powered by internal combustion engines, and Nagoya hopes to attract innovative companies that will help integrate the manufacturing-related technologies accumulated in the region with the most advanced IoT technologies.

Mie Prefecture

This prefecture is one of Japan's major industrial centers with high economic growth rates. In addition to leading the nation in the sales volume of electronic equipment and motor-related products, the prefecture is also rich in tourism destinations such as Ise and Shima with the number of foreign tourists increasing in recent years. Leveraging its advantage of having ICETT, RASC, AMIC and a large number of automotive and electronic parts manufacturers based here, the prefecture hopes to attract R&D institutions and innovative companies in environmental and energy conservation, life sciences, IoT, manufacturing (aircraft and automobiles), leisure services, and hotels. The auto parts importer and seller, Tianjin KW set up operations here in April 2018 while and a Swedish auto forging parts manufacturer also began local operations in 2017.

Matsusaka City, Mie Prefecture

This city is known for being the source of Matsusaka cattle. Its transportation links and rich local resources have attracted many companies in different fields such as food and general machinery manufacturing. In addition to the supply of parts for large companies, industries such as aerospace and health care have also seen considerable development here.

Iga City, Mie Prefecture

In addition to its large health care and machinery industries, this city also has a large concentration of traditional industries with long histories, such as Iga-ware (using local clay and traditional techniques, Iga ware carries a rich tradition that can be traced back to the Nara Period (710–794)) and Kumihimo (a traditional Japanese braid, cord or ribbons made by interlacing strands to bind up the kimono, being popular in the global accessory industry). The city currently lacks an abundance of foreign companies, but hopes to attract more in the areas of technology, human resources, and sales networks to support traditional companies in the future.

Wakayama Prefecture

This prefecture welcomes upscale hotels (by offering financial incentives), ICT companies to form larger industrial clusters, and growing manufacturing companies. In recent years, it has attracted many large foreign-owned IT companies that have established operations in Shirahama.

Kyoto City, Kyoto Prefecture

In addition to being a well-known international tourist destination, Kyoto is also a manufacturing hub. Due to the high concentration of universities and research institutions, Kyoto is popular with multinational companies. The city established the "Foreign Enterprise Investment Promotion Liaison Association" in conjunction with Kyoto Prefecture and Kyoto Chamber of Commerce and Industry and often carries out investment promotion activities overseas by cooperating with JETRO.

Osaka City, Osaka Prefecture

The City of Osaka provides various kinds of support to entrepreneurs through the Osaka Innovation Hub (OIH), which aims to promote innovation in local companies, and has been working to build an innovation ecosystem in Osaka and the Kansai region. In order to build a larger and broader global innovation system, the citys actively introduces Osaka's various initiatives to overseas investors, and creates more opportunities for them to interact with Osaka's entrepreneurs. The city also invites overseas business accelerators and VCs to visit Japan and participate in business talks through the RBC Forum and the International Conference on Innovation "Hack Osaka 2019" (hosted by Osaka City, the Ministry of Economy, Trade and Industry and JETRO). (A number of Chinese companies, such as 3dnest and Codemao, have participated in the event).

In 2018, the Osaka Chamber of Commerce and Industry as well as Osaka Agricultural College opened the urban open innovation facility "Xport" (Cross Port), creating a new model of industry-academia collaboration. These initiatives have attracted startup consulting companies from Hong Kong, the UK, and other countries to Osaka.

The Osaka Business Investment Center (O-BIC), which bridges Osaka Prefecture, Osaka City, and the Osaka Chamber of Commerce and Industry, successfully assisted 42 foreign companies to set up operations in Osaka in 2018, including 21 from China (inc. Hong Kong), and attracted a total of 548 projects related to foreign companies, including 201 from mainland China.

According to O-BIC's public records, it seems that inbound investments in tourism, procurement outlets and real estate agencies have passed the "boom" period. Instead, there has been a significant increase in the number of overseas companies that provide services to Japanese companies or consumers, such as Eco Sea Tech and SEAPA, which provide overseas technology or overseas services to Japanese companies, cosmetics or care products to "the world's most demanding Japanese consumers," and open beauty salons and restaurants. Smart Chinese companies are optimistic about business opportunities in Osaka and have established dispatch companies to provide nursing staff to both China and Japan, trading companies to purchase, import and export maternal and child products, food, cosmetics, and daily necessities, consulting companies to attract Japanese companies to industrial parks in China, Japanese language schools, trade associations (general Corporation Aggregate), payment and settlement companies, and companies selling cell phones and related products (OPPO JAPAN).

Kobe City, Hyogo Prefecture

Kobe has the advantage of combined land, sea and air transportation links and offers a pleasant environment for foreigners to live in with top international schools. After the Great Hanshin-Awaji Earthquake, the city promoted itself as a medical industry hub, attracting 305 medical-related companies or organizations to artificial Port Island, forming the largest medical industry cluster in Japan. In order to increase the vitality of the city and expand employment opportunities, the city is actively promoting the development of strategic industries such as IT, aerospace, and new energy that will lead the future of Japan.

Fukuoka Prefecture

Fukuoka Prefecture is actively attracting overseas companies through "Invest Fukuoka" (Fukuoka Foreign Investment Promotion Center) in order to create clusters in cutting-edge growth industries (semiconductor, IT, automotive, biotechnology, hydrogen energy, robotics, etc.). In addition to providing subsidies for the establishment of companies, new factories and office buildings, the prefecture also actively supports the activities of the Fukuoka International Business Association (FIBA), an organization that involves people from foreign government agencies and research institutions. The prefecture hopes to attract fast-growing companies from Asian countries, and aims to become a leader in innovation in Asia by constantly introducing new technologies or products such as IoT.

Fukuoka City, Fukuoka Prefecture

Based on the "clusters of city" model, its geographical proximity to Asian countries, livable environment, relatively few natural disasters, and abundant human resource, the city focuses on attracting corporate headquarters and companies with high growth potential, such as creative industries. As a "Special Zone for Global Entrepreneurship and Job Expansion," the city applies liberal visa application rules and offers a number of measures to facilitate start-up companies, including start-up visas and tax breaks.

Kitakyushu City, Fukuoka Prefecture

Kitakyushu is home to the first steel manufacturing and automobile-related industry cluster in Japan, starting with the state-run Yawata Steel Works. It is also home to a large number of educational and research institutes in the industrial field, including the Waseda University Graduate School, Kyushu Institute of Technology, and Kitakyushu National College of Technology which are actively involved in industry-academic linkages. Located at the border between Honshu Island and Kyushu Island, the city is an important node for land, sea, and air logistics. It has a variety of transportation links and is relatively free of natural disasters.

Kurume City, Fukuoka Prefecture

Kurume City has long been a city with a strong manufacturing industry, with a high concentration of automobile-related, food processing, production machinery and equipment manufacturing industries. The city has attracted domestic companies by upgrading of industrial zones, business matchmaking, R&D support, and HR training. It is also committed to attracting more foreign enterprises, especially Asian enterprises.

Karatsu City, Saga Prefecture

Focusing on creating an international cosmetics industry cluster covering upstream and downstream segments of the cosmetics industry, the city is promoting exchanges and cooperation between domestic and foreign cosmetics-related companies and organizations through business matchmaking. Asian and European cosmetics companies are a main focus in a range of promotional and investment activities. The city is actively promoting investment by facilitating the establishment of joint ventures between local and foreign companies in the region, developing new products using special local products such as Tsubaki oil as raw materials and expanding foreign markets.

Kumamoto Prefecture

The prefecture has accumulated service industries such as the semiconductor industry, automobile-related industries as well as the BPO (business outsourcing) industry, and is particularly welcoming IoT, semiconductor, and mobility-related companies from East Asian countries that are close by.

In addition to the places mentioned above, other regions are also actively engaged in investment promotion activities. For example, Iwate Prefecture's Appi Kogen Ski Resort incorporated foreign capital in 2016 and has significantly increased foreign visitors (from more than 20,000 in 2015 to more than 70,000 in 2018) by attracting high-income consumers from mainland China, Taiwan and other countries, renovating resort hotels, increasing the number of Chinese-speaking service personnel (from one in 2016 to 18 in 2018), and holding foreign promotion events in cooperation with the Japan National Tourism Organization, and even increased the number of international flights between nearby Iwate Hanamaki Airport and both Taipei and Shanghai Pudong.

Under the leadership of former Mayor Shigeki Nishihara, Makinohara City in Shizuoka Prefecture is promoting the "MIJBC concept" (Made in Japan By China), which seeks to combine Chinese capital and market with Japanese technology and experience to create a "MIJBC" brand of high-quality products, then sell these products to the global market, including Japan and China, and meanwhile to promote two-way investment, trade and cultural exchanges between the two countries. Over the past few years, their unremitting efforts have gradually attracted many local cities such as Shizuoka City to promote this idea, gaining the attention and active participation of people from all walks of life in China. Japan has also offered a series of incentives to attract foreign direct investment. Although the incentives are not as strong as those in China, they show that Japan is keen to welcome foreign investors into its many regions (Table 5).

Table 5 Preferential policies across Japan (updated July 2017)

Region	Subsidies	Overview
Fukushima Prefecture	Support foreign-funded enterprises to invest locally	Subsidies for a portion of rental fees, consultant commission fees, and costs required to establish a base (registration, obtaining residency status, etc.) (Subsidies are set at 75% with a ceiling of 10 million yen per company.) Subsidy target companies are enterprises involved in industries including pharmaceuticals, medical devices, renewable energy and robotics that are setting up manufacturing, R&D and sales facilities in Fukushima for the first time
Chiba Prefecture	Rental subsidies for offices of foreign funded companies in Chiba Prefecture	Rental subsidies are (1/3 for one year with an upper limit of 600,000 yen for 1–5 employees, and 1.8 million yen for 5 or more employees)
	FASuC rental subsidies	Rental subsidies (1/3 for three years, but this measure ended in March 2019)
Chiba City	Subsidies for promoting leasing enterprises to settle in Chiba City	Rent subsidy (1/2 × 3 years ⁎ maximum of 3 million yen cumulatively), reduction of corporate citizenship tax (1/2 for 3 years)
Tokyo	Subsidies for foreign financial enterprises to set up bases	Subsidies for foreign financial companies for part of the cost of setting up a base (up to 1/2 of the cost of legal consultation and other experts; fees paid to employment agencies, up to a maximum of 750 yen)
	Promote the introduction of foreign entrepreneurial talent	Relaxing conditions for "operation/management" residence (6 months) for foreigners who wish to start a business in Tokyo
Kanagawa Prefecture	Rent subsidies "Preferred Kanagawa 100" companies to promote investment	Rent subsidies for factory spaces, research institutes and offices for foreign companies that reinvest in the prefecture (1/3, up to 6 million yen)
Shizuoka Prefecture	Rent subsidy for foreign funded enterprises and other offices	Rent subsidy (within 1/2 × 1 year, up to 500,000 yen)
Niigata Prefecture	Subsidies for foreign funded enterprises	Rent subsidy (1/2 for 3 years) of up to 3 million yen, annual limit of 1 million yen, accumulative for 3 years

(continued)

Table 5 (continued)

Region	Subsidies	Overview
Niigata City	Subsidies for promoting the entry of foreign funded enterprises	Subsidies for registration fees (up to 150, 000 yen per project) and rental fees (1/2 for 2 years), up to 50, 000 yen per month
	"Promotion of foreign entrepreneurial activities" in the Niigata City National Strategic Special Zone	Relax the necessary conditions for "operation/management" residence qualification (6 months of residence) for foreigners who wish to start a business in Niigata City
Aichi Prefecture Gifu Prefecture Mie Prefecture Nagoya City	GNIC foreign-funded enterprises start support system	Support for foreign-funded enterprises to move into the Greater Nagoya area 1. Fees for experts (lawyers, judicial representatives, certified public accountants, tax accountants, administrative representatives, social insurance laborers) required for company registration and visa acquisition (including attorney consultation fees, social insurance-related fees, translation fees for registration-related documents, etc.) 2. Advertising fees or agency fees for talent recruitment 3. Real estate brokerage fees The total amount of 1, 2, and 3 above is capped at 500,000 yen for planned investments of 10 million yen or more, 300,000 yen for those 5–10 million yen, and 200,000 yen for those under 5 million yen, with a registered branch office and operating sales point or experimental research facility
Mie Prefecture	Grants for foreign-invested enterprises to set up Asian bases	Subsidies for 20% of depreciable assets invested (up to 500 million yen) for foreign companies to set up manufacturing bases
	Office rental subsidy	Rent subsidy (1/2 for 3 years) of up to 5 million yen per year
Kyoto Prefecture	Support for foreign enterprises to set up base grants	Registration fees (up to 150, 000 yen per project)

(continued)

In order to attract foreign companies, these regions have developed various incentives.

In addition, there are comprehensive special zones throughout Japan that provide many accommodations for foreign investment (Fig. 23).

Table 5 (continued)

Region	Subsidies	Overview
Osaka Prefecture	Osaka subsidy for promoting the entry of enterprises (subsidy for promoting the entry of foreign funded enterprises)	Partial subsidy for the investment amount (5% of residential purchases or 1/3 of residential rent, with an upper limit) for foreign-funded enterprises with headquarters in Osaka Prefecture (with over 1/3 foreign investment)
Hyogo Prefecture	Reduce corporate enterprise tax	Reduction in corporate tax (1/3 for 5 years)
	Subsidized office rent	Rental subsidy (within 1/2 for 3 years, 1,500 yen/square meter per month, up to 2 million yen per year)
	Subsidy for officially hired new employees	300,000 yen/person for formally hired new employees (600,000 yen/person for formally hired new employees and 300,000 yen/person for informally hired new employees in some promotion areas) (up to 300 million yen)
	Subsidies for market research, establishment of legal entities, etc	1/2 of the subsidy fee (up to 1 million yen for market research expenses and up to 200,000 yen for corporate registration expenses, etc.)
Kobe City	Office rental subsidy for foreign countries and foreign-owned enterprises	[Coordinated by Hyogo Prefecture and Kobe City] Rental subsidy (within 1/2 for 3 years, 1,500 yen/square meter per month, up to 2 million yen per year) [Kobe City separately] Rental subsidy (within 1/4 for 3 years, 750 yen/square meter, up to 9 million yen per year)
Tokushima Prefecture	Subsidy system for foreign investment enterprises and other investment business	Usage fees of various office equipment and communication line (1/2, up to 10 million yen/year), rental fees for real estate such as offices (1/2, up to 10 million yen/year), subsidies for additional employees (500,000 yen/person)
Fukuoka Prefecture	Subsidy for visiting Fukuoka	Partial subsidy for transportation costs (for foreign companies in automotive, IT/semiconductors, biotech, environmental, robotics that are studying to move into Fukuoka Prefecture) 1. Up to 100,000 yen for companies coming from domestic areas outside Fukuoka Prefecture 2. Up to 150,000 yen for overseas companies coming from regions other than Europe and America 3. Up to 200,000 yen for companies coming from Europe and America

(continued)

Table 5 (continued)

Region	Subsidies	Overview
	Subsidies for supporting the establishment of Japanese corporations	Partial subsidy for registration fees (for foreign companies in automotive, IT/ semiconductors, biotech, environmental, robotics (1/2 of registration fees covered, up to 150,000 yen)
Fukuoka City	Entry Subsidy for Fukuoka City (subsidies for offices of foreign countries and foreign-owned companies)	1. Rental subsidy [standard type] (1/4 for 1 year, up to 15 million yen), [large-scale type] (1/4 for 2 years, up to 25 million yen) 2. Employment subsidy [for regular employees]: 500,000 yen per person (Fukuoka residents), 1,000,000 yen per researcher (Fukuoka residents), and 100,000 yen per person for non-Fukuoka residents. [Other long-term employees] 150,000 yen/person for Fukuoka residents, and 50,000 yen/person for non-Fukuoka residents (up to 50 million yen) 3. Subsidy for 1/2 of the setup costs (market research, interpretation, obtaining approvals and registrations, and hiring expenses when establishing the base, up to 3 million yen)
	Start-up rent subsidy (business subsidy for the formation of foreigners' business environment)	Rental subsidy (1/2 for 1 year, up to 70,000 yen per month for housing, and up to 50,000 yen per month for offices)
	Start-up visa (to promote entrepreneurial activities of foreigners)	Relax conditions for "operation/ management" residence (6 months) for foreigners who wish to start a business in Fukuoka City
Kumamoto Prefecture	Subsidy for promoting enterprises to settle in Kumamoto prefecture	Subsidy for invested fixed assets (5% of the investment amount) and newly recruited employees (total maximum of 150 million yen). Subsidies are provided to companies that have opened new or additional offices in the prefecture and have signed a move-in agreement with Kumamoto Prefecture or have signed a move-in agreement with a municipality in the presence of Kumamoto Prefecture

* Examples of autonomous preferential measures exclusively for foreign-invested enterprises
Note Only those measures exclusive to foreign companies and foreign-invested companies are listed
Source Compiled from the websites of each municipality. For details, please refer to the JETRO website at https://www.jetro.go.jp/invest/support.html

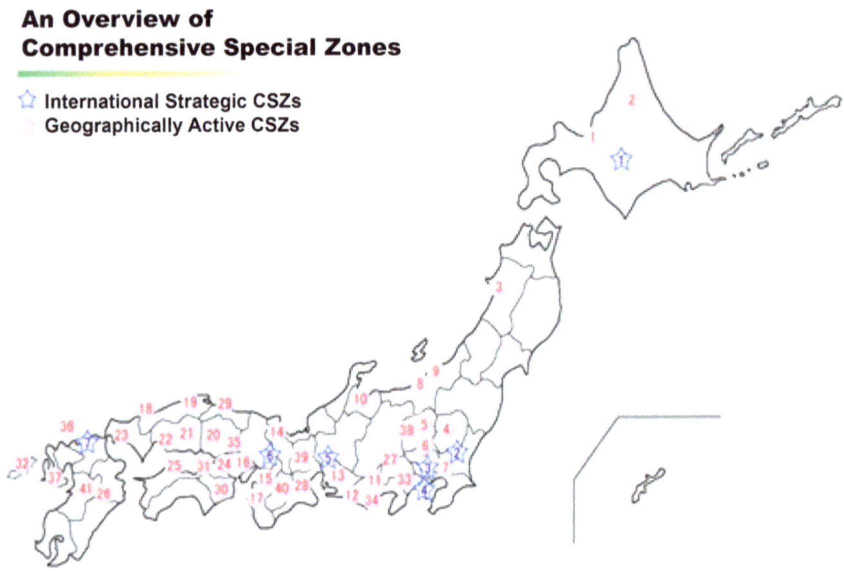

Fig. 23 Japan's comprehensive special zones

Japan's comprehensive special zones are divided into comprehensive special zones with an international strategy (promote industries that will support Japan's future economic growth) and geographically activated special integrated zones (that leverage local resources like education and tourism). Local governments in Japan have the ability to support Chinese companies entering the Japanese market. To avoid any challenges Chinese companies may face when expanding into the Japanese market, local governments and related organizations in Japan can be sought out to provide practical information to Chinese companies interested in expanding into Japan.

Due to the limited length of this report, it is impossible to introduce all the investment and cooperation opportunities in fields including M&A and innovation in Japan. Part of the JETRO Investment in Japan Report, published annually and free to download, will be included at the end of this report for Chinese companies with expertise in these fields. The report contains information on the current state of innovation in Japan and business opportunities for foreign companies in several dimensions. Many foreign companies have set up offices in Japan in recent years including Amazon and Ventre Café, a sister organization of the Cambridge Innovation Center (CIC). JETRO also launched the Global Accelerator Hub Project in June 2018 as part of the J-Startup, a startup support program created under the auspices of the Ministry of Economy, Trade and Industry (METI) and promoted by the government in cooperation with interested companies. The program has held a series of events such as roadshows in Shenzhen and Shanghai and will continue to promote cooperation and exchanges between startups in China and Japan (Fig. 24).

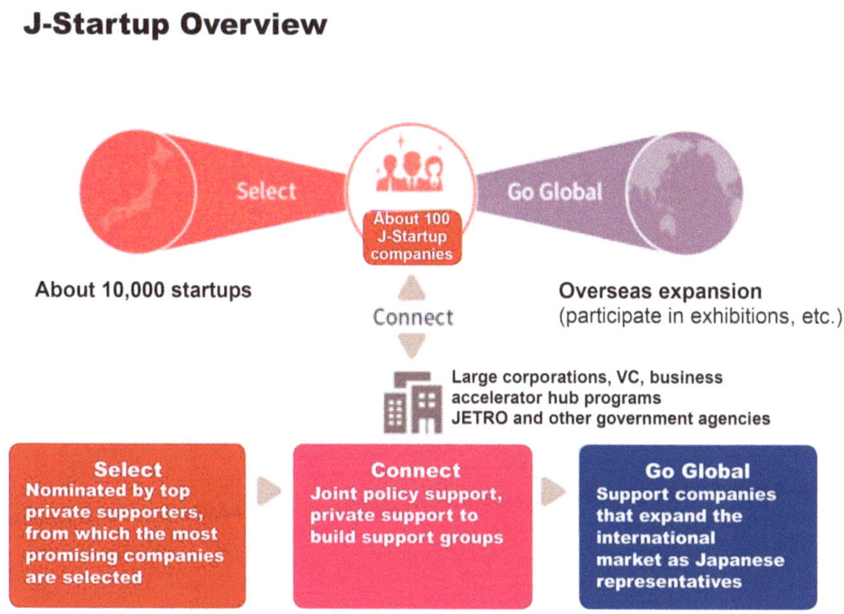

Fig. 24 J-startup overview

In conclusion, with the return of normal relations between China and Japan, as well as many changes both international and domestic, there is bound to be more frequent interaction between China and Japan in the coming years, greatly enhancing economic and trade cooperation, which will drive a transition from quantity to quality. In this process, we hosspe that readers will pay more attention to business opportunities throughout Japan and a range of sectors, which are not covered in more detail in this article, but should not be ignored by Chinese companies in the future.

Jinghao Jin Director of Investment in Japan, Japan External Trade Organization (JETRO) Beijing Office. Currently, he is in charge of consulting and business matching between China and Japan for Chinese innovative companies investing in Japan. He has worked in Sino-Japanese joint ventures (food manufacturing, consulting) in China and Japanese trading companies.

Looking at the Long Term and Overcoming Difficulties of Investing in the US

Weiwen He

Abstract The Trump administration initiated the US-China trade war and the technology and investment restrictions placed on China have resulted in a sharp drop in Chinese direct investment in the US. However, greenfield investment remains a bright spot. While the US strategic and technological debate over China will be long, economic cooperation between the two powers will continue to ensure that trade and investment is on a cooperative track. At the same time, Chinese companies need to be persistent and adapt to changing investment environments in the US. The two governments should continue to talk, and Chinese companies should prepare for greenfield investments that focus on local needs. Despite short-term concerns, investing in the US will continue to offer tremendous opportunities in the long run.

Keywords "Invest in the US" · Greenfield investment · Cooperation

The comprehensive blockade of Chinese technology and technology investment resulting from the Trump administration trade war caused a precipitous decline in investment by Chinese companies in the US in 2017 and 2018. Friction in Sino-US economic, trade, and technology is likely to be a long-term problem and Chinese companies should be prepared for a difficult period in their investment in the US.

1 90% Drop in Chinese Investment in the US in Two Years

According to the Rhodium Group, actual Chinese investment in the US was US$5 billion in 2018, down 82.8% from US$29 billion in 2017. Moreover, the 2107 figure was already down 37% from the US$46 billion in 2016. This two-year cumulative decline was 89.1%. In 2018, Chinese companies in the US divested US$8 billion in assets. Total Chinese investment in the US decreased by US$3 billion to US$145

W. He (✉)
Center for China and Globalization, Beijing, China

H. H. Wang and M. L. Miao (eds.), *The Challenge of "Going Out"*, The Chinese Enterprise Globalization Series, https://doi.org/10.1007/978-981-99-3326-6_9

billion by the end of 2018. Much of the decline in 2017 was due to the Chinese government's calls for a halt to highly leveraged cross-border acquisitions (e.g., entertainment M&A.) The decline in 2018 was primarily due to the Trump administration's sharp tightening of restrictions.

On November 10, 2018, *the Foreign Investment Risk Review Modernization Act* (FIRRMA) pilot program was officially implemented, and the Committee on Foreign Investment in the United States (CFIUS) comprehensively tightened the monitoring of investments involving the Information and Communications Technology (ICT) sector. The Trump administration's blanket blocking of Huawei demonstrates that the US will not allow China to pose a threat to it in the high-tech sector. Several hawkish figures in the White House have even advocated decoupling science and technology in trade between China and the US. As a result, restrictions on Chinese M&As in the US in high-tech, technology personnel exchanges and even visas for Chinese students have been tightened across the board. The June 29, 2019 meeting between President Xi Jinping and President Trump at the G20 Osaka Summit set a general path for the two sides to return to the negotiating table and seek win–win cooperation. Since then, President Trump has also made several goodwill statements and gestures, including the promise that there will be no more tariffs on Chinese products and that Chinese students are still welcome to study in the US. However, there are still many uncertainties about whether the US and China can reach an agreement on economic and trade talks.

2 Chinese Enterprises in the US Running Well Despite Political Shadow

According to the China General Chamber of Commerce-USA, 20% of member companies' revenue in 2018 grew by more than 20% over the previous year, while another 20% grew by less than 20%; 47% of their revenue was flat compared to the previous year, and only 13% had negative growth. In 2019, 83% of the member companies said they would develop their existing business, 54% would explore new areas, and 46% would work on brand creation. Only 3% of the companies said they were committed to learning advanced technologies, indicating the Trump administration had stepped up its technological blockade of Chinese enterprises.[1]

The intensification of economic and trade friction between the US and China has created a great deal of uncertainty in the outlook for Chinese companies in the US. The number of companies that believe the business environment in the US has become worse in 2019 reached 52%, more than double the 23% in 2018 (Table 1):

The table above shows that the proportion of companies that believe the business prospects will deteriorate in the next two years in 2019 reached 23%. This proportion is almost double the 12% of companies that believed this in 2018; before 2017, the

[1] China General Chamber of Commerce-USA: *2019 Annual Business Survey Report Chinese Enterprises in the United States, Jun.10,2019.* www.cgccusa.org.

Table 1 Results of Survey on Business Environment and Immediate Prospects of Chinese Companies in the US (%)

Changes in the business environment	Year	Greatly worsened	Unchanged	Greatly improved	Slightly worse	Slightly better
Prospects for the next two years	2018	0	59	2	23	16
	2019	6	42	1	46	5
	2014	0	19	27	5	49
	2015	0	28	26	1	45
	2016	0	32	10	6	52
	2017	0	35	2	5	58
	2018	0	40	6	12	42
	2019	3	43	1	30	23

Source China General Chamber of Commerce-USA: 2019 Annual Business Survey Report Chinese Enterprises in the United States

proportion was generally single digit. 75% of the companies said they were affected by the tensions between the US and China, and 77% said they were affected by tariff increases. The Trump administration has tightened its scrutiny of Chinese investment and M&A in the US, with increasingly apparent restrictions and blocking of M&A in high-tech sectors in particular. However, most Chinese enterprises in the US start with greenfield investment, reducing this impact. According to the survey, 54% of Chinese companies in the US enter the country through greenfield investments. Another 21% start with a representative office, making a total of 75%. Another 13% prefer to establish joint ventures, and only 9% of the companies enter the US by acquiring assets. Production investment companies mostly enter the US through greenfield investments, such as Fuyao Glass Industry Group Co., Ltd. and Jinlong Copper Co., Ltd., which have not encountered significant obstacles. However, more than 90% of capital investment enterprises enter the US by way of M&A, which creates major difficulties.

3 Greenfield Investment in Manufacturing Remains a Bright Spot

Tensions in US-China economic and trade relations and tight restrictions on Chinese investment in high-technology fields in the US have not affected greenfield investment in the US in ordinary manufacturing industries. On the contrary, investment is actually welcome as long as it can help increase local employment and tax revenue and does not involve sensitive industries.

After investing in the construction of a 60,000-ton per yer copper pipe plant for pipes used in refrigeration equipment in Mexico in 2008, the Xinxiang-based (Henan Province) Golden Dragon Precise Copper Tube Group Inc. (GD Group) invested

US$100 million in a new 60,000-ton annual copper pipe plant (for air conditioners) in Pine Hill, Wilcox County, a remote county in Alabama in 2014. The plant employed 200 people and generated US$45 million in local taxes. As a result, it received strong support from the local government, in addition to US$15 million in subsidies.[2] The state's elected congressmen also helped solve issues around work visas for Chinese personnel to come to the US.

GD Group's construction of a copper pipe plant in the US met the local needs as well as its own. After facing anti-dumping duties in 2004, GD Group set up a factory directly in the US to avoid such issues again, while most of the raw copper is imported from South American countries like Chile, significantly reducing costs. Thus, the plant's location is close to both the origin of raw materials and its sales market, allowing it to avoid tariff barriers.

The US$600 million Fuyao Glass automotive glass plant in Dayton, Ohio, a key manufacturing hub in the US, turned a profit in 2018. Operating income was RMB 3.417 billion, up 58.7% from the previous year and accounted for 41.85% of Fuyao Group's foreign revenue as well as a profit of RMB 246 million. Fuyao's plant in the US was once the source of controversy and criticism in China because many people thought that "Lao Cao" (Cao Dewang, chairman of Fuyao Glass) was "running away". However, producing locally for the target sales market is a straightforward and common practice. In 2011, General Motors (GM) and Fuyao reached a sales agreement. However, one of the prerequisites was to build a plant in the US to ensure supply. This is the same as GM's supply of cars to China, manufactured in China. Its company's global policy is, "make motors where they are sold." The Fuyao plant in the US was welcomed and supported locally because it created 2,000 jobs for locals. The entire plant workforce once voted on whether to form a union, and the result was 444 votes in favor and 868 votes against, showing the trust that the majority of workers had in Fuyao's management.

In 2017, Haier Group acquired the appliance division of General Electric (GE). Then, on October 11, 2018, after the Trump administration began imposing 10% tariffs on imports of US$200 billion in goods from China, and after the Foreign Investment Risk Review Modernization Act had taken effect, Haier announced a US$200 million investment to expand the GE Kentucky plant to expand its washer and dryer production capacity and add a dishwasher production line. Annual demand in the US market for these products was 15 million washers, 7.1 million dryers, and 7.9 million dishwashers. In this context, after the US announced tariff increases on washing machines in March of that year, there was an opportunity for production in the US domestic market.

On June 18, the US Air Force offered to buy 17 drones from SZ DJI Technology Co., Ltd, which, in turn, said it was considering investing in production in the US. This is a good sign and shows that everything should be analyzed on a case-by-case basis as nothing is ironclad. While the US may be tightening its technological restrictions on China, it does not exclude many Chinese practical products that are cost-effective.

[2] Huanqiu, "Interview with Li Changjie, deputy to the National People's Congress and Chairman of Jinlong Group", March 15, 2015, https://finance.huanqiu.com/article/9CaKrnJIF5Y.

This implies that it is still possible for Chinese enterprises to set up factories in the US and sell their products locally if there is a market for their products.

4 US Strategic and Technological Restrictions on China Will Be Long-Term

The sharp decline in M&A by Chinese companies in the US and the tightening of US government restrictions on M&A in sensitive areas are two trends that are likely to continue in the near term. The underlying reason for this is that the Trump administration has positioned China as a strategic rival, reversing the previous stance of increasing mutual strategic trust emphasized by both sides.

The National Security Strategy of the United States of America submitted to Congress by the US National Security Council on December 18, 2017, explicitly positioned China as a strategic adversary. The 2018 President's Trade Policy Agenda[3] submitted by United States Trade Representative (USTR) on February 27, 2018 supports this. This Agenda proposed five pillars of US trade policy, the first of which is US strategic security, explicitly stating that China is a strategic adversary. Under this premise, US trade and investment policy toward China will likely include containment and suppression.

The US-China trade friction over the past year has shown that the US government cannot tolerate China as a major country on the Communist Party-led path to socialism, which may replace US dominance in economics. It has also shown that it will neither tolerate the challenge posed by China's high-tech and high-end manufacturing industries nor the Belt and Road Initiative reconfiguring a US-led international order. Under this backdrop, the USTR's 301 investigation report on China criticises China for "forced technology transfer" and "theft of intellectual property", which has prompted the US to strictly prevent Chinese companies from merging into high-tech sectors in the US (e.g., information and communication technology, new energy, biotechnology) and security-related fields (electronic payment and finance). This policy will not change in the short term, and Huawei's withdrawal from the US market shows that instead of fighting against such barriers, it is better to change strategy for the time being.

Given this trend, we should respond in two ways. Firstly, the Chinese government should resolutely oppose unreasonable restrictions by the US government and protect the legitimate rights and interests of Chinese enterprises. At the same time, it should reach some kind of agreement on two-way investment through economic and trade negotiations, forcing the US to relax such restrictions. Secondly, the Chinese enterprises affected by the US-China trade war should undertake specific analyses of specific projects and make efforts to find opportunities to circumvent any issues.

---

[3] <2018 Trade Policy Agenda and 2017 Annual Report>, www.ustr.gov.

5 There is Still a Way Out for Investment in the US

The Trump administration's strategic positioning of China and its investment and technology restrictions on China caused a significant decline in Chinese companies' investment and M&A in the US. This will likely continue for a while, but this is only one side of the story. The economic complementarity between China and the US is something that no politician can change. US-China cooperation, including investment cooperation, will remain the fundamental aspect of US-China economic and trade relations.

According to statistics released by the Ministry of Commerce, by the end of 2017, Chinese companies had invested US$67 billion in the US across 46 states, creating 140,000 jobs. As this is in line with US economic and public interests, it will continue to receive solid support.

The Chinese market has become an essential component of global sales, profitability and growth for high-tech companies in the US, which means that their cooperation with China cannot be isolated by the Trump administration's trade policies either. This cooperation is generally a two-way street. For one thing, US high-tech companies must set up R&D centers in China to expand their sales. For another thing, they often also need to set up China-oriented support centers (R&D, research, promotion) within the US, and such support centers often require the participation of Chinese companies.

Since the Trump administration's efforts to bring manufacturing back to the US have not worked, it is an excellent opportunity for Chinese companies to invest in manufacturing in the US. Faced with the uncertainty of market prospects brought by the Trump administration's unilateral tariffs, Chinese companies can be strategic about locating assembly and completion of some products for sale in the US or directly investing and producing them in the US.

6 Exploration of Specific Ways and Means

First, the Chinese government needs to continue negotiating with the US to safeguard the legitimate rights and interests of Chinese enterprises. Meanwhile, the US should significantly relax foreign investment access and strive to resume negotiations on a Bilateral Investment Treaty (BIT) and provide basic legal and institutional safeguards for enterprises to invest in the US.

Second, enterprises investing in the US should avoid sensitive industries for the time being and focus more on non-sensitive industries such as general machinery, electrical appliances, auto parts, household consumer goods, logistics and trade. It is also advisable to enter the US market by conducting greenfield investment or setting up representative offices in these areas.

Third, it is recommended that Chinese companies adopt greenfield investment strategies, specifically in manufacturing. The investment plan should be based on three factors: whether it meets both the needs of the local US market and the enterprise's own needs for overseas expansion; whether it is feasible; and whether the risks are controllable.

Fourth, Chinese companies should consider greenfield investments in steel, auto parts, and general machinery in the "Rust Belt". With their rich experience in corporate transformation, China can help these traditional US industries upgrade and drive economic growth. If positive results are achieved in this area, it will benefit the enterprises and play a positive role in easing economic and trade relations between China and the US.

Fifth, Chinese enterprises should not aim too high. They should cooperate with local governments and seek to establish close working relationships with, for instance, mainstream banks and law firms that undertake localized investment and operation. The majority of local and business communities in the US do not follow Washington's policies, and their main concerns are the development of the local economy, employment, and taxation. As long as Chinese enterprises can cooperate with US local governments, they can contribute to the US economy and states.

As the current and near future will be difficult for US-China economic and trade relations, Chinese companies should create sound response plans. At the same time, we must carefully analyze opportunities for US-China cooperation and seek to expand investment opportunities in the US. In the long run, the current difficulties and detours are only temporary setbacks. As long as they remain determined on investing in the US, there will be a bright future ahead for Chinese enterprises and the people of both China and the US.

Weiwen He Former Economic and Commercial Counselor at Chinese Consulates General in San Francisco and New York, Non-resident Senior Fellow of CCG.

Notable "Going Out" Case Studies

Geely's Path to Becoming a Global Corporation

Jihua Ding, Lingchen Guo, and Zhile Wang

Abstract Global corporations can provide insights for Chinese companies seeking for "go abroad". One such example is Geely Auto. Geely has implemented a global strategy that builds a global value chain around R&D design, manufacturing assembly, and marketing services. It has set up a global governance structure to support these services, including a company culture of harmony and inclusiveness. As a result, Geely is on its way to becoming a global company.

Keywords Global corporations · Global strategy · Global governance · Global corporate culture

1 Background

Since the 1990s, and driven by a new round of economic globalization, a quiet revolution has been taking place in the business world—transnational corporations have been transforming into global corporations to adapt to the global market—implementing global strategies to create global value chains, establishing global management and governance structures, and assuming global responsibilities of economy, society, environment, and compliance. Compared with ordinary multinational companies, the globalization of companies serves to enhanced their global index (the average of the ratio of overseas assets, overseas sales and overseas employees to total assets, total sales and total employees), moving their focus to overseas markets. These companies use global strategies, governance structures, and various cultural philosophies to form a global mindset and business model.

In the 1990s, continuous technological breakthroughs in the auto industry and increasing pressure to lower production costs led to the auto industry's globalization. The globalization of marketing and services has globalized the manufacturing

J. Ding (✉) · L. Guo · Z. Wang
Beijing New Century Academy On Transnational Companies, Beijing, China

H. H. Wang and M. L. Miao (eds.), *The Challenge of "Going Out"*, The Chinese Enterprise Globalization Series, https://doi.org/10.1007/978-981-99-3326-6_10

and assembly process as well as R&D and design. In this way, each link within the automotive industry chain has transcended the geographical barriers of individual countries and has been distributed globally and appeared in all major markets worldwide.

As promoters and integrators of globalization in the automobile industry, many multinational automobile companies have carried out large-scale cross-border M&A and restructuring projects, which have changed the pattern of the global automobile industry. These global industry integrators have transitioned from multinational companies to typical global corporations and include companies like General Motors, Toyota, Honda, and Volkswagen, which are influential and control the global automotive industry chain and value chains.

Geely Auto entered the automotive sector in 1997. With a global mindset and business model, Geely has become one of the most influential local Chinese enterprises in the global automotive industry over the past 20 years. Geely ranked 343rd on the Fortune 500 list with US$31.4 billion in revenue. In the 2017 China Top 100 Multinational Companies and Multinational Index, produced by the China Enterprise Confederation, Geely ranked 19th with overseas assets of RMB 129.2 billion, overseas revenue of RMB 145.2 billion, and 26,546 overseas employees, as well as a multinational index of 59%. This clearly shows that that Geely is becoming a global corporation.

2 A Global Strategy to Promote Global Development

At a time when global automobile companies are laying out their plans for the Chinese market, Geely remains eager to participate in the global auto industry market.

2.1 A Development Strategy Combining Endogenous Organic Growth and Outward M&A Expansion

When it was first founded, Geely produced models like Null, Meiri, and Youliou. The company later designed and produced the Jingang, Yuanjing and Free Cruiser. Continuous growth made it possible for Geely to carry out outward cross-border M&A expansion while also studying and introducing advanced foreign technologies.

In 2006, Geely Auto established a joint venture with Manganese Bronze Holdings to produce the iconic London Taxi in Shanghai, holding 19.97% of shares. In 2013, Geely acquired all of Manganese Bronze Holdings' shares in London Taxi (later renamed LEVC, London Electric Vehicle Company). In 2009, Geely acquired DSI, the world's second-largest maker of automatic transmissions. In 2010, Zhejiang Geely Holdings reached an agreement with Ford to take full ownership of Volvo Cars and became China's first multinational automotive group. This was a landmark event in the globalization strategy of private Chinese automotive companies.

Through the acquisition of DSI, Geely acquired important automatic transmission technologies and after its acquisition of the LEVC, Geely entered the new energy field; and with its acquisition of Volvo, Geely fully participated in the production and R&D, and since then has also made great strides in its development, making several breakthroughs in technology and management.

In 2017, Geely entered Malaysia to acquire 49.9% equity of Proton Holdings Berhad and 51% equity of Lotus Cars, which made it an exclusive strategic partner. Yet another step forward in its globalization strategy, Geely acquired the brand, achieved technology output and fully developed the Southeast Asian market.

This outward M&A approach to growth has enabled Geely to learn from decades or even centuries of experience and acquire technology from advanced companies. At the same time, Geely is also developing technology with cutting-edge partners in the global automotive industry chain through various forms of strategic cooperation and by setting up new R&D centers and design centers worldwide. These actions have greatly promoted Geely's growth.

2.2 *Building a Global Value Chain Around R&D and Design, Manufacturing and Assembly, and Marketing Services*

After Geely acquired Volvo, it established a global layout and global value chain.

First, global R&D promoted synergy between Geely and Volvo in R&D. The companies established China Euro Vehicle Technology (CEVT) in Gothenburg, Sweden, in 2013. This partnership resulted in the creation of a mid-size vehicle Compact Modular Architecture (CMA) platform and related components that could meet future needs of the global market.

Second, in terms of global procurement, before acquiring Volvo, Geely had few opportunities to cooperate with major international suppliers. However, Geely's procurement scope has broadened to include many top international suppliers since the acquisition. The partnership between Geely and Volvo also worked well in terms of procurement and resulted in a global procurement system that both companies use.

Third, in terms of global manufacturing Geely has introduced new renowned manufacturing processes at its domestic bases and followed Volvo's factory and management standards since the acquisition. Geely has also expanded into South American and North American markets. In 2015, Volvo established a new plant in Berkeley County, South Carolina, to produce the next-generation compact sedan S60 for the US market.

Fourth, in global sales the partnership between Geely and Volvo enables the companies to use each other's existing sales and service networks. This has resulted in Geely exporting automotive products to 60 countries and regions worldwide, with more than 400 sales and after-sales service centers overseas. Meanwhile, Volvo is optimizing and upgrading more than 2,000 of its sales networks and service systems in Europe and North America.

2.3 *Building Its Own Brand System by Combining Self-Created Brands and Acquired Brands*

Geely encourages independent design and production of its brands, strengthening the competitiveness of "Geely" cars, but it has also engaged in international cooperation and cross-border M&A, acquiring several companies such as Volvo. This has enabled Geely to form a multi-brand development strategy with local and well-known international brands, building an independent brand system with many products.

Today, it is increasingly difficult for a company to create a globally renowned brand entirely on its own, which means that Geely has made the right choice in acquiring well-known brands. Through M&A, Geely has acquired ownership of well-known brands such as Volvo, changing Geely's image as a poor quality, low-cost car manufacturer.

In recent years, Geely's global brand influence has grown. Despite the overall slowdown in Chinese auto exports, Geely's exports have continued to increase. In 2014, Geely vehicles were chosen as designated cars for the APEC Senior Officials Meeting in China, increasing public recognition of the Geely brand. In 2015, the first batch of Geely Borui foreign affairs protocol cars were officially delivered to the Diaoyutai State Guest House in Beijing, making Geely the designated automobile provider for foreign affairs protocol vehicles and cars for ambassadors. In 2017, Geely ranked first among the top 15 Chinese brands in the "2017 Top 100 Global Automotive Brands" list published by Brand Finance, a British brand value and strategy consulting firm, and ranked 24th in the overall list.

3 Building a Governance Structure That Adapts to Globalization

To adapt to global development, Geely has reshaped its management and governance structure:

First, Geely has created a globalized shareholding structure. A key element of this globalization of equity structures is that MNCs have transitioned from utilizing shareholders' resources and being accountable to shareholders in one country, to absorbing shareholders' resources and being accountable to shareholders worldwide.

During his early days in the auto industry, Li Shufu was already determined that his family would not work at Geely. In the following ten years, after its listing in Hong Kong and cross-border capital M&A cooperation, Geely has successfully transformed from a typical family-owned enterprise to a modern joint-stock company.

Second, Geely has developed a globalized governance structure. The acceleration of Geely's globalization process, especially after the acquisition of Volvo, means that non-local members hold positions on Geely's board of directors and in senior management. Volvo has established a scientific three-tier structure of corporate governance: shareholders, a board of directors, and management. The board members are representatives from their own fields located worldwide, with Li Shufu as the chairman. To ensure a strong partnership between Geely and Volvo, senior executives of both companies can nominate candidates for the board of directors of Geely Group.

Third, a global management structure provides an integrated "New Geely" with a dual-track organizational and management framework to oversee two independent companies (i.e., Geely and Volvo). As a shareholder in both Geely and Volvo, Geely Group maintains management principles of "full authorization, strict supervision, clear assessment, fairness and transparency". Geely Group has also established a "Volvo-Geely Dialogue and Cooperation Committee" to ensure timely, efficient, and unhindered discussions between the two parties.

4 Cultivating a Corporate Culture That Adapts to Globalization

On the path to becoming a global company, Geely has always sought to build a corporate culture that meets global development needs. According to Li Shufu, Geely has worked to create a global corporate culture that transcends national boundaries, ethnicities, and religious beliefs. He believes that such a culture is conducive to the the company's progress, innovation, and adaptation to global development. Geely's culture is also proactive in living up to its corporate responsibility and seeks to uphold the principles of fairness, lawfulness, and transparency.

4.1 A Basis in Compliance Culture

In 2014, Geely established a compliance management system. But why was this needed? Li Shufu believes that compliance is a prerequisite for sustainable corporate development and a key to the interdependence and legal competition of the global economy. He sees compliance as a tool for corporate survival and building a global corporate culture. For these reasons, Li Shufu demands that Geely comply with the law of "going global". He has said that "For a company to grow in globalization …… (it must consider) how to go further on the road of compliance. Compliance is like being on the highway; if you want to drive, you have to understand and obey the traffic rules, and improve your driving to avoid traffic accidents. This is the only way can enterprises achieve their strategic goals and go far. Otherwise, enterprises won't know when something goes wrong and will suddenly go belly up, failing in global competition."

The implementation process is made up of four steps: the first step is to identify the compliance risks the company faces; second is to establish a compliance management system covering all levels of employees and businesses within the company; third is to establish a control mechanism to guarantee efficient compliance management; the last step is to promote the formation of an ethical compliance culture with persistent spirit and determination throughout the entire company.

4.2 *Making Inclusive Culture as a Prerequisite*

Companies must accept and acknowledge efforts by their employees to establish an indusive global corporate culture. So what exactly does inclusive culture mean? According to Li Shufu, the famous sociologist Fei Xiaotong once said that: "Each nation has its own set of criteria for evaluating beauty; and in the process of cultural exchange, each of them gradually accepts the 'beauty' of other nations, and then forms further identification with other national cultures and establishes common values, eventually reaching the 'beauty' that people aspire to." Inclusive culture means that we must accept individuality and promote teamwork. Geely is cultivating a multicultural corporate culture in its global development by incorporating this.

Firstly, Geely combines globalization with localization. Geely recruits staff from all around the world and employs local talent in the countries where it invests.

Secondly, Geely seeks to incorporate different cultural identities by carrying out many cross-border mergers and acquisitions, which are often in developed countries. This requires a humble attitude and the desire to understand each other's culture, discover differences, and integrate.

Thirdly, Geely promotes cultural integration by developing communication and mutual trust. Geely's acquisition of Volvo has resulted in a strong partnership. Since acquiring Volvo, Geely has followed European business practices by allowing managers at all levels to form a sense of "ownership". Further, Geely advocates a culture of "harmony and difference" to encourage ideas that support the company's development. Geely is committed to conducting responsible business practices in its multinational operations, taking the initiative to take on economic, social, environmental and compliance responsibilities to promote sustainable development.

4.3 Placing Enterprising Values at the Core

The main reasons for Geely's competitiveness are innovation and entrepreneurship. This is made possible by Geely's corporate culture, which motivates employees. The key to the successful implementation of Geely's global strategy lies in recognising the talent and work ethic of its employees.

First, Geely insists on the core value of "Happy Life, Geely Drive". In 2008, Geely made "Happy Life, Geely Drive" its core value and aimed to make its cars "the safest, most environmentally-friendly and most energy-efficient vehicles".

Second, Geely encourages innovation and entrepreneurship. Li Shufu has driven Geely's continuous growth. As Premier Li Keqiang said during a visit to Geely Holding Group on November 20, 2014, "As a national brand that makes the country proud, the most remarkable thing is that Geely Auto has gone global and acquired globally renowned automobile companies. Geely Auto's experience marks the epitome of China's continued economic development." This pioneering spirit has also spurred Geely's domestic and overseas growth. The company initially produced spare parts by hand, but has since become a global auto manufacturer.

Adaptation is essential in globalization and Geely provides a reference point for other Chinese companies that are planning to "go out" and engage global markets. The creation of a unique culture that incorporates not only the native culture of Chinese companies, but also learns and incorporates local cultures by listening and observing local structures and communities is a key part of Geely's success. It is also essential to feel free to re-imagine a company's image and even position in other markets and other contexts as this gives companies a greater range of opportunities to expand overseas and increases their rate of success. However, perhaps the most important aspect of Geely's success is its corporate values, which it has maintained throughout its process of growth and expansion.

Jihua Ding Ph.D., Director of Research and Consulting Department, Beijing New Century Academy on Transnational Corporations.

Lingchen Guo Ph.D., Director of Research and Consulting Department, Beijing New Century Academy on Transnational Corporations.

Zhile Wang Director of Beijing New Century Academy on Transnational Corporations, fellow of the Research Institute of Ministry of Commerce.

Building the World's Most Competitive Professional Supplier of Auto Glass: A Case Study of the Fuyao Group

Jingru Zhao

Abstract Founded in 1987 in Fuzhou, China, the Fuyao Group began its journey toward "globalization" in the early 1990s, moving into Hong Kong, Singapore, the United States and Canada. Today, Fuyao has factories in Europe, America, Australia, and Asia, and has become the No. 1 automotive glass supplier in China and No. 2 in the world. This paper examines Fuyao Group by dividing its process of "globalization" into three key stages: opening up international sales by allying with Saint-Gobain, overcoming overseas anti-dumping lawsuits, and fulfilling corporate social responsibility. By discussing Fuyao's focus on improving quality and standards, enhancing brand influence, establishing an international business philosophy, and speeding up upgrades to its industrial processes through smart manufacturing in the process of going global, this paper aims to serve as a reference for other Chinese enterprises.

Keywords Fuyao glass · Anti-dumping · Social responsibility · Manufacturing transformation

1 Milestones in the Globalization of Fuyao Group

Fuyao Group (Fuyao) has steadily increased its presence in the European and American markets, setting up a factory in Russia in 2011 and in 2014 establishing a wholly-owned subsidiary in Ohio. In July of the same year, Fuyao acquired Mt. Zion, owned by the glass giant PPG, leading to the official creation of Fuyao Glass Illinois Co., Ltd.. According to Fuyao's financial report, in 2016, operating income and net profit both set new records at RMB 16.62 billion and RMB 3.92 billion respectively. Fuayo's growth rate also hit a new three-year high.[1] Today, Fuyao is the second largest professional automotive glass supplier in the world (Table 1).

[1] Fuyao Glass Annual Report 2016.

J. Zhao (✉)
MiraclePlus, Beijing, China

H. H. Wang and M. L. Miao (eds.), *The Challenge of "Going Out"*, The Chinese Enterprise Globalization Series, https://doi.org/10.1007/978-981-99-3326-6_11

Table 1 List of major milestones in Fuyao group's "Globalization" experience

Time	Events
1987	Established as Fujian Yaohua Glass Industrial Co., Ltd. in Fuzhou, Fujian
Early 1990s	Entered the Hong Kong, Singapore, the US and Canada
1993	Listed on the Shanghai stock exchange
1994	Announced a joint venture with Saint-Gobain
1997	Bought back shares, and ended Saint-Gobain joint venture
1995	Built warehouse in the United States
1998	Closed US warehouse, switched to direct sales
2000	Received "Global supplier excellence awards" from Ford Motor Company
2002	Anti-dumping lawsuits in the US and Canada
2004	The United States Court of International Trade ruled in Fuyao's favor in anti-dumping case
	Purchased float glass production line from PPG
2005	Signed automotive glass supply agreement signed with Audi
2006	Fuyao Europe GmbH registered in Heilbronn, Germany
2007	Set up just-in-time delivery center in Heilbronn, Germany
2008	Fuyao Japan Corporation registered in Japan Awarded "Supplier of the Year 2007" by General Motors Corporation
2010	Established Fuyao Hongkong and Fuyao Automotive North America
2011	Established China Fuyao (Russia Kaluga) Glass Industry Co., Ltd.
2014	Established a wholly owned subsidiary in Ohio
	Acquired PPG's Mt. Zion (US) and established Fuyao Glass Illinois Co., Ltd.
2015	Global offering of Fuyao H-shares, forming "A + H" model on domestic/overseas capital platforms
	Dayton plant in US produces first piece of automotive glass
	Mt. Zion's float glass production line launched to supply raw glass

1.1 Alliance with "Saint-Gobain" Paves the Way to International Sales

In 1993, Fuyao already had more than 40% of the domestic market and was officially listed on the Shanghai Stock Exchange (SSE). At the time, Fuyao was the only company in Fujian Province listed on the SSE. Instability brought about by the rapid development of the domestic auto glass industry, the weak rise of domestic auto production, and the advantage of low labor costs in China, caused Fuyao to look to the huge potential of overseas markets. Meanwhile, the French conglomerate, the Saint-Gobain Group, was planning to enter the Chinese market in the form of a "Sino-French joint venture". After two years of negotiations, the two companies formally signed a contract in early 1996 to establish Wanda Automobile Glass Industry Co., Ltd.

Partnership with Saint-Gobain provided Fuyao with sufficient capital, advanced production technology and management experience, and the opportunity to expand into overseas markets. However, Saint-Gobain wanted to follow its global customers into the Chinese market by providing parts, which meant that if Fuyao expanded overseas that Saint-Gobain would loose market share, so Saint-Gobain did not hesitate to raise the price of Fuyao's exports, thereby limiting its overseas development.

This move by Saint Gobain challenged Fuyao's plans to expand overseas. In 1996, Fuyao invested land purchases and warehouse construction in the US where it began wholesale distribution. However, after only three years, it lost millions of dollars and at the end of 1998 Fuyao quickly changed the focus of its US business from warehouse sales to direct sales, clearing its inventory and related assets.

However, this came too late and Fuyao's net profit plummeted from US$48,045,900 before the joint venture to US$405,400 in 1996 and then shrank to about US$-17.9 million in 1998. The following year, banks refused to issue loans to Fuyao and, doubled with the fact that the return on net assets fell below 10%, this meant that Fuyao lost its allotment of equity and the qualification to raise funds from the stock market for the next three years.

It was clear that this alliance could not be maintained and in May 1999, Fuyao paid US$30 million to buy back all of its shares in Saint-Gobain in exchange for Saint-Gobain's market share in China after five years, eliminating a powerful rival for Fuyao in the Chinese market. Fuyao immediately bounced back and two years after the share repurchase, Fuyao's profits doubled, accounting for 13% of the market share in the US. In 2002, Fuyao began to take over Hyundai Kia's (China) export business and started to use an OEM (Original Equipment Manufacturer) strategy to enter the international market.

1.2 *Overcoming Anti-dumping Lawsuits*

In March 2001, at the request of three glass producers, including PPG, the US Department of Commerce began an anti-dumping investigation of 31 Chinese auto windshield producers,[2] among which Fuyao Glass was the largest. At that time, Fuyao accounted for 12% of the market share in North America. In 2002, the US Department of Commerce ruled that windshield glass exported by Fuyao to the US for automotive repair would be subject to an 11.8% anti-dumping duty. In April of the

[2] According to the statistics of the US Department of Commerce issued by PPG and other three glass manufacturers, in 1998, the US imported 650,000 m^2 of Chinese windscreens, with an average price of $26.84/$m^2$; and by 2000, the imports tripled to 2.4 million m^2, but the price dropped to $18.50/$m^2$.

same year, Fuyao Group and its subsidiary the US Green Yung Glass Industry Co. filed an expensive formal lawsuit with the US Court of International Trade.[3]

In 2003, the US Court of International Trade granted eight of the nine claims in Fuyao Glass' appeal and returned the case to the US Department of Commerce for reconsideration. In 2004, the US Department of Commerce ruled that Fuyao Auto windshield was no longer suspected of dumping.[4]

This was, in fact, not the first time Fuyao had faced anti-dumping accusations by foreign businesses. In late 2001, the Canadian International Trade Tribunal (CITT) also received a complaint from PPG and notified the Chinese auto glass industry that it would carry out an anti-dumping investigation. Fuyao immediately decided to actively respond to the lawsuit the very day it received the notice. In August 2002, the CITT ruled that there were no sales infringements by Chinese auto glass manufacturers in Canada, and the Canada Customs and Revenue Agency made a final decision to reduce dumping tariffs on Fuyao glass by 24.09%. Fuyao won the anti-dumping lawsuit, and Cao Dewang, the chairman of Fuyao, was called "the first person to win the anti-dumping lawsuit after China's accession to the WTO" by the media.[5]

1.3 Corporate Social Responsibility a New Issue

In the first half of 2017, Fuyao's US plant became the focus of attention: in November 2016, Fuyao Glass fired Dave Burrow and John Gauthier, vice presidents of the Moraine plant. In January 2017, Burrow filed a lawsuit claiming personal damages, punitive damages against Fuyao, attorneys' fees and court costs of at least US$442,000. However, Fuyao had employed 2,000 American employees in Moraine, which exceeded the 1,500 agreed with Moraine and the Ohio government and made Fuyao a well-liked local enterprise. Pay raises for workers further increased support for Fuyao. In April 2017, the Fuyao plant had just announced a collective pay increase of 14–15% on top of the US$17 hourly rate for employees at the Dayton plant.

---

[3] In order to respond to the anti-dumping case, Fuyao hired GDLSK, the most famous anti-dumping lawyer among American lawyers, as its representative to respond to the anti-dumping investigation. The form documents filled out were several hundred kilograms, the deposit withheld by the U.S. Department of Commerce was $5 million to $6 million, and the attorney's fee was nearly $3 million. Fuyao responded to the anti-dumping lawsuit with four main reasons: first, the main raw materials for more than 65% of Fuyao's export products are purchased from abroad, so the cost is fair; second, being essentially a foreign private listed company, there is no doubt about Fuyao's the market-oriented operation; third, Fuyao glass accounts for 60% of the number of similar products exported from China to the North American market, while the sales account for more than 70%, so Fuyao did not export at a lower price than its domestic counterparts; fourth, according to the authoritative financial report of the internationally renowned Arthur Andersen, Fuyao's export price in 2000 was much higher than its domestic market price, so there is no suspicion of dumping.

[4] The US Department of Commerce announced the final dumping rate of only 0.13% for Fuyao auto windshields.

[5] Wang Qi, "Cao Dewang,a tired winner", *Chinese Entrepreneurs Magazine*, December, 2004(12).

As one of China's earliest manufacturers that had "gone out", Fuyao has bound to face challenges integrating with local culture and American regulatory practices and standards as well as trade union conflicts and employee lawsuits. In 2014, Fuyao acquired PPG's Mt. Zion plant. While PPG has said during negotiations that the union at the plant could disband after the acquisition, Fuyao believed that Chinese companies should respect local cultures and people rather than seek temporary gains. This prompted Fuyao to fulfill its promise to raise salaries and retain both the union and the entire management team.

Before Fuyao had established its wholly owned subsidiary in Ohio to produce auto safety glass, the original plant had been closed in the wake of the financial crisis, leaving thousands of local workers unemployed. Fuyao Glass purchased the factory for US$200 million, creating more than 1,500 local jobs and in 2015. Dayton, Ohio named the road where the local Fuyao plant was located "Fuyao Avenue" to thank Fuyao Group for its contribution to the economy and the livelihoods of local people. In January of the same year, Fuyao donated US$7 million to the University of Dayton to support the development of its China Institute.

From the first day it "went out", the Fuyao Group has always made corporate social responsibility a focus of its business operations. This has enabled it to gradually develop a sense of corporate social responsibility and awareness of the need to protect worker rights, while also attaching importance to WTO rules. Fuyao's actions show that it has taken practical actions to give back to society and local people, actively engaging in public service to fulfill its social responsibilities. By doing so, Fuyao has achieved abundant socioeconomic benefits.

2 Inspirations from Fuyao Group's "Globalization"

2.1 Focusing on Quality and Standardization to Build an International Brand

"The '1:10:100 Rule': it only costs '1' to solve the problem immediately; it costs '10' to cover it up for fear of being held responsible; and it costs '100' times more if it becomes a customer complaint." For more than 30 years, eye-catching quality assurance slogans like these have been proudly hung above Fuyao Glass production lines.[6]

In the early 1990s, Fuyao realized that quality control was the first step in "going global". From that point forward, Fuyao introduced Finnish world-leading tempering furnace technology and began to study the layouts and designs of foreign factories to optimize product quality. Cooperation with France's Saint-Gobain enabled Fuyao to train its staff on glass production line workflow and technical expertise. In 1999,

[6] He Ke. Let every piece of glass shine with the luster of quality. *China Quality News*. Oct. 28, 2016.

Fuyao established a product R&D center to design and develop VPL equipment, vertical tempering furnaces, G5, and other industry-leading products. In 2006, Fuyao began producing LOW-E coated glass and broke foreign monopolies in high-quality auto glass.

In March 2016, Fuyao introduced the "Taguchi Method", a robust design technology, to carry out the first phase of the project, advancing the focus of quality control to the design stage. The 13-h chemical tempering process is an important process in locomotive glass production. However, long processing times and external factors such as temperatures and raw materials are more likely to affect the quality. Fuyao analyzed and compared 18 experimental variables and finally reduced the tempering time by three hours, which made production more efficient and ensured quality, generating an additional RMB 1.2 million in sales a year.

Fuyao's insistence on quality has helped it obtain VDA6.1 certification, Germany's highest standard quality management system, and QS9000, the standard certification in the global auto parts industry, making it the largest supplier of the world's eight largest auto manufacturers.

2.2 *Evolving International Management Philosophy*

Fuyao has always led Chinese manufacturers in terms of their international business philosophy and the management system adopted during its partnership with the Saint-Gobain Group has remained in place.

In 2016, Fuyao Group adopted a rare "lean management" model both in China and abroad, developing its "FPS" strategy. In 2016, a famous domestic lean management consulting company cooperated with Fuyao Group to define the company's strategy to "use the power of the entire group to introduce comprehensive lean management". Chairman Cao Dewang personally supervised this top-level change in management and all employees were trained in FPS with the vision of making Fuyao Group a global leader in the automotive glass industry, known for its "high quality, low cost, flexible delivery and ability to learn".

2.3 *"Changing the System with Wisdom" to Transform Traditional Manufacturing*

Cao Dewang's listing in Forbes China cites his slogan "Let Industry 4.0 settle in Fuyao", which he coined and his implemented in the company. Since 2010, China's manufacturing industry has become less profitable due to the rise in popularity of the Internet and driven a transformation from traditional manufacturing to "new manufacturing". Fuyao keenly seized this opportunity by making the leap from "manufacturing" to "smart manufacturing". In 2016, Fuyao sped up its implementation of smart production and committed itself fully to building a world- and industry-leading smart manufacturing model.

First, Fuyao established automated production lines to improve customer experience and internal operational efficiency. Second, Fuyao created digital links and enterprise management systems at all levels. Third, Fuyao achieved "human–machine-material" interconnection by building a smart manufacturing system. In addition, in 2016, Fuyao integrated "smart manufacturing" into its "Red Five Stars" quality management model, integrating CRM, PLM, MES, SRM and ERP data, and achieving interconnectivity in "production, supply and sales, as well as people, property and things" throughout the supply chain.

The Fuyao Group Research Institute has a world-class magnetron sputtering coating laboratory, the most extensive antenna indoor testing darkroom in Asia, an advanced robotics laboratory, testing and analysis center of a thin film property, and cutting-edge optical, mechanical acoustic laboratories, creating a smart manufacturing laboratory suited for the "Industry 4.0" era. In 2016, Fuyao's Smart Plant Construction Project was selected as a Pilot Demonstration Project for Smart Manufacturing by the Ministry of Industry and Information Technology.

3 Summary: Building an International Brand that Represents Chinese Industry

In 2017, China's economy continued to transform and develop, but its automotive industry exceeded all growth expectations. 2017 was also a critical year for Fuyao to "go global" as the company worked to expand name recognition and influence. Fuyao dramatically improved its capabilities in international management and business administration thanks to a combination of wise decisions, the promotion of information technology and big data platforms, improvements in automated manufacturing, and its global shared R&D platform. Fuyao also sought to actively and effectively meet its obligations in terms of corporate social responsibility and strengthen employee awareness in terms of the responsibilities and risk in environmental protection. In the future, Fuyao Group will continue to strictly control quality and standards, implement its "Industry 4.0" model, and adhere to the principle of "customer-orientated" service to grow into an international brand and a model representing Chinese industry.

Jingru Zhao Assistant researcher at CCG, an Honors Master of International Relations and a Master of Arts in Diplomacy at the Australian National University.

Center for China and Globalization (CCG)

Founded in 2008 and headquartered in Beijing, the Center for China and Globalization (CCG) is China's leading global non-governmental think tank. It has more than ten branches and overseas representatives and over 100 full-time researchers and staff engaged in research on globalization, global governance, international economy and trade, international relations and global migration. CCG has also become a hub of exchange between prominent figures in intellectual, policy advisory, diplomatic, and business communities at home and abroad.

CCG is the first Chinese think tank granted Special Consultative Status by the United Nations.

CCG offers a nationwide post-doctoral research program. CCG is also a member of the Belt and Road Think Tank Alliance, a founding member of the US Research Think Tank Alliance established by the Ministry of Finance. CCG also holds the annual China Inbound & Outbound Forum which is widely influential in China.

While cultivating its own research teams, CCG has also built an international research network of more than 200 leading experts in China-related and global issues, engaging in ongoing research on China and globalization from an international perspective. CCG also makes policy recommendations on development and global governance in many countries, making us a think tank that provides new ideas and perspectives for domestic and international audiences. CCG also plays an active role in non-governmental exchanges and "Track Two Diplomacy", and has become a valuable platform for the promotion of mutual understanding between China and the rest of the world.

After over a decade of development, CCG has grown into a significant think tank with global impact that promotes China's globalization process. In the 2020 "Global Go To Think Tank Index Report" released by the University of Pennsylvania, the world's most authoritative think tank ranking, CCG was again recognized as one of the world's top 100 think tanks, ranking in 64th place globally. CCG was the first Chinese non-governmental think tank to achieve this feat and is consistently

H. H. Wang and M. L. Miao (eds.), *The Challenge of "Going Out"*, The Chinese Enterprise Globalization Series, https://doi.org/10.1007/978-981-99-3326-6

considered a leading Chinese non-governmental think tank in authoritative think tank evaluations at home and abroad.

CCG Publications

Huiyao Wang and Lu Miao, *Strategies for Chinese Enterprises Going Global* (Singapore: Springer, 2023).

Huiyao Wang and Lu Miao, *Understanding Globalization, Global Gaps, and Power Shifts in the 21st Century: CCG Global Dialogues* (UK: Palgrave Macmillan, 2022).

Huiyao Wang, *The Ebb and Flow of Globalization: Chinese Perspectives on China's Development and Role in the World* (Singapore: Springer, 2022).

Huiyao Wang and Lu Miao, *China and the World in a Changing Context: Perspectives from Ambassadors to China* (Singapore: Springer, 2022). Huiyao Wang and Lu Miao, *Transition and Opportunity: Strategies from Business Leaders on Making the Most of China's Future* (Singapore: Springer, 2022).

Huiyao Wang and Alistair Michie, *Consensus o*r Conflict?: China and the World in the 21st Century (Singapore: Springer, 2021).

Huiyao Wang and Lu Miao, *Handbook on China and Globalization* (Cheltenham: Edward Elgar Publishing, 2019).

Huiyao Wang and Lu Miao, *China's Domestic and International Migration Development* (Singapore: Springer, 2019).

Lu Miao and Huiyao Wang, *International Migration of China: Status, Policy and Social Responses to the Globalization of Migration* (Singapore: Springer, 2017).

Huiyao Wang and Lu Miao, *China Goes Global: How China's Overseas Investment is Transforming its Business Enterprises* (London: Palgrave Macmillan, 2016).

Huiyao Wang and Yipeng Liu, *Entrepreneurship and Talent Management from a Global Perspective: Global Returnees* (Cheltenham: Edward Elgar Publishing, 2016).

Huiyao Wang and Yue Bao, *Reverse Migration in Contemporary China: Returnees, Entrepreneurship and the Chinese Economy* (Basingstoke: Palgrave Macmillan, 2015).

Huiyao Wang, *Globalizing China: The Influence, Strategies and Successes of Chinese Returnees* (Bingley: Emerald Group Publishing Limited, 2012).

Wenxian Zhang, Huiyao Wang & Ilan Alon, *Entrepreneurial and Business Elites of China: The Chinese Returnees Who Have Shaped Modern China* (Bingley: Emerald Publishing, 2011).

The Chinese Enterprise Globalization Series

- Huiyao Wang and Lu Miao, *Strategies for Chinese Enterprises Going Global* (Singapore: Springer, 2023)

This book carries out comprehensive research on the underlying problems in the globalization of Chinese enterprises. It also proposes practical solutions for dealing with difficulties in the legal sphere, legislation, international talent development, and financing solutions for Chinese firms going global. In light of the great opportunities and space that the Belt and Road Initiative has created for outbound investment, this book also looks at the future development of BRI.

The insights contained herein will help readers understand the current state of Chinese enterprises in overseas development and has important reference value of enterprises looking to gain a better understanding of foreign investment strategies, make the most of opportunities, face challenges and take their development to the next level.

- Huiyao Wang and Lu Miao, *The Globalization of Chinese Enterprises: Trends and Characteristics* (Singapore: Springer, 2020).

Drawing on nearly 3000 data samples, using both quantitative and qualitative research methods, this book presents unique insights into the features and patterns of Chinese enterprises' globalization. The analysis provides a useful reference for enterprisesthat have already gone global and those that plan to.In particular, this book investigates challenges confronted by Chinese companies when doing business in foreign countries. It summarizes research covering three angles, namely: the current situation, causation analysis and corresponding solutions, and recommendations for firms, government agencies and other institutions. This book provides a comprehensive overview to help readers to grasp the broad picture of the international expansion of Chinese enterprises. It has important reference value for enterprises to help devise foreign investment strategy, seize opportunities, and navigate challenges in the course of globalization.

Index

H. H. Wang and M. L. Miao (eds.), *The Challenge of "Going Out"*, The Chinese Enterprise Globalization Series, https://doi.org/10.1007/978-981-99-3326-6

MIX
Papier aus verantwortungsvollen Quellen
Paper from responsible sources
FSC® C105338

If you have any concerns about our products,
you can contact us on
ProductSafety@springernature.com

In case Publisher is established outside the EU,
the EU authorized representative is:
Springer Nature Customer Service Center GmbH
Europaplatz 3, 69115 Heidelberg, Germany

Printed by Libri Plureos GmbH
in Hamburg, Germany